Imagining Organizations

Routledge Studies in Management, Organization and Society

This series presents innovative work grounded in new realities, addressing issues crucial to an understanding of the contemporary world. This is the world of organised societies, where boundaries between formal and informal, public and private, local and global organizations have been displaced or have vanished, along with other nineteenth century dichotomies and oppositions. Management, apart from becoming a specialized profession for a growing number of people, is an everyday activity for most members of modern societies.

Similarly, at the level of enquiry, culture and technology, and literature and economics, can no longer be conceived as isolated intellectual fields; conventional canons and established mainstreams are contested. **Management, Organization and Society** addresses these contemporary dynamics of transformation in a manner that transcends disciplinary boundaries, with books that will appeal to researchers, student and practitioners alike.

Imagining Organizations

Performative Imagery in Business and Beyond

Edited by François-Régis Puyou, Paolo Quattrone, Chris McLean, and Nigel Thrift

Routledge
Taylor & Francis Group
NEW YORK   LONDON

First published 2012
by Routledge
711 Third Avenue, New York, NY 10017

Simultaneously published in the UK
by Routledge
2 Park Square, Milton Park, Abingdon, Oxon OX14 4RN

*Routledge is an imprint of the Taylor & Francis Group,
an informa business*

Typeset in Sabon by IBT Global.
Printed and bound in the United States of America on acid-free paper by IBT Global.

Library of Congress Cataloging-in-Publication Data
Imagining organizations : performative imagery in business and beyond / edited by François-Régis Puyou . . . [et al.]. — 1st ed.
    p. cm. — (Routledge studies in management, organizations, and society ; 14)
    Includes bibliographical references and index.
    1. Business.   2. Organizational change.   3. Visual communication.   I. Puyou, François-Régis, 1978–
    HF1008.I46 2011
    338.7—dc22
    2011002810

ISBN13: 978-0-415-88064-0 (hbk)
ISBN13: 978-0-203-80790-3 (ebk)

Contents

PART III
Publicity: Brand Icons and Humor

PART IV
Inscriptions, Emotions, and Passions

Figures

Imagining Organizations
An Introduction

Paolo Quattrone, François-Régis Puyou,
Chris McLean, and Nigel Thrift

Images and visuals enter our lives in many different forms and through various events and occasions. As we walk down the street of a new city, we navigate our way through an assortment of visual practices and objects (e.g., maps, signs, people giving directions, colored lines, etc.). Each day we are bombarded with images relating to our everyday lives such as our health (e.g., x-rays, scans, no smoking signs, graphs and images linking heart disease, obesity, what we eat, and life expectancy). Within the workplace we therefore engage in many different practices of imagining on a daily basis. A moment of reflection can produce a long list of examples of organizations relying extensively upon a myriad of images and pictorial representations such as budgets, schedules, reports, graphs, organizational charts, project models, scans, surveillance, plans, visual standards, to name but a few. Managing and organizing can involve making sense of abstract slogans and planning future strategies with the aid of diagrams and planning devices; accounting relies heavily on written numeric records, tables, graphs and accounts; and health care involves the assemblage of a vast array of forms, assessments, scans, medical reports and interventions. Organizations thus endure through, and thanks to, these many various visual representations and their related practices. In other words, forms, images, visualizations and assemblages of all kinds underlie the process of organizing, a process by which organizations are constantly made and re-made.

So, why is a greater understanding of the role of images and visualizations so important in organizing? And, how can we learn more about the relationships between imagining and organizations?

Studies of organizing require a greater sensitivity and identification of the ". . . . key practices that can allow organizations to minimally cohere in space and minimally reproduce in time such that they are still deserving of the name" (Thrift, 2004). This includes reflecting on the process and performances, which underlie images and *imagining*, and the role of certain practices, relations, and inscriptions underlying this organizing process. We can draw on the work of many different authors who provide alternative ways of examining issues of repetition, process, performance, and these complex relations. We may refer to the idea of actor networks from studies by Latour, Law and Callon, or the concepts of difference and repetition and virtual/actual developed by Deleuze, Bergson, and Tarde; or finally Actual Occasions from the work of Whitehead. While each of these can provide particular insights into ideas and issues relating to these areas of enquiry at a broader level, we require more specific understandings of those complex relations between process, performance, repetition, and the role of signs, practices and inscriptions underlying such a process of Imagining Organizations. We believe that inscriptions have a key role in prompting and sustaining organizing processes for they can be seen as *acts of engagement* (Fabbri, 1998; Jones et al., 2004), that is, they are actions themselves, and as actions, then it is important to understand what effects they produce and how they affect people and organizations (Thrift, 2007). Thus for us, imagining does not happen only in the mind, as a pure cognitive process, but in networks of actants, among which inscriptions play a key role that we aim to investigate.

In order to clarify our thinking and identify some issues that we believe are crucial when *Imagining Organizations*, a short recount may help.

Imagine this scene. A lecture theatre of a business school is packed with Master of Business Administration (MBA) students hungry to hear more about the latest techniques to master the turbulence and volatility of financial markets. You can feel excitement in the room. People rush into the theatre to get the best seats. Students prepare their notepads and pens. The chair is anxious to obtain order and silence. He attracts the audience's attention and introduces the distinguished speaker. Once the lecture begins, the clarity and beauty of the formulas shown on the screens thrills the imaginations of dozens of people and you can almost see the ideas on how they plan to exploit this new knowledge floating in the air. The lecture is a crescendo of interest, the speaker is interrupted with questions, and his witty replies prompt sympathetic laughs. The Question and Answer (Q and A) session lasts longer than the time available, and the chair has to tempt people with the promise of a glass of champagne in the foyer of the school to make them leave the room. The lecture ends with a long and roaring applause, and everyone is now ready for the drinks and more debate and discussion in the foyer. That day the guest speaker was a finance guru who made millions managing a hedge fund. A week after the lecture, he was charged with serious misdoings and resigned. A reverend who was invited to attend the lecture recounted this experience to one of the editors of this book and commented: "What I saw reminded me of a priest arousing the masses with the idea of a new God: finance. It also made me wonder why managers are now able to engage the audience more than the clergy, which has done this for centuries". So what are the engagement mechanisms that allow people to coalesce technologies and managerial techniques of various kinds in networks of contrasting and changing agencies and allow specific organizing and organizations to emerge? Yet (think, for instance, of the year 2000 (Y2K) bug or the illusions created by beliefs in market efficiency as testified by the recent financial crisis) how is that utterances, visions and representations that later reveal themselves as completely illusionary work?

Within this illustration, the reverend rightly points to the power of certain regimes of truth and how the supposedly neutral and scientific techniques and calculations utilized in stock exchange markets and religious practices share the need for certain ritual and performative practices. While the specific practices of enunciation underlying such truth production may differ, the processes of engagement and attraction are similar in the way they allow the co-existence of difference uses, meanings, and effects alongside apparent sameness of forms and methods. The market for business solutions offers plenty of material to reflect on this apparent paradox: the Balanced Scorecard, Enterprise Resource Planning Systems (ERPs), and one of the oldest practices of this kind, i.e., accounting, are successful because they are so malleable and contribute to attract and manage diversity that they rarely present the same features (in terms of structure and functionalities) when implemented in different organizations, or utilized by different corporate functions and divisions (see, for example, Orlikowski, 2000; Quattrone and Hopper, 2006). Understanding how this happens is a key theoretical issue for academics to understand but also a very practical task in making sure that organizations 'succeed', i.e., happen, as the Latin etymology of the word teaches us (from *succedor*, i.e., to happen). In other words, we need to focus on how organizations are performed via acts of engagement and relations and the combination of homogeneity and heterogeneity through a process of difference and repetition, multiplicity, and alteration.

Addressing these problems requires a shift from a focus purely on entities to how to combine entities and processes, singularity with multiplicity and difference. For example, in contrast to viewing organizations, as some objective, coherent, discrete, and clearly observable entity existing in a stable set of relations in some singular reality, we need to become sensitive to problems of reifying them and develop alternative tools, concepts and approaches that avoid this problem. While this shift from nouns to verbs (imagining, organizing, informing, etc.) provides the basis to study images and organizing in the context of the many associations, relations, and mediations in which they are seen to act, we also need to avoid the problem of reifing processes and relations.

In order to explore these issues in further detail, we will focus on four specific areas of interest (see Figure I.1), which underlie research associated with the theme of *Imagining Organizations*. The first examines ideas of visibility and invisibility in relation to the performative role of apparently hidden spaces, disjunctures, and discontinuities in producing further spaces, outcomes and effects; the second concerns the importance of performance and action in and around imagining and how these combine repetition in relation to process and multiplicity; the third relates to the role of images in prompting emotions, visions and outcomes in relation to icons, brands, advertising and publicity, and; finally, the fourth, examines how we can interrogate signs and inscriptions as powerful means of organizing, rather than as passive effects of organizing efforts. As illustrated in Figure I.1 below, these four areas also link to the specific sections and chapters within this book and how they each contribute to debates and discussions surrounding these areas of study.

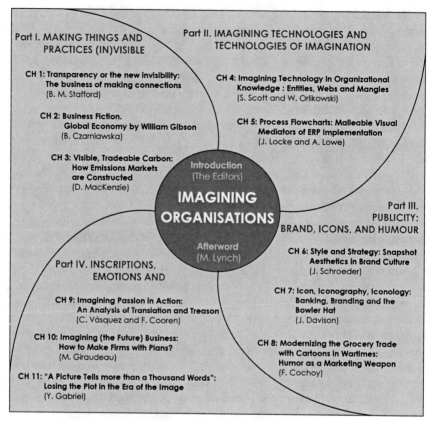

Figure I.1 The content of the book.

PART I: MAKING THINGS AND PRACTICES (IN)VISIBLE

When exploring the role and relations which underlie practices of inscribing and representing (be these PowerPoint slides used by a finance guru in a lecture theatre, production reports, formulas, or other kind of images used in an organizational context), one also needs to consider how in this process of making things visible, many other invisibles become referred to and called into action. This relationship between visibility and invisibility is the first theme dealt with in this book.

How can we develop ways of delving into these spaces, which appear to subsist and provide further moments of attraction, engagement and action that go well beyond some notion of 'original design' or the intentionality of designers? If we take the example of the speech recounted above, one way of attending to this issue would be to explore the role of what is left unspoken and invisible in the speech in creating certain spaces (openings and closings) to be colonized by the audience. Rather than viewing representations as spaces to be 'seen,' an alternative could be focusing on the margins of these representations (see Camille, 1992), that is, on the imagining process prompted by what is referred to by images and visions but not explicitly defined. These constitute further openings and spaces of action that ignite a continual process of engagement in particular events. For instance, when talking about 'efficiency,' the Chancellor of a world-famous university once said: "I am not against efficiency, as far as I can still keep the tutorial system as it is." In other words, everyone may relate to some notion of 'efficiency' (and many find it difficult to argue against it, see Hansen and Mouritsen, 1999) and see in it what the notion seems to refer to. However what becomes interesting concerns the ways in which such 'truths' are produced and what underlies the prompting of certain actions, images, and practices of organizing. How the notion of 'efficiency' is made real depends on the deployment of specific organizational and calculative solutions, which are left at the margins of the definition but are crucial in making this abstract notion appealing for they leave room for the appropriation of the concept by the final user. This is why, in order to understand why images and visualizations are powerful, it may be more interesting to concentrate not only on what they make visible and try to represent but also on what appears to be left out of the picture. This includes examining those apparently missing forces, actions and moments of vitality underlying these imagining events of 're-presenting' (i.e., making present again, Carruthers, 1990; Latour, 1986). These many forces and energies which engage and attract others and lead to such repetitions through difference and multiplicity are what typifies organizing and organizations[1].

These issues are explored by the chapters within Part I in terms of rethinking ways of engaging in these ideas of performance, practices, and invisibility. This commences with the chapter by Barbara Maria Stafford who addresses the issue of the secretive capturing and use of personal information by data amassing companies. Such companies benefit from the growing involuntary exposure of isolated consumer's preferences and sources of interest on the Internet to connect buyer's offline and online interests. Despite the myth of online transparency and democracy, Barbara Maria Stafford argues that no one really knows the kind of *ars combinatoria* used by those modern physiognomics to categorize information. While no taxonomist is able to classify the life forms that participate to the invisible entanglements of visible data on the Web, Barbara Czarniawska review of the famous novelist William Gibson, provides some interesting and original ways of rethinking the circularity of influences between popular culture and lived culture. By reviewing literature on fictions, she highlights how this may shed lights on actual practices on the margins of economy. For example, can this exploration depicted by W. Gibson provide ways of relating to data trends which are largely ignored our out of the reach of more traditional research approaches? Do these help in describing a present that 'hadn't been very evenly distributed yet,' and how 'netrunners' provide ways of seeing patterns in oceans of data? Finally, Donald MacKenzie studies performances, visibility, and invisibility through the construction of emissions markets. This includes making greenhouse gas emissions economically visible in relation to prices and the way such markets operate through opaque boundaries between 'politics' and 'science.' The black-boxing of critical scientific matters subject to controversies, such as the calculations of Global Warming Potential can be seen as making different greenhouse gases comparable and seen as facilitating political action in favor of the environment.

PART II: IMAGINING TECHNOLOGIES AND TECHNOLOGIES OF IMAGINATION

The reference to invisibilities and the practices and performances that these may prompt links to our second theme of representation and imagining. Such a focus on process and performance is important when considering the ways in which business practices and organizing are always subject to change and alteration (see Czarniawska-Joerges and Sevón, 2005, in relation to the translation of global ideas). For instance, it also allows us to explore how certain performances can provide the image of stability, but also the possibilities of change. In other words, it is this process of assembling difference in many forms, spaces and actions that enables organizing and organization to stay the same and differ at the same time (Jones et al., 2004). The idea of 'per-form-ance' existing *around* and *in* images is therefore a key aspect that this volume wants to explore, as a performance is a series of actions (*-ance*) through or around (*per-*) a *form*. We believe that it has never been as important as today to make use of a greater understanding of images and their quasi-liturgical aspects in creating believers (see Quattrone, 2009) in order to explore the worlds that surround us and to recover a vision of what organizations and business were, are, and could become. Think for a moment the apparently unchallengeable beliefs in 'markets,' 'efficiency,' and how these beliefs had a tremendous role in the recent developments concerning the banking crisis.

For a performance to happen, specific spaces for action and mediation are required. In many organizations these spaces could be constituted by various platforms which prompt and around which, some performance happens. The Balanced Scorecard, Total Quality Management, Six-Sigma, and other business solutions best sellers all constitute spaces that host various forms of performance. Information technology in its many forms provides a particularly interesting venue to explore how organizations and the platforms themselves are imagined. Both the chapters in Part II provide a detailed exploration of these process and performances of imagining and organizing in relation to the role of information technologies. In particular, they examine the role of images in mediating our understanding and relations to objects, as well as shaping our visions of organizations and organizing practices, especially in situations which may appear unclear and undefined.

The first chapter in Part II by Susan Scott and Wanda Orlikowski describes how current images of technology in organizational literature are not axiomatically neutral. The dominant images of technology as 'entities' and 'webs' are seen as directing the researchers' analytical gaze by assuming a clear separation between humans and materiality. While the image and methodology guided by the idea of the 'mangle' is proposed as a way of engaging in the visual palette in order to combine social and technological agencies. The following chapter by Joanne Locke and Alan Lowe develops this idea of performance further in their study of flowcharts and the implementation of ERP. This includes exploring the of role flowcharts as specific forms of inscription and translation devices. In particular, they focus on the ways in which representational practices such as flowcharts draw certain actors into the project, enable certain forms of communication between individuals and between groups, and achieve degrees of 'interessement' and enrollment for software also in the making. In this sense, they are technologies of imagination and allow the diffusion of human agencies between a network of actants that cannot be limited to the human mind.

PART III: PUBLICITY: BRANDS, ICONS, AND HUMOR

Publicity and marketing not only subsist in an arena of many different images and imaginings but also give life to many more. They are the focus of Part III of this book in which the performative role of images in the forms of icons, photographs, advertising, and publicity are explored through detailed cases. This includes the divergent practices underlying the specific cultures, values, and aesthetics that support strategic orientations. For instance, Jonathan Schroeder uncovers the strong connections between pictures and corporate strategy through his analysis of the 'snapshot aesthetic.' Photographic styles in this form are examined in terms of their 'staged spontaneity' and how they are related to ideas of authenticity and proximity. The chapter by Jane Davison also provides an example of how certain visual rhetoric may be connected to a brand through specific aesthetic and cultural codes. The Bradford and Bingley's bowler hat provides a wonderful example to illustrate the rich cultural associations and the links between iconology and iconography of hat styles and shifts in company business models. This highlights the potential crossover between culture and commodities and intangible value transfers. Finally, through a study of cartoons in the trade press journals' *Progressive Grocer*, Franck Cochoy explores how humor contributes to a performative rhetoric that can transform business practices. Cartoons make the readership of 'practical minded hard working men' look at the world differently by giving them an idea of what the future of grocery could be with a deliberate twist mixing leisure with apprenticeship.

That images call for a performance is something well known since medieval times. However, we have a tendency to forget this. Bissera Pentcheva's work (2006), reminds us that images are always performance and call for a bodily experience that goes beyond the eye. She shows, through her historical works, how the praise of icons in the basilica of San Marco in Venice involved a series of precise actions that had a two-fold effect. First, they involved the whole body (not just the eye): as the believer was asked to light a candle and move in front of its light in order to create a game of light and shades on the icon; second, that these movements changed the image on the icon itself. Thus not only images call for actions and create a whole body experience but also performing them made the image itself change. This raises the question of how we understand rationalities not as something limited to 'reason' and what we positively 'see' (think of the obsession with measuring of contemporary sciences, organizations and whole societies as in Power, 1997) but as visual schematizations that involve, are sustained, and generate affect, emotions and passions. This therefore links to our final area of enquiry in relations in imagining business.

PART IV: INSCRIPTIONS, EMOTIONS, AND PASSIONS

The question of how to explore the issues of process and performance in relation to images links to our fourth and final theme of signs and inscriptions in Part IV of the book. This includes examining those semiotic spaces in which specific relations, practices, and organizing perform particular orderings and regimes of truth. First, in order to explore ideas of imagining in terms of process, performance, and repetition, we need to go beyond the belief that images and representations hold specific and intrinsic meanings to be conveyed and a specific or inner truth. As outlined in the collection of chapters in this book, inscriptions can take a variety of forms within the organizational setting. Such studies thus provide the basis to explore the performative role of inscriptions within an array of complex and shifting associations, relations, and mediations, which underlie the imagining and organizing process. Take for instance the case encountered by one of the authors of this introduction when studying a newspaper printing factory: the production director explains how the 'boards do the talking' (e.g., production boards, containing tables and charts, quality, health, and safety boards, etc.). He describes that when someone enters the factory and sees the boards: "Nobody needs to speak because as soon as someone walks onto the factory floor they should know exactly how well the factory is performing" (Production Director, 2007). What does the image of the 'talking board' portray, and how can we study specific imagining and organizing events, such as the daily production meeting, in which various managers assemble around these boards?

Such a study allows us to think about how we conceive ideas of time and space in relation to such an event. For example, even though underlying these inscriptions, techniques and tools (e.g., production reports, downtime and waste figures) there may be a sense of linearity and geometric space, how can we produce accounts which do not rely on linear and successive ideas of time and space with objects existing in some realist form out-there? One way may be to rethink time as co-existing (past, present, future) through such events (e.g., production meeting) and the role of signs (e.g., production figures and charts) in generating flights of time and spaces[2] (Deleuze, 2004). In other words, this allows us to rethink ideas of representation and relations, which promotes the idea of a sucession of linear presents, existing in relation to another in a real series which refers back to some original term (which remain in some specific place or point). In contrast it is the process of perpetual disguise and displacement, which is inseparable from the heterogeneity and multiplicity that underlies such an event. Therefore, how can we explore repetition in terms of an event that relies on the performance and assemblage of many differences and relations?

Accounting and other numerically based practices of organizing specifically provide an excellent arena to explore the role and complexity of inscriptions in terms of this process of repetition and difference and the imagining process. A multitude of accounting-based inscriptions underlies the process and practices of sense-making in organizations. This may relate to a variety of strategies, visions, and actions of organizing; however, little attention has been paid to the imaginative power of inscriptions. Even less attention has been devoted to the visual nature of numbers, which has a long history and roots that intersect various realms from rhetoric and the art of memory to meditative and religious practices[3]. The word 'hierarchy,' for instance, originates from *hiereus*, 'priest' (and *hieros*, what is 'holy') and *arkhe*, 'rule,' thus revealing a link between a key organizing principle (hierarchy) and the 'tree' (an image developed in medieval times to aid memorization; see Bolzoni, 1995; Höpl, 2004; Quattrone, 2009). Similarly, the word 'inventory', comes from *inventio* (the first canon of rhetoric), 'record' comes from *recordor* (to remember), and 'formula' comes from *forma* (a visual shape). The word 'calculation' is not exempt from this visual nature either: *calculus* (calculation) is a synonym of 'account' and accounts are those *loci*, i.e., visual spaces, where transactions are stored in order to prepare their inventory (Quattrone, 2009). Thus, to make calculations and prepare inventories relate to the ability to re-configure these visual spaces, these accounts in forms which respond to practical and always changing calculative problems. Even the word most loved by those who believe in the *homo oeconomicus* has a visual nature: 'rationality' comes from the Latin word *ratio*, which more than 'reason' meant 'schema,' 'ordering device,' or an 'account' (Murray, 1978). And if one is not convinced of these unex-plored links, then one may look at the Balanced Scorecard (one of the most popular strategic management solutions, see Kaplan and Norton, 1996; Nørreklit, 2003) and see how it shares its shape and functioning with one of the most common rhetorical images: the wheel (see Busco and Quat-trone, 2009).

While these words today refer to the human ability to make objective calculations, what is more interesting is how they reveal a reliance upon forms of visualization and imagination, which have to do more with solving pragmatic problems and performing 'scientific truths' rather than scientific truth as existing independently from them. Those who believe in the power of rationality should never forget how accounting techniques and finance models rely heavily on, and are, 'forms' and as such their validity is relative to specific relations, contexts, and nests of relationships of which they are part. If one wants to understand how inscriptions contribute to turn people into 'believers,' into organizational members who are engaged by missions and strategies, then all of these roots are to be re-discovered. "Words have a history" (Long, 2001), however, this can become lost in some accounts, such as the work neoclassical economics.

The first chapter in Part IV, by Consuelo Vásquez and François Cooren, seeks to explore the imagining process by examining the role of specific inscriptions, in the form of posters. Within this paper they offer a semiotic reading of these images as both representing organizations and generating passions. By identifying images as 'spokesobjects' we are shown how the deceived expectations about 'presentification' (i.e., the process by which something or someone is made present to someone else), is assimilated to treason. The production of passionate reactions is examined in this chap-ter as posters to communicate about a series of public events is discussed. Rather than opposing passions to rationality, the authors explore of mobi-lization of disappointment in relation to specific images and the translation of interests and ideas of rationality within these complex sets of relations. The chapter by Martin Giraudeau also seeks to explore the role of specific inscriptions in the forms of business plans in bringing together entrepre-neurs and investors in 'a market for virtualities'. He highlights how busi-ness plans through specific performances, relations, and practices provide ways of imagining future businesses in the making. Finally, Yiannis Gabriel highlights the importance of rethinking how we engage in studies of images and emotions in comparison to textual narratives. He argues how images differ from textual narratives in terms of their emotional triggers as they convey immediate perception and are deprived of plots (as opposed to sto-ries with definite characters, beginning, middle, and end). Indeed, Yiannis Gabriel suggests that images privilege 'suffering' over 'peripeteia' and 'dis-covery,' which are difficult to represent within our culture. A culture which is mostly ocular-centric and rather than living our lives through narratives we live through images directly incorporated into our experience.

The book is closed by an afterword by Michael Lynch. Rather than attempting to summarize this eclectic and diverse collection of ideas and thoughts, Michael Lynch seeks to understand the possible relations between imagining in the context of organizing and organizations and science and technology studies (STS). In particular, he highlights the potential of this work in developing new cross-disciplinary spaces where theory and practices mix with unpredictable results.

IMAGINING AN EDITED BOOK:
RHETORICAL WHEELS, PERFORMING CONTENT,
AND REFLECTING ON THE WHOLE PROCESS

The visual representation that constitutes our table of contents (Figure I.1) is widely used in various declinations in daily organizing practices (think of the Balanced Scorecard, see Busco and Quattrone, 2009). However, despite having long historical roots (as it was discussed at length in Toscanella, 1560; see Bolzoni, 1995), its organizing power and engaging effects go largely understudied. More interestingly, it was used to inventorize, and to 'figure out,' new knowledge. We thought that it was therefore pertinent to the aims of this book to briefly discuss its features, to illustrate how it helped us to order our thinking and final shape of this book, and, possibly to help the reader to find other connections among chapters and parts that we have not thought of, those possibly made invisible though our editorial choices.

The rhetorical wheel used in Figure I.1 is a circular pictorial representation that helped medieval and early modern orators organize and deliver their speeches. The orator was set to define the topic to be discussed, e.g., love, and then to prepare an inventory of cards, that is, a number of pieces of paper upon which s/he (but, sadly, only 'he' at that time) could define various subtopics that in his/her views defined the concept of love (e.g., passion, affect, etc.). Then s/he placed the main topic at the centre of the wheel and surrounded it with, say, four cards taken from the inventory previously made in an order that s/he thought could be appealing to the audience. We can also see this form of pictorial and relational style of device in practices such as mapping techniques, spider diagrams, semantic maps, etc. The wheel was one of many rhetorical 'machines' (as defined in Bolzoni, 1995) that intertwined with techniques known as 'the art of memory' (Carruthers, 1990, 1998; Yates, 1966) helped remember and communicate knowledge, but, more interestingly, its discovery.

The functioning of these machines can also be understood if one looks back at the etymology of the first canon of rhetoric, the *inventio*. The *inventio*, as recalled above, originated the word 'inventory'[4] but also, and more interestingly, the word 'invention'. And in fact:

the goal of rhetorical mnemotechnical craft was not to give students a prodigious memory [. . .], but to give an orator the means of wherewithal to invent his material, both beforehand and—crucially—on the spot. Memoria is most usefully thought of as a compositional art. The arts of memory are amongst the arts of thinking, especially involved with fostering the qualities we now revere as "imagination" and "creativity." (Carruthers, 1998, p. 9)

The *inventio* was therefore the precondition for inventing new knowledge and develop innovative arguments, as the number of possible cards' combinations is normally so high that it always offers new connections and knowledge to the user of the rhetorical machine.

During the process of producing this edited book, we faced the same problem and profited from the same opportunity. These include the vast, albeit limited, number of possible combinations we had for ordering the 11 chapters (e.g., one estimation produced 39,916,800 possibilities). The wide array of perspectives and approaches underlying each of the chapters further complicated the process. Thus, to help limit the possibilities, we contemplated certain sets of practices we could use to make connections and assemble papers together into some form of 'coherent' ordering.

We decided to build captions relating to each chapter containing the chapter title, the author's name, and a short summary of its content (three to five lines). Reducing the complex argumentations and rich connections within each chapter to a few lines of text in one way felt like an over simplification, but in another way it allowed us to display all 11 contributions on one side of A4 paper. This enabled us to glance at all the chapters, and we started to trace arrows between sentences and words from different captions where they appeared to share 'common' topics or concepts. In this way we began to link ideas and contributions together visually. The imagining process enabled a process of generating many different connections, openings, and closings. This produced a very complex and complicated nest of arrows and relations. During the next stage, the connections, which linked more clearly to the developing themes of the book, were given more weight (i.e., the arrows turned into red ones). This enabled another process of 'simplification' that allowed us to look beyond the apparent 'chaos' and 'mess' of the current image and suppress other connections, leaving the red ones remaining. To tidy the image up and limit the crisscrossing of red arrows, we began moving the captions around. This produced clusters of chapters sharing strong connections between them. At this stage, we began to process the captions more as images than extended text, as the captions stood in for these new orderings of chapters and sections. Once we agreed on a satisfactory form the arrows and summaries were removed and the process (e.g., summaries, arrows, traces, etc.) became less visible. This was then replaced with the initial table of contents containing section headings and chapters. Further discussions and revisions followed during the writing and re-writing of the introduction, and chapters continued to move and alter their position. The rearranging of chapters also continued when the wheel in Figure I.1 was designed as the power of new and different connections developed producing further possibilities and forms (e.g., section groupings and introduction).

This process of mapping and the related practices (e.g., spider diagrams and writing; wheels, hierarchies, etc.) may remind you of your own research experiences in terms linking ideas, concepts, and empirical findings in order to create spaces for drawing things together and producing new and interesting links and connections. All the intensities, actions, and interactions, which underlie this imagining process, clearly do not adopt some linear and teleological form of development, however, the role of specific inscriptions and mediations (such as the mapping process) is an interesting aspect to explore when performing such orderings and performances. For instance, the captions, themes, arrows (black and red), A4 format, practices of shifting in and out from text to captions, the wheel, as well as the various other intensities, relations, and practices all contributed to performing such orderings (e.g., the table of contents). However, how do we re-present the imagining and organizing process which captures the specific processes and performances in making 'things' present and producing further spaces and openings for further action, as well as closings and exclusions? And, while the selection of chapters and connections via themes has influenced the way in which the book has been performed and continues to be performed, there are still many possibilities surrounding this book?

This again returns us to the power of such inscriptions and how we understand this role in terms of ideas of spaces, times and actions (Latour, 2005) and how we view the roles of inscriptions, signs, complex nests of relations. We thought that choosing a rhetorical wheel as represented in Figure I.1, could provide you with the possibility of creating your own ordering and place with the vast number of combinations that the 11 chapters offer to you. As readers you may select to access the book in a wide range of ways as there are clearly many different ways of reading a book. You may, for example have already skipped through the pages and smiled at Yiannis Gabriel's passage on 'opportunistic' reading by academics (Chapter 11). Serendipity, intuition, and your own personal interests in relation to the chapters' titles may actually guide you through the 11 independent chapters and the Afterword. Some of the references in a chapter may have suggested a paper of interest, or you may recognize a key author or set of references, and these will constitute further opportunities to extend the inventory of 'cards' available to you in inventing new knowledge when dealing with *Imagining Organizations*. Either way we hope you find this book interesting and stimulating. As argued by Johns (1998) a book is a book if it is read, if there is a performance around it, otherwise it is something else, a piece of furniture, something to jar the door open, or a dust collector.

In conclusion, through the varied and insightful chapters which follow, this book will explore this new and emerging realm of *Imagining Organizations* by combining different disciplines and approaches. This book seeks to provide a new disciplinary space in which to experiment and capture the significant role that images and other forms of engagements play in the performance of all kind of organizational activities. It aims to provide a focal point for the growing mass of studies which explore how various artifacts draw on the power of the visual for them to become global phenomena appropriated by various users in diverse contexts. It is a space to encounter and perform our understanding and engagements with this complex area of enquiry, by exploring how organizations are imagined, invented, inventoried, ordered, and constantly re-invented through this imagining process.

NOTES

1. The crystal image also provides a way of engaging in possibilities which arise not through the realization of something in potential but though relations and intensities folded through specific events. Discontinuities, disjunctures, and the apparently unconnected, become assembled through the performative space of the actual/virtual.
2. This relates to Deleuze's concept of the crystal image and memory as discussed in *Proust and Signs* and *Cinema 2: The Time-Image*.
3. As a Benedictine accountant, Angelo Pietra (1586), already pointed out in 1586: "numbers *are* figures."
4. In the context of art of memory practices: "[i]nventoried materials are counted and placed in locations within an overall structure which allows any item to be retrieved easily and at once" Carruthers, 1998, p. 11.

REFERENCES

Bolzoni, L. (1995). *La stanza della memoria. Modelli letterari e iconografici nell'età della stampa.* Turin: Einaudi (J. Parzen, Trans., *The Gallery of Memory: Literary and Iconographic Models in the Age of the Printing Press.* Toronto: University of Toronto Press).
Busco, C., and Quattrone, P. (2009). How management practices diffuse: the Balance Scorecard as a rhetorical machine. Working paper presented at the seminars of the accounting department of Harvard Business School, Manchester Business School, Babson College and the EAA annual congress, Tampere.
Camille, M. (1992). *Image on the Edge: The Margins of Medieval Art.* London: Reaktion books.
Carruthers, M. (1990). *The Book of Memory: A Study of Memory in Medieval Culture.* New York: Cambridge University Press.
———. (1998). *The Craft of Thought: Meditation, Rhetoric. and the Making of Images. 400–1200.* Cambridge: Cambridge University Press.
Czarniawska-Joerges, B., and Sevon, G. (2005). *Global Ideas: How Ideas, Objects and Practices Travel in a Global Economy.* Malmö: Liber and Copenhagen Business School Press.

Deleuze, G. (1989). *Cinema 2: The Time-Image*. (H. Tomlinson and R. Galeta, Trans.) Althone Press.

———. (2003). *Proust and Signs*. University of Minnesota Press.

Fabbri, P. (1998). *La svolta semiotica*. Bari: Laterza.

Hansen, A., and J. Mouritsen (1999). Managerial technology and netted networks. *Organization*, 6(3): 451–471.

Höpl, H. (2004). *Jesuit Political Thought: The Society of Jesus and the State, c. 1540–1630*. Cambridge, England: Cambridge University Press.

Johns, A. (1998). *The Nature of the Book: Print and Knowledge in the Making*. Chicago and London: University of Chicago Press

Jones, G., Mclean C., Quattrone, P. (2004). Spacing and Timing. *Organization*, 11(6), 723–741.

Kaplan, R. S., and D. P. Norton (1996). *The Balanced Scorecard: Translating Strategy into Action*. Boston, Havard Business School Press.

Latour, B. (1986) Visualization and cognition: Thinking with eyaes and hands. In H. Kuklick and E. Long (Eds.), *Knowledge and society: studies in the sociology of culture, past and present* (pp. 1–40). London: JAI Press.

———. (2005). *Reassembling the Social. An introduction to Actor-Network Theory*. Oxford: Oxford University Press.

Long, P. (2001) *Openness, Secrecy,Authorship : Technical Arts and the Culture of Knowledge from Antiquity to the Renaissance*. Baltimore: London: Johns Hopkins University Press.

Murray, A. (1978). *Reason and Society in the Middle Ages*. Oxford: Clarendon Press.

Nørreklit, H. (2003). The Balanced Scorecard: What is the Score? A Rhetorical Analysis of the Balanced Scorecard. *Accounting Organizations and Society*, 28(6), 591–619.

Orlikowski, W. (2000) Using Technology and Constituting Structures: A Practice Lens for Studying Technology in Organizations. *Organization Science*, 11(4), 404–428.

Pentcheva, B. V. (2006) The Performative Icon. *The Art Bulletin*, 88(4), 631–646.

Power, M. (1997). *The Audit Society. Rituals of Verification*. Oxford, England: Oxford University Press.

Quattrone, P., and Hopper, T. (2006) What Is IT?: SAP, Accounting, and Visibility in a Multinational Organisation. *Information and Organization*, 16(3), 212–250.

Quattrone, P. (2009). Books to Be Practiced. Memory, the Power of the Visual and the Success of Accounting. *Accounting Organizations and Society, 34*, 85–118.

Thrift, N. (2004). Thick Time. *Organization, 11*(6), 873–880.

———. (2007) *Non Representational Theory. Space. Politics. Affect*. London and New York: Routledge.

Yates, F. A. (1966). *The Art of Memory*. Chicago: University of Chicago Press.

Part I
Making Things and Practices (In)visible

1 Transparency or the New Invisibility
The Business of Making Connections

Barbara Maria Stafford

> 1.
> Money is talking
> to itself again
> in this season's
> bondage
> and safari look,
> its close out camouflage.
> Hit the refresh button
> And this is what you get,
> Money pretending
> That its hands are tied.
> 2.
> On a billboard by the 880,
> Money admonishes
> "Shut up and play."[1]

"In those days I would wrap myself up in someone else's personality, a set of clothes that I not only tried on but wore, as if I had none of my own—I did but they didn't yet fit; I was lost in the folds or I was too bound, or the colors weren't right: too faded, mismatched—I preferred someone else's" (Treat, 2009, p. 116).

The classicist Richard Seaford recently made the fascinating argument that the sixth-century Greek *polis* was the first society in history (with the possible exception of China) to be pervaded by money. He interprets this innovation as having had the unsettling repercussion of generating a sense of limitlessness responsible for suffusing and eventually undoing the city-states. Further, he identifies the revolutionary aspect of the notion as being that universal power resides not in the individual but in some elusive circulating material substance. Significantly, in the wake of this invention, a novel moral economy came to underlie both the abstract system of Ionian philosophy (that is, the possessive idea of the cosmos as a Zeus-ruled dominion) as well as the birth of tragedy (with its solitary heroes alienated from their closest kin and from the predatory gods, whose playthings they become.)[2]

Curiously, however, he does not link this extreme isolation of the individual, flailing away in a tyrannical and arbitrary monetary society, to the reverse of the same coin. I mean the fact that bottomless insatiability, personal greed, and the launching of succeeding epochs of "everlasting uncertainty and agitation" was predicated precisely on a supposedly *connective* system of business exchange. Today, the atomic unit of consumption resides not in metallurgy but in the physics of intangible data. Digital information supposedly allows you to fulfill all your needs, deregulating and disintegrating the integrated subject through text snippets and other fractioning rituals. Involuntary distribution and redistribution within a vast information technology (IT) system is not the same thing as voluntary performance.

But, ironically, Seaford's stark vision of the destruction of internal depth by the external forces of accumulation and the rise of indeterminacy no longer derives merely from devaluing speculation. I suggest, instead, that the contemporary resistance to any unitary or integrative category is paradoxically the product of an age of bundling connectivity. Our era is obsessed with figuring out and secretly managing the isolated consumer's relationship to clicks. This simulation of the partial user—partial because it omits imagination, kinesics (body language), paralanguage (pitch, tone, and wordless noises), and other ambiguous nonverbal cues such as the emotional power of touch—coexists alongside the exaggerated rhetoric about the Internet as an open, not opaque, communicative tie that always binds. Our culture is characterized, then, not just by its hostility to closure but by the questionable myth that countless fragmentary selves are transcendently gathered together in some hypermediated communal space that they democratically control.

Apparently, this libertarian belief in the individual as free agent continues to reign despite the sea change in the way consumers currently encounter the Web. Machine intelligence has moved from the grand vision of anthropomorphic automata and carnivalesque devices to innumerable "Turks" concealed inside the online Chess-Player's mysterious cabinet (Riley, 2009, pp. 368–369). Public debates and distraught concern over online privacy have spiraled as data companies proliferate.

Telemarketers have always known a great deal that we would rather not have them know about how we conduct our offline lives: income, credit score, debt, home ownership, favorite charities. But the ongoing and exponential explosion of the browser universe—with its free-floating digital bits begging to be coupled—has reached terrifying proportions. Some of these data-amassing companies (such as Acxiom and Datran Media) are beginning to closely connect buyer's offline with their online interests. As a *New York Times* front-page story recently proclaimed business is literally getting "deeply personal."[3]

Despite the obfuscation, a strong visual presence is central to conducting business on this occluded and darksome NET and not just because of the prevalence of advertising. Its true clout derives from a specious business ethics bandying about the fetching concept of "transparency" while muddying the Web's oceanic depths. Not a day goes by without further revelations concerning behind-the-scene market manipulations, Ponzi schemes, the liquidation of securities, various hedge-fund ruses, global intrigue, or just one more civil fraud case. Fiction apparently trumps plausibility every time.

For the moment, I want to single out the pivotal image of connectivity from this treacherous swamp. The electronic technology enabling invisible "behavioral tracking"—in which marketing companies lurk and log activities such as the Web pages users visit, the ads they click, and the terms they search for, then consolidate them into an "identity" that gets sold to linking marketers—is itself not new. Unseen tracking procedures involve a cookie being placed surreptitiously on the hard drive of a computer so that the unsuspecting user now roams the Internet cookie in tow, unknowingly announcing what sort of consumer he or she is. What gets innocently declared are things like one's age group, income level, home address, magazine subscriptions, and even public records. Persistent cookies, it seems, make it almost impossible for any user to go online without eventually being tracked, profiled, and quietly compared and connected to other unaware users—unless a deliberate effort is made to discover and delete or disable them.

Just as people who eat a lot of raw jalapeno peppers eventually become desensitized to mouth burning and eyes stinging, one has to wonder if there is such a thing as chronic economic desensitization. One neural theory about the development of a dietary tolerance—to capsicum in the case of red hot chilis—is that a neurotransmitter gets depleted so that people respond less vigorously to the initially painful ingredient the more they are exposed to it.[4] Is there a similar numbing effect in the matter of our growing exposure and becoming accustomed to hidden linking practices? The conjunction of volatile online with offline data occurs when it is least expected, for instance while someone routinely registers on a Web site or intentionally or even unintentionally just clicks onto a marketer's e-mail message. To be sure, the two leading companies claim that the cookie data they collect is anonymous and sold as such to advertisers on Facebook or Yahoo. Yet who has not been struck, when browsing those sites, by the aptness of the personalized pop-ups directing products to one's own real-world shopping habits!

Of course, sophisticated buyers should not be surprised that any time they release information into the great beyond of the Internet, that someone or, more likely, some thing, will automatically collect it. But it is also true that the ideal of a much-vaunted transparency refers only to the user's access to information, not to what is done to it behind the scenes. Even if no information gets posted, maintaining a low profile is a challenge. Internet security specialists sagely advise that the best rule of thumb is that you prevent private data from getting out there in the first place. But how does one manage this feat given the fact that on Snitch.name, for example, users can enter their own name or someone else's and watch as the site culls information from dozens of search engines, social networks, and directories?[5] As Paul M. Schwartz, a privacy expert and law professor at the University of California, Berkeley states "Interactive media really gets into this creepy Orwellian thing, where it's a record of our thoughts on the way to decision-making . . . We're like the data-input clerks now for the industry."[6]

Additionally, one must reckon with other clandestine optical technologies, as well as the problems attending them. These, too, involve worrisome linkages made by invisible tracking devices. Walt Disney Company's secretive new research facility in Austin, Texas, uses eye-tracking goggles to reveal how users respond to variable-sized ads. What ties these two selling phenomena together is disguise masquerading as transparency. Data-gathering and consolidating companies, as we have seen, measure and deduce online and offline habits from how many times people click on advertisements as well as on other items. Deception, in the case of the Disney research, derives from a different level of concealment. It is not the user's appetite—ostensibly for this or that television sports program (created by American Broadcasting Company (ABC), Entertainment and Sports Programming Network (ESPN), or Disney XD)—that is being tested but, rather, his reaction to how small product banners can visually become and still draw the viewer's attention.

This is clearly a pressing problem in a barracuda-competitive market saturated with smart machines (the Web, digital video recorders [DVRs]), overturning how we view television and thus shredding the entertainment industry's formerly successful money-making (from commercials) model.[7] But what of developing brain research on something even more elusive: all those millions of people who do not pause to click at all but whose eyes nevertheless flit across the screen. What can one tell about their neural activity while they are watching commercials?

Many of the favorite sites on the Web are supported by advertising. Art, film, media, and design historians, as well as visualists more generally, should therefore take note that behavioral psychology as well as neuroscience is trying to find out what sorts of *configurations* draw and hold the viewer's attention in a range of differently scaled electronic media: spanning banner ads, prerolls (those shots that play before a video), animated ads, live-action, and watermark ads.

To add to the dizzying complexity, this heterogeneous experiential media gets performed on variable and increasingly more intimately sized platforms, ranging from large plasma screens, to bookish Web pages, to sleek cell phones. There is a new physiognomics implicit in such law-seeking scientific research. This semiotic analysis of corporeal signs was redefined in its modern form as well as *systematized* in the late eighteenth century by Johann Caspar Lavater. Supposedly rigorously scientific, Enlightenment physiognomics minutely analyzed the arrangement of facial structure to a deeper explanatory and predictive purpose than had been done in antiquity and, notably, again during the seventeenth century.

Its aim was to seize an individual's most private inner characteristics from inadvertently betraying outward marks and to prognosticate from them about future actions.[8] Behavioral tracking thus is a sort of online physiognomics. To be sure, present-day analysis does not seek to probe the anatomical shape of the skull, or the tilt of a nose, or the wrinkles creasing a forehead. Rather, it attempts to make precise behavioral forecasts from a digital "portrait" whose revealing habits have been covertly assembled.

This patching together of elusive *patterns*—the electronic traces left by our paths of noticing—creates a decentralized and distributed subject. Not only is eye-tracking equipment deployed. A vast armamentarium of medical apparatus further dismembers the individual beholder: heart rate monitors, skin temperature readings, and the analysis of facial expressions via probes attached to cranial-maxillary muscles. Seizing whatever still remains invisible or inscrutable in the contemporary world demands, among other things, the collection of ever more intimate data concerning the kinds of images capable of capturing and retaining the fickle viewer's wandering gaze. Just like the behind-the-scenes maneuvering with concealed cookies, then, to sell ultrafast new media platforms entails ever-finer analyses of unsuspecting viewers' cognitive and perceptual functions and, ultimately, must deploy stealth devices.

Given this sharp-sighted media climate, Viktor Mayer-Schoenberger worries about the loss of "social forgetting" and the interminable recording of our every moment in a networked society rife with archived blog postings and dating sites. His chief concern is that we have created so many amnesia-proof tools that perhaps we need to design software that grows misty, erases like human memory, and can ultimately forget. In his book, *Delete: The Virtue of Forgetting in the Digital Age*, he refers mainly to social software where embarrassing things we said or ridiculous images we created years earlier might come back to haunt us since electronic files are so easily retrievable (Mayer-Schoenberger, 2009). Although intentional forgetting is a wonderful concept, it does not get at the problem of the exponential cobbling together and merger of online with offline data and the use of this information by businesses that have no intention of ever committing it to oblivion.

This brings me back to the Greeks. The hubris of predictability saturates the media industry caught up in trying to determine exactly the changing ways people consume visual or experiential media. But consider the lessons learned from earlier mass media, like television reporting or film and video documentaries, and their relevance to the new personalized or "tailored" media of exposure. We cannot predict the specifics of disasters, for example, but we can anticipate them. Hence, businesses take measures to protect themselves against hurricanes in Miami and earthquakes in Tokyo. The valid assumption, based on prior experience, is that, given enough time, bad things will undoubtedly happen.

But, what of events that are so infrequent and unpredictable that it would be uneconomic, if not foolhardy, to take prior action against them? The likelihood of two airplanes demolishing two of the largest structures in the world is so small as to be indiscernible, but it did happen. No one could have predicted that (with the exception of the uncommunicative terrorists). Perhaps *something* of the physical and urban extent of the impact, however, could have been foreseen.

The impact on the surrounding businesses could also be have been assessed. Businesses, both those in the Twin Towers and those nearby, might have been able to predict the destruction of their premises and the simultaneous unavailability of former space, transportation, and telecommunications. So one might conclude that companies could have planned for some of the major impacts, if not the causes, of such an event.[9] But at the personal and relational level—for those who died—no degree of predictability would have sufficed.

So the question to ask is not how probable an event is, but rather what the response would be to the failure of any of the necessary conditions for running a business, such as access to and use of buildings, computer systems or vital records, availability of people, ability to communicate or travel, and preservation of health and safety. We may not know what will constitute failure if such things occur, but a company is derelict in not recognizing, prioritizing, and mobilizing in the face of predictable surprises. Should the same guidelines not hold for Internet security? And should the same precautionary standards not be applied to guard against deluding promises of transparency and stealthy Internet "connective" procedures?

But there is a larger issue bedeviling the public, greater than stalking or categorizing media surfers, or trying to predict precisely what sorts of advertising designs will be effective in the future. It is the migration of the neurosciences into the marketing sector, more generally. Observing and analyzing the minute decision-making behavior of the unaware consumer is as nothing compared to the eruption of lightning fast, so-called "flash" stock trading techniques, worrying not only the Securities and Exchange Commission (SEC) but economists worldwide. Blink-like, high-frequency computerized trading allows a semi-private "dark pool" of traders—comprising a collection of select investors—a 30-millisecond glimpse at buy or sell orders before they get routed to everyone else.[10] Like many supposedly transparent and public connective dealings fostered on the Internet, this sort of trading is anonymous as well as institutional, involving large investors and big blocks of shares. Again IT favors faster and riskier interactions based on the invisibility of dark pool members and the inscrutability of their intentions to an audience that does not have fair access.[11]

But there are positive initiatives to be noted as well—beyond the dubious computer science currently operating on Wall Street reaping billions for the invisible few. These point to the potential for massive gathering and integrating of data as a *visible* phenomenon: following the flow of ideas across cyberspace on sites and blogs or opening up new frontiers for diverse applications. Instead of powerful algorithms automatically executing millions of orders a second and scanning dozens of private and public marketplaces simultaneously—confounding smaller investors by issuing and almost immediately canceling orders—media clouds are for everyone. Although the impact of cloud computing (third-party data hosting and service-oriented computing) has cybersecurity implications, it holds the potential for more open interaction between true stakeholders. It affirms that the Web provides a tremendous resource not just for measuring what millions of people will buy but for observing how they interact.

Certainly, the recent data surge has foregrounded the need for a sophisticated clustering of what is merely the raw material of knowledge. The Internet, private networks, virtual private networks, and a host of other technologies are weaving the planet into "a massively complex 'infosphere.'" But as Joseph F. Coates—one of emerging technology's most acute observers—aptly remarks "The Internet is [also] a mess, open to all kinds of uses, misuses, antisocial material, irksome intrusions from ads, identity theft, international swindles, and on and on . . . For these reasons, as well as the potential for national security interventions and general hell raising, it is time to plan, design, and execute over the next five to seven years a replacement for the Internet."[12]

Given the current flood of disconnected data, I have not been denying the urgent need to find and perform conjunctions. Rather, I have been addressing the soft underbelly of a false connectivity: the secretive capturing and coordinating of personal information about an individual—spanning the online and life worlds—by manufacturers and sellers that covertly categorize or brand them. One might think here of Ray Kurzweil's prediction concerning the "Singularity's" event horizon: the moment "when our artifacts will be so intelligent that they can design themselves, and we will not understand how they work."[13]

On the other hand, the trawling of vast troves and new realms by the computer has also created the need for a novel statistician capable of making sense of the results.[14] Just as there is a requirement for taxonomy in the natural world—the sorting, naming, and recognizing of deep-seated, even universal, patterns characterizing myriad organisms [15]—the strange and confusing Internet awaits its taxonomist to classify its artificial life forms and to chart its Darwinian *ars combinatoria*. Perhaps even a deep-seated categorizing function, akin to that classifying natural objects but dedicated specifically to organizing synthetic entities, will be discovered within the temporal lobes of the brain. These anchoring neural regions help us avoid being at sea when inundated by a deluge of conflicting spatialized information. Conceivably the most exciting research discovery might yet be that *no* distinction obtains between noticing and sorting real and virtual phenomena. Ordering and understanding the multiple dimensions we inhabit thus opens the alluring prospect for reconnecting them physically, mentally, and ethically.

Consider, for example, the exciting development of a robust, comprehensive, and reliable database—available to the public—that is able to track the daily rhythm of the global news cycle over time. Mediacloud.org. allows you to *watch* the *shaping* of vibrant issues or the *forming* and mutating of contagious ideas before the eyes. Viewers can see, pursue, and evaluate the evolution and variation in coverage around an actual situation from carefully mapped findings. This sort of link analysis is exciting because, while the data is collected by the computer, it requires an intelligent and attentive viewer to evaluate the competitive reports swirling around the cloud of events arising on any given day.[16]

True, graphs can display the lasting power or disappearing act of a specific news item, but they cannot flesh them out. It might help to imagine this protean visual process as resembling the recursive performance of doing/undoing recorded by Bill Viola in his two-part video, *Dissolution*. This mesmerizing work shows a man and a woman whose nebulous features lift and resolve themselves over and over again into clarity before once more subsiding indistinctly back into a pool of rippling water.[17]

Similarly, the automatic scanning of hundreds of sources proves that an elusive item or situation cannot be delivered or redelivered enough times. This looping out and coming back invites questions posed by thinking individuals to what is, after all, merely a variable media landscape. Media Cloud is still in its early stages. Nonetheless, it already declares itself as a *tool* for imaging how an idea sketchily starts and then coalesces as it travels through the intricate byways of the public sphere. What is made visible in this case is not the collecting mechanism but that the collected information requires human agency. Like Viola's constantly shifting imagery, this animated database forces us to see what is both inside and outside the computational box. It, too, segues from the presentational to the abstract, summoning us to reconnect embodied with disembodied data.

Time has a way of bringing good ideas back to our conscious awareness. While realizing that businesses need to encourage innovation, far-sightedness, and investments in virtual technologies, I want to bring to the fore an overlooked visual medium. Even in quick message board land, there is nothing more illuminating than face-to-face exchange, assisting in the interpretation of one person to another in real-life situations.

In light of the ambiguities and subterfuge surrounding Internet business and social networking, it is fascinating that Cindy Sherman became famous by pretending to be someone else. She is a notable early practitioner of "extreme impersonation," i.e., those performance hoaxes made notorious by Web perpetrators and pranksters.[18] I want to conclude my reflections on the new online invisibility masquerading as transparency by reflecting on how randomness (Mlodinow, 2009) not only rules our lives but also eludes the predatory digital connectionist. As we have seen, robots increasingly administer the daily operations of electric grids and stock markets. What humanly created chaotic performances, then, are capable of eluding this smart equipment? What thought processes do we undergo when chance confronts us and, more to the point, how do we craft and make them visible?

Perhaps no one since the American Gilded Age writer, Edith Wharton, has so superbly conjured the transformation of the self with makeup, wigs, even prosthetics, and skillful lighting. Cindy Sherman's photographic work challenges the perception that humans are immune to change. Like the early-twentieth-century author, she uncovers ingrained patterns of behavior in order to visualize and then help us to abandon an unthinking status quo. Consider, for example, Wharton's description of the second Mrs. Peyton: "a scented silvery person whose lavender silks and neutral-tinted manner expressed a mind with its blinds drawn down toward all the unpleasant-nesses of life" (Wharton, 2001, p. 7).

Visual art as well as literature has much to offer the millennial genera-tion of digital media users. Instant messaging and a raft of Web sites are building communication communities as complex, involved, random, and evasive in terms of personal revelation, as those existing entirely in the outside world. So, perhaps, there is a telling link after all binding the hal-lucinatory labyrinth of artificial life to the maze of reality, one unsuspected by the spying and encrypting marketers.

Sherman's alternative lifestyle rehearsals should be considered as a kind of drastic physiognomics, perfectly suited to our contemporary prankonomy. After all, the leap from prank to scam, from sham to fraud, from being hood-winked to getting gamed, is not great! These abundant reimaginings of a per-sonal situation, the potential for success as well as failure began in the late 1970s. Back then, she pioneered the tongue-in-cheek *Untitled Film Stills* (69 black and white images of Sherman impersonating 69 different characters ranging from office worker, bimbo, high school girl, femme fatale, and so on). Such clever disguises—now routinely featured straight-faced on those Faux-toshops called social networks (craigslist, YouTube, or Facebook)—should be regarded as the first salvo in the use of the single-image "constructed" photo.

But what originally was a Vogue-ish or playfully fashionable dress-up occasion for a consummate performance artist has evolved into non-stop acting from which there is no escape. In the age of Twitter, everyone is a digital mountebank; everyone is a credulous mark. In this media swamp, Sherman's subsequent work remains remarkable because it shows the gaps between the arcane props—wigs, mannequin heads, fake body parts, false teeth, plastic toys, hilarious novelties, thrift-store outfits—and the indelible person lurking underneath the paraphernalia.

In her latest series of fictional female portraits, Sherman probes deeper into the ruses that produce a shifty reality. In her hands, the frightening shape of actuality never ceased being an uncharted region of conjecture. But after three decades, her physical experiments with the body have become extended to include her own experience of aging. Sherman's long habit of visualizing identity enhancement continues to produce an imaginative world that is both familiar and strange. The fourteen pictures in the artist's current show (now on world tour) significantly no longer use 35-mm film but digital technology.[19] Seeing the results of role-playing suddenly became much easier: enabling the generation of test color prints of the composition and the quick addition of adjustments or the deletion of details.

It may seem we have drifted away from the issue of connectivity. But, in fact, the new worry in the business world is also about social compari-sons creating a dysfunctional and fragmented workplace. Apparently, it is envy—not just greed—that is the big problem. According to Jackson Nickerson and Todd Zenger of the Olin Business School at Washington University in St. Louis, nothing risks stirring up more discord in an organization than a sense of entitlement or the "self-serving bias."[20] Collaboration, that is, a real sense of connection to a group, is undercut by perceptions of superiority or specialness that are not founded on genuine accomplishments. Envy, significantly, is dialectical at root. This intrinsically comparative passion is also acutely critical: seeing in another person what is not to be found in oneself. Like Sherman's vulnerable show-off characters, this duality makes for satire and compassion, cruelness and tenderness, and humiliation and nobility.

Her new work is so emotionally powerful because it is not caricature. The artist goes through with her fictional figures what they attractively and unattractively go through themselves. Each subtly "doctored" image presents Sherman as representing a woman of a certain age, as she has created or willed herself to be seen by a youth-seeking audience that, like herself, is *critical* of the visible results. Unlike the morphed imagery—or smoothed and "improved" data—frequently found on the Internet, there is no question of seamless masking here. Rather, as Wharton remarks about her heroine Kate Orme in the short story, "Sanctuary," it is more as if "the pink shades had simply been lifted from the lamps, and she saw him (her fiancé Denis Peyton) for the first time in an unmitigated glare." (p. 18). Sherman, like Wharton, reminds us—and it is reminder that might be heeded by the online world of business—about the tactics of *exposure*.

Here is Wharton again: "[E]xposure does not alter the features, but it lays an ugly emphasis on the most charming lines, pushing the smile to a grin, the curve of good-nature to the droop of slackness. And it was precisely into the flagging lines of extreme weakness that Denis's graceful contour flowed . . ." (Wharton, 2001, pp. 334–335). Exposure is letting the viewer see simultaneously, and in a flash, the core of a person and what has happened to him or her. This relentless stripping action resembles a raking strobe light shed both on a physical as well as a moral process.

This brings me back to money. It is not coincidental that what is exposed to Wharton's perceptive protagonist is that in this convoluted tale about a brother's suicide and his despairing and now dead mistress and their child, that "the [inheritance] money, of course, had made a difference." In fact, the previously baffled Kate Orme suddenly sees that there had been no real struggle in the mind of Denis who "stepped happily into affluence" over the body of his deceased stepbrother and his irregular menage.

Sherman similarly startles us with the anguish of discovery through the broken defenses of self-presentation. Her over-50 affluent women, dressed to kill, exert on the beholder both the concrete pressure of the undeniable facts of inexorable aging and the valor of the battle waged against it. Her art of exposure models one antidote to Internet fraud—by declaring the perplexity of any situation. To be sure, each of Sherman's images presents a poised and controlled woman coming from a wealthy social class: variously bejeweled, elegantly attired, majestic in stature, or carefully coiffed, and standing in an obviously elite museum or fine home setting. But there is always the telling point, the sign of psychological fragility leaking around the carefully guarded edges. What makes her work so strong, effective, and even ethical is this double-presence of artifice and reality.

Enhancement, then, does not necessarily mean absolute simulation. Even grand adornments and massive amounts of cosmetic surgery do not add up to a single sustainable illusion. Like Wharton, Sherman practices an interventionist inlay style. Strategies of avoidance or denial vanish at the interstices where untidy truth gets exposed: these are characters who have all "paid some price." I am proposing that, analogously, the invisible entanglements of data on the Web might become more transparent when the implicit as well as the explicit allows itself to be summoned from the morass and made visible.

NOTES

1. Armantrout, R. (2009, August 3). Money Talks, *New Yorker,* 63.
2. Seaford, R. (2009, June, 19) World Without Limits. The Greek Discovery That Man Could Never Be Too Rich. Commentary, *Times Literary Supplement,* pp. 14–15.
3. Clifford, S. (2009, July 31). Ads Follow Web Users, and Get Deeply Personal. *The New York Times,* pp. A1, A3.
4. Ray, C. C. (2009, August 11). Red Hot Chili Peppers. *The New York Times, Science Times,* p. D2.
5. Sarno, D. (2009, August 18). Little escapes the Internet's Eye. *Chicago Tribune* , p. 15.
6. Clifford, "Ads," A 3.
7. Barnes, B. (2009, July 27). Watching You Watching Ads. *The New York Times,* pp. B1, B6.
8. On Lavater, see Stafford, B. M. (1991) *Body Criticism. Imaging the Unseen in Enlightenment Art and Medicine.* Cambridge, MA. and London: MIT Press, pp. 120–129.
9. Jean-Philippe Pastor, PHONEREADER Library. http://www.frenchtheory.com/ (last accessed April 2011). Also see the journal French Metablog with different posts.
10. Duhigg, C. (2009, July 24). S.E.C. Starts Crackdown on 'Flash' Trading Techniques. *The New York Times,* pp. B1, B8.
11. Duhigg, C. (2009, July 24). Traders Profit with Computers Set at High Speed. *The New York Times,* pp. A1, A13.
12. Cetron, M. J., and Davies, O. (2009, September–October). Ten Critical Trends for Cybersecurity. *The Futurist* pp. 42–43.
13. Cetron, M. J., and Davies, O. (2009, September–October). Ten Critical Trends for Cybersecurity. *The Futurist,* p. 41.
14. Lohr, S. (2009, August 6) For Today's Graduate, Just One Word: Statistics. *The New York Times,,* pp. A1, A3.
15. Yoon, C. K., (2009, August 11). Reviving the Lost Art of Naming the World, *The New York Times, Science Times,* pp. D1, D4.

16. Cohen,P. (2009, August 5). Hot Story to Has-Been: Tracking News via Cyberspace. *The New York Times,* pp. C1, C8.
17. From the exhibition *Unbounded: New Art for a New Century,* Newark Museum, Summer 2009. See newarkmuseum.org/museum_default_page. aspx?id=7532 (last accessed April 2011).
18. Leckart, S. (2009, September). The Age of the Prank. *Wired,* pp. 89–93.
19. Kazanjian, D. (2009). A Brave Face. *Vogue,* August, pp. 150–153.
20. Wagner, C. G. (2009, September–October). Bad Attitudes, Bad Business. *The Futurist,* p. 18.

REFERENCES

Mayer-Schoenberger, V. (2009). *Delete: The Virtue of Forgetting in the Digital Age.* Cambridge, MA: Harvard University Press.
Mlodinow, L. (2009). *The Drunkard's Walk. How Randomness Rules Our Lives.* New York: Random House.
Riley, T. (2009). Composing for the Machine, *European Romantic Review,* 20(3), 368–369.
Treat, J. (2009). Little Bitches. In *Meat Eaters and Plant Eaters, Stories* (p. 116). Rochester, N.Y: BOA Editions.
Wharton, E. (2001). Sanctuary. In M. Howard, M. (Ed.), *Collected Stories* (pp. 334–335). New York: Library of America.

2 Business Fiction

Global Economy by William Gibson

Barbara Czarniawska

> Cyberspace. A consensual hallucination experienced daily by billions of legitimate operators, in every nation, by children being taught mathematical concepts ... A graphic representation of data abstracted from the banks of every computer in the human system. Unthinkable complexity. Lines of light ranged in the nonspace of the mind, clusters and constellation of data. (William Gibson, *Neuromancer* (NR), 1984, p. 67)

Interviewed by Scandinavian journalist Sindre Kartvedt (1994/1995), Gibson admitted that he had coined the word "cyberspace," and added that it had already been incorporated into the *Oxford English Dictionary*. A talent for predicting the future—even the ability to shape the future with his works, had been attributed to him, but this was not how he saw it: "I always assumed that I was writing about the present anyway ... The future was already here. It just hadn't been very evenly distributed yet" (Kartvedt, 1994/1995, p. 55).

This chapter was written on the assumption that Gibson's work contributes to a more even distribution, bringing to light the images of economic activities that do exist, although less known or only partially represented in the literature of fact. I have chosen his work rather than that of the other well-known representative of cyberfiction, Neal Stephenson, because Stephenson, a Master of Business Administration (MBA), has a distinct theory of the global economy incorporated in his work. A confrontation with such implicit economic and management theories would also be of interest, but the focus in this volume is on images. Gibson is more of an ethnographer; the global economy forms a background for his plots—a taken-for-granted image worth exploring.

Although I am unaware of another analysis of business activities in Gibson's work, my choice of it can hardly be seen as surprising. As Douglas Kellner put it, it is "William Gibson and the cyberpunks who have carried out some of the most important mappings of our present moment and its future trends" (1994, p. 299).

I begin by sketching a general image of the global economy in Gibson's works, followed by a presentation of its main actors: freelancers, corporations, and products and services. To facilitate reading, I use abbreviations of the titles of Gibson's works, a complete list of which can be found at the end of the text.

THE ECONOMIC LANDSCAPE

In Gibson's universe there are two centers: Japan and the Boston-Atlanta Metropolitan Axis (BAMA or the Sprawl). The rest of the globe consists of many small countries. Even California is divided into two parts: NoCal and SoCal. In later works Gibson indicated that the Japanese center may be moving toward Moscow (Russians start showing up in *Virtual Light* (VL), and by *Idoru* (ID) there are Russian gangsters, prostitutes, and designers)—or perhaps China. Costa Rica is a data haven—the cyber equivalent of Switzerland, hiding data rather than money—whereas Cyprus is the tax haven for Russians[1].

Cash is already illegal in Gibson's Japan by 1984 (NR: p. 13), but some old paper currency, like the New Yen and United States (US) dollars show up now and then. Credits chips are used (*Count Zero* [CZ]: p. 43), as they are in the factual world.

Money-laundering businesses flourish, particularly in Singapore and Hong Kong. One of the cyberspace cowboys pays a money-laundering company a yearly percentage that is likely equivalent to what he would have paid in taxes (CZ: p. 172). In one of Gibson's latest books, *Spook Country* (SC), a whole container of money that was to be used to provide help to the Iraqi government and had been stolen; the "good guys" contaminate it with cesium to prevent laundering.

The main actors are the multinationals (including the Mafia); the military; the banks; small businesses and single entrepreneurs; and last but not least, the freelancers. The black-and-white markets are entangled beyond separation, as are the criminal and legal activities. The main industries are biotechnology; narcotics; the pop music industry, and entertainment in general; and, obviously, information technology, at the service of all the other industries.

There are myriad small businesses, usually old-fashioned and shady, like JULIUS DEANE IMPORT EXPORT (NR: p. 21). The bridge between San Francisco and Oakland is full of such businesses: tattoo parlors, gaming arcades, magazine stalls, betting shops, sushi bars, pawnbrokers, herbalists, hairdressers, and bars (*Virtual Light* (VL): p. 66). Many serve as covers for freelancers, temps, or agents of big corporations.

To use economic terms, it can be said that Gibson describes what Baumol at al. (2007) have defined as "good capitalism" (that is, good for the growth and prosperity of US): a combination of entrepreneurial and big-firm capitalism.

The authorities and public services are few, and they usually lose when in conflict with the other actors. There is an energy utility, Eastern Seaboard Fission Authority (which for a while could actually be seen on http://eastern-seaboardfissionauthority.com, now (29 March 2011), accessible to gamers only); it delivers electricity, but also checks on potential competitors who attempt to dabble in nuclear power (*Mona Lisa Overdrive* [MLO]:p. 83). The BAMA Transit Authority runs public transportation, and includes the

Turing Registry, which issues Single Identification Numbers (SINs; MLO: p. 64) and the Turing Police, controlling the development of Artificial Intelligences (NR, CZ).

In virtual reality, there are cities and countries, some replicating the actual ones, some products of Gibson's fantasy. Among the latter, Walled City deserves special attention. It is a multi-user domain that went secret after regulations and monitoring had been introduced into cyberspace and developed in a complex world of its own—Gibson's clear warning against any attempt to regulate cyberspace. Many young people (33,000 people originally; ID: p. 184) live primarily in Walled City, rarely returning to the physical world (ID: p. 125). They learn languages there, make designs, work, and play. But Walled City has no address, and one can enter by invitation only.

There are the vestiges of the old world in Gibson's world—there is mention of governments, churches, and airlines; but because they are not important to the plots of the stories, I am omitting them. His invented universe is relatively stable, however; I am able to discuss it thematically or according to actors because both themes and actors come back in several of his works. Actors—human and otherwise—develop, age, and remember previous events.

There is an enormous number of ecological, "green" activities and technologies in Gibson's world, accompanied by an equally enormous amount of garbage, waste, and pollution. The former is concentrated primarily where rich people reside, the latter among the poor.

There is another element of his universe worthy of mention, although it seems to be taken for granted. Saskia Sassen (2001) has suggested that one of the phenomena caused by ongoing globalization is increased connectivity: more and more places becoming more quickly connected to one another. In Gibson's universe, it is not only places that are undergoing this process; it is also people, machines, and organizations. Connectivity permeates the whole world, from top to bottom:

> Case had always taken it for granted that the real bosses, the kingpins in a given industry, would be both more and less than people. . . . He'd always imagined it as a gradual and willing accommodation of the machine, the system, the parent organism. It was the root of street cool, too, the knowing posture that implied connection, invisible lines up to hidden levels of influence (NR: p. 243).

The point is that what seems to be hierarchically structured is, in effect, circular; thus there are no ultimate levels of influence, only many dispersed centers that connect and disconnect as needed. And not only real bosses, but everybody in Gibson's works is more and less than human; they are all cyborgs, they have all been remade by biotech, and most of them are on drugs. In this, Gibson's vision is reminiscent of Huxley's (1924) *Brave New World* but with the opposite result: the consequence is extreme individuation rather than conformity.

Individual characters are central for Gibson's narrative, but their impact on cyberspace, which is dominated by supercomputers, artificial intelligence devices, and data banks, is minimal. And, as Allucquere Rosanne Stone (1992/2007, p. 444) pointed out, "[t]here is no reason to believe that the cyberspaces being designed at NASA or Florida will be any different."

FREELANCERS AND TEMPS

> He was a perpetual outsider, a rogue factor adrift on the secret seas of intercorporate politics. No company man would have been capable of taking the initiatives Turner was required to take in the course of an extraction. No company man was capable of Turner's professionally casual ability to realign his loyalties to fit a change in his employees. Or, perhaps, in his unyielding commitment once a contract had been agreed upon. (CZ: pp. 128–129)

The freelancers deserve special attention in this text, for two reasons. In the first place, the phenomenon of freelancers and temps has received recent attention in the management and organization literature (see e.g., Bergström and Storrie, 2003; and Barley and Kunda, 2004). Although the phenomenon has been presented in a relatively objective manner by the researchers, who pointed out the good and bad sides of freelancing and contingent employment, their opinions about the world of practice were overwhelmingly positive. Freelancing meant the death of bureaucracy, a liberation of talents, and a free field for creativity—and the sacrifice of security seemed like a worthwhile tradeoff (Storrie, 2003). The 2008/2009 financial crisis has brought the reality of freelancers and temps much closer to the one presented by Gibson: desperate, aging, in search of employment, and living without a security net. Yet even Barley and Kunda's book, based on a 1999 study, and published after the crisis of those times, ended with the conclusion that the phenomenon will remain and that the drastic changes brought about by the global economy are on the way. Happy or desperate, the freelancers and contingent workers are supposed to become a stable characteristic of the contemporary world, just as they are in Gibson's works.

There is a second reason for freelancers to be worthy of special attention: they are actually the main heroes of Gibson's stories, as the quote at the beginning of this section amply illustrates. They come in several variations.

Cyberspace Cowboys and Ronins

Freelancers are either cyberspace cowboys, or "ronins,"[2] and most often cyberpunks, dressed in black leather jackets. The difference is not large. Console cowboys shoot when necessary, and ronins are hi-tech experts. The prototype of the cyberspace cowboys is Johnny Mnemonic (JM, first love of ronin Molly [JM, NR, MLO]), whose freelancing career dwindled as he became a memory deposit for other people. In time, and with Molly's help, he turned it into an asset and the basis of a small company that he ran with Molly and a super-intelligent dolphin called Jonas.

The most advantageous contracts for freelancers come from big corporations. If the contract has been fulfilled to everybody's satisfaction, they will deposit their pay into Swiss bank accounts and then erase their traces from the corporate memory (*New Rose Hotel* [NRH]: p. 112). If not (and there is usually a hitch, to keep the plot going), they would cancel their credit and often attempt to kill them or damage their brains (NRH: p. 14). Such was the fate of Molly's second lover, Case, who became "just another hustler, trying to make it through" (NR: p. 11), before he was bio-repaired to enter yet another contract.

The freelancers usually begin as highly talented young forces. Their fate changes, either because of their hubris, which propels them to take on the corporate giants, or, if they began their working lives in military, state or corporate bureaucracies, because of a betrayal from those higher up (NR: p. 104). Age is their enemy: 28 is old for a console cowboy (*Burning Chrome* [BC]: p. 170), so the goal is to make big money and to get out of freelancing (BC: p. 178). Longevity is no more than five years (CZ: p. 172). This career path is reminiscent of the young people of Silicone Valley and of Wall Street, who made big money and retired to their vineyards, their ecological farms, and other places of calm and wealth. In Gibson's work, and probably in real life as well, they usually fail. Still, they overreach themselves—not from greed, but because of their search for a secure life. When they succeed (temporarily; Gibson is not into happy endings), like when they demolish Chrome's brothel in BR, they would give the bulk of the money to charities and keep only 10% of it, paying 60% for laundering service (BR: p. 188). There are exceptions: Wig from CZ became rich by stealing obsolete software being sent to the Third World, "incidentally bringing about the collapse of at least three governments and causing untold human suffering" (CZ: p. 173). But he later atones.

When contracted, usually paired with ronins, console cowboys hack into corporate cyberspace, in a double sense. They "cut the ice," that is, break through the protective software (ICE—Intrusion Countermeasures Electronix, BC: p. 169), an action accompanied by an actual intrusion, which usually follows the pattern of a bank robbery. Both parties risk death: cyberspace cowboys from "black ice" that kills the intruder (BC: p. 182) and ronins from actual weapons.

Another freelancer job is that of a corporate extractor, mentioned in the initial quote of this section—a variation of headhunter. The corporate extractor specializes in corporate "shifts": moving top executives, and more often top researchers, from one corporation to another (CZ: p. 14). The operation begins with an extraction, followed by a medical cleansing, in case the employee has a cortex bomb or some other security device implanted (CZ: p. 132). This step is followed by relocation, usually accomplished by permission and with the cooperation of the person involved. If thefts of hardware, software, and bioware are modeled on bank burglaries, a corporate extraction is patterned on a guerilla attack (CZ). Additional complications may arise when corporate defectors are uncertain of their intentions.

Freelancers can also abduct celebrities, such as show-business stars, for ransom or in order to ruin the show (MLO: p. 198).

Pattern Recognizers

Pattern recognition is more than a job; it is an ability possessed only by certain persons. Because this ability is in great demand, pattern recognizers can easily find employment on a temporary basis (ID) or they can freelance (*Pattern Recognition*, PR). These cyberspace dowsers, a.k.a. "netrunners," often present themselves as "researchers"; they are able to see patterns in oceans of data, and locate critical nods—those that presage future developments (ID: p. 25). This ability may be a result of an experimental drug (ID) or a childhood experience (PR). They are subject to a kind of attention deficit, which allows them to peruse an enormous amount of data rapidly, like dedicated zappers, and arrive at a pattern.

Another type of a dowser contracted by advertisers is the "coolhunter," who recognizes patterns in the world of global marketing (PR: pp. 2, 8). Allergic to fashion and labels (Naomi Klein's *No Logo. Taking Aim at the Brand Bullies*, 2000, was published three years before PR), Cayce is "a very specialized piece of human litmus paper" (p. 13), probably because of some "tame pathology" of hers (PR: p. 94). She can be contracted by advertisers or manufacturers who want her to keep track of street fashion, but she is not managerial material.

> . . . Cayce is not someone you hire to run an agency in London. Not someone you hire to run anything. She is hyper-specialized, a freelancer, someone contracted to do a very specific job. She has seldom had a salary. She is entirely a creature of fees, adamantly short-term, no managerial skills whatever. (PR: p. 61)

But there is not only a lack of skills operating here; freelancers usually look at corporate employees with contempt. They call them "lifers" because they sign indentures (CZ: p. 145), and see the world of lifers as tribal (CZ: p. 128). The executive trainees at the computer corporation Ono-Sendai, for example, undergo a "tearful graduation ceremony" (MLO: p. 119), during which they demonstrate loyalty to their zaibatsu, an obvious allusion to the Japanese corporate rituals from the 1980s. A freelancer who has been forced to accept a stable employment is a loser (ID: p. 2).

Temps

The situation of temps differs slightly from that of cyberspace cowboys and ronins. Like them, they need a job, but they are not as strongly opposed to employment. The temps can have been freelancers or can become freelancers when they come into conflict with their company. One such company is IntenSecure, which specializes in "rentacop" services (VL: pp. 6, 9). Security is needed everywhere—in corporate buildings and gated communities alike (VL: p. 31). Rentacops wear the uniforms of their company (VL: p. 58), and are not allowed to carry guns—only stunners—although they do not always obey the law (VL: p. 59). They receive information from the same source as the police do: a Southern California Geosynclinical Law Enforcement Satellite, popularly called Death Star (VL: pp. 13–14). "They said the Death Star could read headlines on a newspaper, or what brand and size of shoes you wore, from a decent footprint" (VL: p. 275). IntenSecure is also connected, probably illegally, to the even bigger DatAmerica (VL: p. 119).

The couriers and messengers own their own equipment and work on commission. They are required because the seamless web of communication between offices can be seen as porous: there is always the risk that a message will be intercepted, unbeknown to the sender (VL: pp. 97–98). Moving through city traffic, they are prone to accidents, but the company that hires them is not responsible for their insurance. Nanofaxes, which could replace messengers, appeared later in Gibson's work (ID).

CORPORATIONS

There are zaibutsus, the "normal" multinationals, and there is Yakuza—a corporate criminal organization, which is a merger of the Mafia, Cammora, and other criminal groups. As in the real world, however, the difference is only in legality. Yakuza is a true multinational, owning satellites and space shuttles (BC: p. 8). Like every other corporation, Yakuza is a part of the information economy, able to trace any individual if necessary, following all the bits and pieces that every person leaves in the cyberspace (BC: pp. 16–17). Kombinat (ID: p. 3) is a later addition: a Russian hybrid of government and the Mafia.

As for the zaibatsus, they control entire economies (NRH: p. 103), even whole continents in the inter-corporate sea (NRH: p. 106). Their survival depends not on people, but on information. The point is, however, not an accumulation of information as such, but of the information edge. The information is represented in the matrix—in an abstract representation of the relationships among data systems (BC: p. 169), usually in a graphic form. Thus the Mitsubishi Bank of America has green cubes, the Military has spirals (NR: p. 69), and the London Stock Exchange's roof is connected with the roofs of all neighboring City units on the Web (MLO: pp. 270–271).

If corporations expand or merge, it can be seen graphically on the Web (MLO: p. 254). Legitimate employees can access their employer's sector of the matrix; the hackers have to cut the ice first—the ice walls that are invisible to the employees whose work is thus protected.

The corporation is a life form, independent of the lives of people who comprise it (NRH: p. 107). What life form? Describing the multinational Tessier-Ashpool (T-A), but also other corporations in NR, Gibson used the metaphor of a wasp's nest: "hives with cybernetic memories, vast single organizations, their DNA coded in silicon" (NR: p. 242). As Gibson explained:

> Power, in Case's world, meant corporate power. The zaibatsus, the multinationals that shaped the course of the human history had transcended old barriers. Viewed as organisms, they had attained a kind of immortality. You couldn't kill a zaibatsu by assassinating a dozen key executives; there were others waiting to step up the ladder, assume the vacated position, access the vast banks of corporate memory. (NR: p. 242)

The metaphor of a hive is not unknown, but it is more often used in a benign version of a beehive. Bees may be hierarchical and totalitarian, but they produce honey; wasps merely cause pain and carry danger.

Anachronisms, Still Going Strong

Tessier-Ashpool is nominally a public company, but its shares had not been in the open market for centuries (NR: p. 95). Shy of the media, it owns—discreetly—many things, including the Freeside Orbital Resort. It hides itself partly through a chain of ownerships—Bockris Systems GmbH, Frankfurt, is owned by Reinhold Scientific AG, Berne—and with the removal of three more companies, T-A is revealed (NR: pp. 157–158).

It started with the marriage of a Tessier heir to a fortune based on biochemistry patents; she married an Ashpool, a son of the owner of a large engineering firm from Melbourne—a marriage that was a merger (MLO: p. 133). They soon divested themselves of their previous holdings, investing in orbital properties and shuttle utilities. At that time, the orbital space contained some military stations and the first automated factories owned by cartels. The owners of T-A established a data haven in the orbit—badly needed by some sectors of the international banking community. The community repaid in generous loans, so that T-A was able to build Freeside Orbital Resort—of lunar concrete (MLO: p. 134). The orbital archipelago expanded, and Freeside became more and more prosperous. It contains every conceivable type of pleasure and business necessity: data banks, gambling places, spas, and so on and so forth. Only a patent trial revealed that T-A continued to invest heavily in research, focusing particularly on Artificial Intelligence.

Tessier-Ashpool resembles other corporations, but with a difference: it remains a family-owned company, and thus is an anachronism. The members of the family who run the company are either cryoned or cloned and thus immortal. While cryopreservation is an actual fact, it takes little effort to see cloning as a metaphor for the type of cloning that exists in today's corporations, whether family-owned or not. The "anachronistic" character of the company is signaled in NR by a series of Victorian props and accessories: the offices, the studies, and the clothes of Ashpool senior. All of this is well mixed with the newest computers and biotechnology—but, after all, Gibson and Sterling had already managed to create a Victorian computerized world in *The Difference Engine* (1990). This blend of the 1800s and the 2000s is more than textual ornamentation: the offices of factual corporations feature both ultra-modern and antique furnishings.

Tessier-Ashpool, with its Victorian, vampire-like character, must succumb to the new world, but as its last members become perfectly capable of using cyberspace for their own purposes, the corporation lives much longer than its formal shape. They are "a very late variant on traditional patterns of aristocracy, late because the corporate mode doesn't really allow for an aristocracy" (CZ: p. 145). Still, the difference between a clan-owned and a publicly owned corporation is not large: there is always somebody, with or without a blood tie, to step in if somebody else dies or retires.

Another anachronism is Virek (CZ: pp. 144, 195), whose prototype is Howard Hughes: an individual who is immensely rich, who lives in a gigantic vat, and who tries to achieve immortality by entering cyberspace. If he fails and dies, "you'll see Virek and Company either fragment or mutate, the latter giving us the Something Company and a true multinational, yet another home for capital-M Mass Man" (CZ: p. 145). Virek attempts to fight off approaching death, not only by biotechnical means but also trying to buy out Maas Biolabs. Maas Biolabs, feeling too strong already, refuses the offer.

Biotech

Then there are corporations like Maas Biolabs GmbH[3], which started as a research lab, and which is "small, fast, ruthless" (NRH: p. 108). A small lab in the beginning, it was soon acquiring other companies, and establishing its facilities worldwide (Maas Biolabs North America, CZ: p. 27). The research labs are like prisons for their employees: situated in desert places, separated from the world, under heavy security. They are dispersed in this way so no single attack can wipe out the entire research faculty at once. Face-to-face meetings are avoided if possible. It is Maas Biolabs that starts producing biochips and biosofts (described below). Mass Biolabs is in constant and ruthless competition with the Japanese Hosaka. Its activity requires utmost secrecy, although Maas Biolabs expends many resources on public relations.

Chains

Lucky Dragon, with its parent corporation located in Singapore, is the equivalent of the 7-Eleven store in Gibson's world (*All Tomorrow's Parties* [ATP]: p. 7). Lucky Dragon Global Interactive Video Column connects all

Lucky Dragons, so that upon entering or leaving the premises, clients can see the franchises to which the local store is connected at the moment. The night security guards at Lucky Dragon are expected to patrol the curb in front of the location during the night, a measure recommended by an in-house team of US cultural anthropologists (ATP: pp. 7–8).

For security, the guards are issued a fanny pack (a small bag worn around the waist) that can be turned into a bulletproof vest (ATP: p. 9). The stores are located in specially designed modules, the newest of which have a graffiti-eating finish (smart material, ATP: p. 86). If a guard decides that a customer is carrying a suspicious-looking bag, the bag will be collected and the customer is given a logo tag. The logo tags are too big and too heavy to carry them, so customers cannot forget they are carrying them and go out, which helps to keep the costs down (Lucky Dragon obviously has learned from the actual hotels, see Latour, 1992).

Lucky Dragon has its own Lucky Dragon International Bank, with ATMs at every possible location with the ability to pepper spray customers who behave strangely. In case of more serious attacks, like putting a crowbar into the money slot, the machine will mist customer and itself with water, thus electrocuting itself (ATP: p. 89). Identification takes place via palm contact followed by a personal identification code (at present, the choice is fingerprints or the iris of the eye).

Employees are given medical coverage and other perks—at least in theory. When one of the guards quits, having given written notice, the location manager fires him, citing numerous violations of Lucky Dragon's policy, and thus reducing his last paycheck (ATP: p. 23).

Infotainment Industry

Sense/Net is the main media company in the earlier works, with many branches and product variation. It works somewhat like traditional television, using security temps:

> . . . Turner's employer had contracted to provide security for a Sense/Net simstim team who were recording a series of thirty minute segments in an on-going jungle adventure series .. . . He'd set up a liaison between Sense/Net and the local government, bribed the town's top police official, analysed the hotel's security system, met the local guides and drivers and had their histories double-checked, arranged for digital protection on the simstim team's transceivers, established a crisis-management team, and planted seismic sensors around the Sense/Net suite-cluster. (CZ: p. 129)

But for a few details, this quote could have described an actual practice. Equally realistic is the description of the celebrity cult (cf. Rojek, 2001; Jenkins, 2008), the basis of Sense/Net operations. It starts with simstar Tally

Isham in NR, continues with Angela Mitchell and her double Mona Lisa (CZ, MLO), and culminates with idoru (ID). There is also the more serious Net/ Knowledge, which shows documentaries (MLO: p. 108); later, there is a specialized unit called Real One (ATP: p. 33). Behind Sense/Net, however, there is an Artificial Intelligence called Continuity; otherwise, Sense/Net would be too complex an entity to survive alone (MLO: p. 265).

Whereas Sense/Net works on producing celebrities, Slitscan works on destroying them (ID: p. 5). In the eyes of its executives, celebrity is "a subtle fluid, a universal element, like the phlogiston of the ancients, something spread evenly at creation through all the universe, but prone now to accrete, under specific conditions, around certain individuals and their careers" (ID: p. 7). Thus it must not last long: a celebrity should—if necessary, with the help of Slitscan—"murder someone, become active in politics, admit to an interesting substance-abuse problem or an arcane sexual addition" (ID: p. 7). Slitscan is the tabloid of Gibson's world.

Slitscan employees do not have desks; they have computers and telephones. They have virtual meetings, or meetings in small conference rooms, called the Strategic Business Unit. All employees have personal lockers where they keep their personal belongings, and it is forbidden to take printouts outside of the company and to use Post-its. Secrecy is critical, and all computer memories and phone calls are monitored (ID: p. 29).

> Slitscan was descended from "reality" programming and the network tabloids of the late twentieth century, but it resembled them no more than some large, swift, bipedal carnivore resembled its sluggish, shallow-dwelling ancestors. Slitscan was the mature form, supporting fully global franchises. Slitscan's revenues had paid for entire satellites and built the building . . . in Burbank.
>
> Slitscan was a show so popular that it had evolved into something akin to the old idea of a network. It was flanked and buffered by spinoffs and peripherals, each designed to shun the viewer back to the crucial core, the familiar and reliably bloody altar that one of . . . the co-workers called Smoking Mirror (ID: p. 39).

Its programs affected elections, markets, laws, research, and, of course, the making and unmaking of lives and careers. It has also provoked the emergence of a meta-tabloid (ID: p. 67), dedicated to a counter-investigative journalism—a show about shows like Slitscan (here Gibson is obviously sarcastic).

Advertising and Marketing

The issue of public relations and marketing gains more space with subsequent books. As early as his writing of MLO (p. 127), there is mention of a company that provides names for new companies. It checks the names of existing companies (which becomes more and more difficult, as are more and more companies are founded and the good names are taken) but also checks their meaning in various languages so that they are not ridiculous or obscene. Alas, this service is still lacking in the factual world, or if it does, it does not work very well.

By PR, the first novel with action occurring in present times, the advertising company, Blue Ant, and its owner, Hubert Bigend, are at the center of events (PR: p. 6). The services of Blue Ant, which are many and varied, include corporate identity creation; one of the two largest manufacturers of athletic footwear asked Blue Ant for help with its falling sales, for example. Blue Ant diagnosed the company as requiring rebranding, ordered a new logo from the graphic design partner company, and contracted a dowser to check if the logo design would work (PR: pp. 9, 62).

According to Bigend, advertising and espionage are two sides of the same coin:

> I want to make the public aware of something they don't quite yet know that they know—or have them feel that way. Because they'll move on that (. . .) They'll think they've thought of it first. It's about transferring information, but at the same time about a certain lack of specificity. (PR: p. 63)
>
> Intelligence . . . is advertising turned inside out. . . . Secrets . . . are cool. . . . Secrets . . . are the very root of cool (SC: p. 106)

Adrian Forty (1986) would probably agree, at least concerning design and advertising. In his opinion, successful design makes explicit what people at a given time and in a given place implicitly know and feel.

Still according to Bigend, "[f]ar more creativity, today, goes into the marketing of products than into the products themselves" (PR: p. 67). And, although the scientists in the physical world are still undecided, Bigend is a firm believer in subliminal advertising (PR: p. 69).

As to the company itself, although it is constantly growing, its owner is described as "a hands-on micromanager" (SC: p. 75). The company's successes are ascribed to the fact that Bigend's mother was a member of Situationist International,[4] and therefore possessed an artistic sensibility. According to Bigend, however, the company's successes depend on his ability to find the right person for the task at hand—thus an intense use of freelancers. Relatively small in terms of permanent staff, Blue Ant is globally distributed. Its older offices in New York and in London's Soho (PR: p. 6) are complemented by the impressive headquarters being constructed in Los Angeles (SC: p. 100–101), designed with an intention to unsettle visitors ("Unsettled is good," SC: p. 101). There is a suite of offices in Beijing, but until an office has been established in Montreal, an enormous apartment in Vancouver can be used by the Blue Ant visitors to Canada (SC: p. 236).

Blue Ant has also a sub-unit called Trans, which is an abbreviation for either translation or transgression—nobody but Bigend knows. Trans contracts attractive freelancers, who go to clubs and restaurants and chat with unsuspecting people—usually of opposite sex. When certain products or services are mentioned in conversation, the Trans temps say they like it, too. Thus positive reinforcement from an attractive person of the opposite sex is calculated to reward the opinion of the target person. The goal of this operation is not necessarily the purchase of the product; the goal is for the target person to recycle the information to others (PR: pp. 84–85). Discovering—by chance—a guerilla marketing technique consisting of mysterious footage (it is not obvious what is being marketed), Blue Ant manages to enroll it for its own services (SC).

PRODUCTS/SERVICES

One of the conclusions that one can draw from Gibson's works is that the distinction between "products" and "services" no longer exists—that they blend into one another, even as hardware and software are becoming less and less separable.

Entertainment

In the business of entertainment, there are at first Apparent Sensory Perceptions (ASPs; JM: pp. 36–39), which later become simstims (simulated stimuli, BR: p. 183). In Gibson's world, it is possible to enter into someone else's bodily perceptions, but at present there are just the attempts to extend to tactile perceptions the sense perceptions of people dealing in cyberspace.

In subsequent stories, simstims become more and more sophisticated. In CZ, a recovering corporate extractor spends time in a ROM-generated simstim construct of an idealized 19th-century New England childhood (CZ: p. 9). Simstims are circulated via telephone (courtesy of Bell Europa, for example; CZ: p. 24), and, most importantly, become a product of the media corporation, Sense/Net. Their omnipresence becomes confusing to people who are not sure what is reality and what is the simstim construct. It is no coincidence that Douglas Kellner (1995) analyzed Gibson's work, together with that of Jean Baudrillard; both Gibson and Baudrillard suggested the possibility of dissolving borders between reality and its representations. But, Gibson adds, mirrors were the first step on this road (CZ: p. 197).

In later works, simstims give way to virtual worlds. Some of them—similar to Second Life—are the places where the teenaged singer-celebrity fans meet (ID: p. 11). Some sites can be carved from previous corporate websites (ID: p. 109). A virtual guide for a physical city in MLO becomes, by the writing of ID, a virtual guide in a virtual city, which uses representation fragments, but assembles them at will (ID: p. 43).

The infotainment business also continues to perfect its tools: ATP features a system of cameras carried by balloons that can enter distant places and change position as required by the operator (ATP: p. 34). Such balloon cameras, albeit less sophisticated versions, are used in archeological photography, among other areas.

The top invention is idoru (from aidoru–the Japanese word for "idol"), an Artificial Intelligence that produces a hologram of a woman singer ("a personality-construct, a congeries of software agents," ID: p. 92), which is, in fact, a synthespian (a computer-generated actor).[5] She was preceded—in physical and virtual realities—by constructs that were syntheses of the traits of most popular Hollywood starts, but she is different. Not only do her looks differ—they are non-racial, like some avatars (Gustavsson and Czarniawska, 2004)—but her performance is also unique, in that she is a kind of virtual Zelig.[6] She is an aggregate of subjective desires, an articulated longing (ID: pp. 178, 237). Important as she is, she also has a corporate identity: Famous Aspect (ID: p. 235). She is an emergent system, a self continuously iterating on the basis of its experiential input (ATP: 163). Thus capable of development, she grows in directions that were not foreseen by her constructors, who were aiming at an entertainment product.

In Gibson's latest novels, situated in the present time (PR and SC), there is another virtual reality (VR) product, based on the possibility of geohacking, made available in May 2000, when civilians were allowed to access the Global Positioning System (GPS) Coordinates (SC: pp. 20–21). Apart from myriad opportunities to trace, situate and follow people and things, this created a new form of art: the annotated space (SC: p. 32), a kind of locative media.[7] Viewers equipped with VR helmets can see virtual monuments in annotated spaces–shrines to celebrities who died in those places (SC: pp. 32–33), a piece of art (a sea of poppies, SC: p. 219) or a company advertisement (SC: p. 64).[8] A router must be installed in the given place, (SC: p. 39), and the helmets are required, but one day we will internalize the interface, at which point we will be able to do without such equipment (SC: p. 65).

Biotech

Narcotics are omnipresent; almost everyone is on drugs—myriad extremely sophisticated drugs that can strengthen or weaken each other. Opium is the religion of the people in Gibson's worlds, though one of his characters says that heroin is the opiate of the masses (ATP: p. 7). Actually, there is no religion, or rather there are a great many sects holding eclectic sets of beliefs. Among many exotic sects, one is exceptionally so. Its followers believe that the world will end when the total weight of the human nervous tissue on the globe reaches a specific point (ID: p. 145). It is also suggested that astonishing developments in cyberspace (especially, if cyberspace were to become sentient) will likely be explained by the existing interpretative templates of mythical and religious kinds, and it is not accidental that it is vodou, slaves and rebels' religion (CZ: pp. 111, 173; MLO: pp. 138, 263, 615; SC).

The drug market is represented as a perfect market: users are driven away by dealers that offer a poor product or exorbitant prices (ATP: p. 137).

Body parts are also bought and sold on the open market (CZ: p. 9). As for artificial body parts, Gibson dedicates a great deal of attention to optical enhancing devices in all of his works. Molly (JM, NR, MLO) has build-in mirror shades (later one of the cyberpunk symbols), and most characters desire or own "Zeiss-Ikon eyes" (BR, CZ: p. 131): vat-grown, optically perfect organs, which have been further developed to serve even as cameras (recoupable after the death of the owner).[9]

Virtual Light glasses constitute a step beyond these lines; they have EMP, electromagnetic pulse drivers around the lenses, which can be connected directly to the optic nerve (VL: p. 128). They allow the wearer to see the name of every object in English and Latin, and any related information that can be digitized. They were originally built for blind people–they deliver data to the optic nerve without the need for such optic devices as eyes (VL: p. 135). Thus a blind owner of these glasses sees, instead of a holograph of idoru, a "big aluminum thermos bottle" (ID: p. 179)

Biochips, a product of Maas Biolabs, are based on a betterment of hybridoma technology.[10] These hybrid cells, working as miniature biochemical factories, are linked and incorporated into chips—thus biochips (CZ: p. 127; already, in fact, in existence). These biochips can be implanted for various purposes, although the future seems to go in the direction of grafting, which means that they can develop further within the body.[11]

Hi Tech

Within hardware, the new portables, called Sandbenders, are of particular interest. They are made by Native Americans living in a commune on the Oregon coast. Their covers are renewable coral, rock crystal, turquoise, or fossil ivory nut; aluminum parts are recovered from old cans, and panels are made of linen permeated with resin (ID: p. 45). An interface designer and her husband, an ecologically minded jeweler, invented them. Heavier than the usual portables, they are cult objects, especially as it is easy to exchange their electronics (ID: p. 138). Sandbender software used by teenagers is a virtual development of the Playmobil figures.[12]

Outside the world of toys are, for example, Squids—"Superconducting quantum interference detectors" (JM: p. 9); used originally in submarines to detect enemy cybersystems, they likely exist in reality. All the ICE systems, or firewalls, belong in this category as well.

As mentioned previously, ICE stands for Intrusion Countermeasures Electronix (BC: p. 169). The sophisticated ICE has several layers of defense; it can defend against the intrusion of such authorities as audits and subpoenas, and it can defend itself against viruses (BC: p. 175). In this case, however, Gibson's terminology failed to catch on; in present parlance, ICE is called a firewall—but the idea is the same. In the texts, it is the Artificial Intelligences that produce both ice and icebreakers, and the Turing Police try to prevent them from doing anything else.

More exotic, if not to say bizarre, is a ROM personality matrix, based on a person who is brain dead (flatlined) (NR: p. 97). One of the funniest applications of this technology takes the form of a cube containing the personality of former corporate executive (MLO: p. 174), which can be asked and can answer questions. If this idea seems far-fetched, one should consider the ideas of the ultimate robot specialist, Hans Moravec, who predicted in 1984 that by 2004, the "mind" could be transferred from the human brain to a machine without a loss of consciousness.[13]

A further developed version of the personality matrix is biosoft. In the factual world, it is the software used for biological research; in Gibson's world it is used to enter the coded memories of another person. An aleph[14]-class biosoft (MLO: p. 163) contains a flatlined person's consciousness, as well as the consciousness of others; an entire virtual world, being an abstract of the whole of cyberspace, with its own security net, so that the users of the cyberspace cannot enter it at will (MLO: p. 218).

Nanotechnology finds more and more applications. Nanoassemblers are able not only to build an entire city (Tokyo after the earthquake) but can also reassemble an object sent by a nanofax (ATP: p. 195). Nanofax AG offers a technology that reproduces physical objects at a distance. Nanofaxes exist, and were in use before the novel was published, in fact. The technology is called stereolitography, and it creates a three-dimensional plastic model from a three-dimensional computer-aided design (CAD-drawing).[15] Nanofax experimenters are as yet unable to fax a logo statuette, as planned by Lucky Dragon in the novel.[16] Even fiction is placed under legal constraints, however nanofaxes may not reproduce functional hardware or nanoassemblers (ATP: p. 195).

Other Products

There are great many other products described by Gibson, which are not of central importance for his plots, but are of interest here because they mirror either products currently under development or the popular wishes of technology users.

One such product is the portable "vacation module": a camper fully equipped for the needs of the vacationer, and placed by a cargo lifter into the most advantageous place on an attractive beach, where it can turn to follow the sun and thereby receive maximum energy from its solar panels (CZ: p. 72). There also are intelligent houses that can be required to speak in a desired tone of voice (MLO: p. 56) and smart cars that drive themselves and dispatch information about the passing sights. A machine called

Investigator is indeed good news; it is a remote manipulator for handling toxic spills and nuclear plant clean-ups (MLO: p. 259).

Gibson's software rental complexes (NR: p. 73) are the obvious predecessors of Internet cafés, which, according to Wikipedia, did not exist before 1991.[17] Another example of reality catching up with Gibson's imagination is the motion bike: the one in ATP (p. 32) can be configured into a dozen different bikes. Ten years later, I was able to buy one at a reduced price that can be configured into thirteen.

THE IMAGE AND ITS RELEVANCE

One striking thing about the global world depicted by Gibson is what appears to be the disappearance of the middle classes, for the extremely rich and the new hi-tech proletariat populate Gibson's world. Perhaps this is but a textual strategy, as the tension between the two offers more exciting plots than does one more exegesis of the middle classes. When interrogated about this phenomenon in an interview for Amazon.com, conducted at the occasion of publication of SC, however, Gibson answered

> There's something I was aware of when I was writing this book, because I had the cause to go back and look at the parts of *Neuromancer*, is that thing about the world in *Neuromancer* is that there is no middle class. There are only very, very wealthy people, and desperately poor, mostly criminal people. It's a very Victorian world, and when I was writing *Spook Country* I kept running against that feeling that the world I'm actually trying to predict is becoming more Victorian, not less. Less middle class, more like Mexico, more like Mexico City. And I think that's probably not a good direction (www.williamgibsonbooks. com/source/qu/asp (accessed September 9, 2010).

In this statement, he seems to agree completely with his colleague Neal Stephenson, who described just such a new Victorian, hi-tech world in The Diamond Age or, *a Young Lady's Illustrated Primer* (1995). Much as this description could fit the US and Mexico, it seems that the opposite phenomenon is occurring in the—previous—welfare states in Europe, such as Scandinavian countries, Germany and France. A growing middle class pushes out the rest. The rich flee to no-tax countries, whereas the poor live off welfare or fly to Afghanistan. It could be that the contemporary world will witness a new stratification, where certain classes will keep to certain places in the world.

Is there a theory behind Gibson's descriptions, after all? If so, it is difficult to slot it into the existing categories. I agree with Bukatman (1993/2007) that Gibson's books, in spite of the rather black picture of the global world that he is painting in them ("the future as nightmare" says a cheerful quote on the cover of NR), need not be perceived as dystopic. There is always some kind of redemption for the cyberpunks, mostly through love, compassion, and solidarity. This textual strategy is known, however, from earlier works on proletariat.

Can Gibson's ethnographies be counted among critical studies, then? They do, after all, portray a world of "warring imperial corporations, universal commodification and a disenfranchised underclass," as Parker et al. (1999, p. 582) have remarked. Perhaps—were it not for the fact that cyberpunks really want to become these very, very rich people, even if their human decency prevents them from reaching this goal. If there is an accusation, therefore, it is against the human race rather than the capitalist system.

In general, Gibson is praised by its critics for his "street-smart refusal to moralize" (Hitchings, 2003). As Kellner formulated it, Gibson's world is basically "postpolitical" (1994, p. 315); in the words of one Gibson's characters, ". . . politics. That particular dance, . . . that's over" (VL: p. 98). This world is also "posteconomics"—there are no economists in it. Perhaps the author did not know enough about economics or was not interested. At any rate, his global economy is based on technically sophisticated but relatively simple markets, which do not require economists in order to function. Their knowledge has likely been incorporated into machines: global arbitrage engines, for example (ID: p. 154). What is always present, however, is war—past, ongoing, or potential.

In this world, economy, culture, and technology are intertwined so that their borders can no longer be detected. As Gibson says, however, popular culture is a testbed of our future (ID: 238), and some business scholars agree (Czarniawska and Rhodes, 2006; Parker and Rhodes, 2008).

Gibson frequently claims that his worlds are not worlds of the future but of the present. Indeed, apart from some as yet nonexistent products, the image he presents is recognizable. It is as if the margins of the center of the global economy, the one we perceive through the media, have been highlighted, sometimes cruelly. It is not, however, the landscape we usually explore in our mainstream business studies, which follows well trodden tracts. Perhaps rightly so. But there is no doubt that there was a need for the margins to be known as well, if for no other reason than that they may move toward the center in the future. But are fictive depictions of any use in a research endeavor?

In the first place, there is the circular character of contemporary culture to be considered (Johnson, 1986/1987). In this circuit, the media and popular culture represent the lived culture, but the lived culture also takes inspiration and actualizes ideas from the media and popular culture. Gibson's work contains many examples, not only of cyberspace; it would need a truly historical detective work to establish if certain concepts and terms were used first by Gibson or by biotechnologists or computer specialists. There is no one-to-one correspondence, but the circuit is certainly in operation. A striking example is the term "infotainment," used originally by Neil Postman (1985) with contemptuous irony, and now a taken-for-granted technical term to be found everywhere—including Gibson's works.

Commenting on *Neuromancer*, John Clute (2003) has noted that by the time of writing the book, Gibson was quite ignorant of computer technology, writing by hand, and

> ... if the world in 2003 in some ways resembles the world he created ... it is because the world, and the writers who articulate the world, have imitated Gibson. It is surely not the other way around: Gibson, by his own testimony, was too incompetent to imitate the world. (Clute, 2003, pp. 71–72)

Parker et al. (1999, pp. 580–581) quoted several examples of science fiction influencing actual management practices, often mediated by management consultants. Science fiction is used as a resource for strategic planning scenarios, and the ideas of cyber-marketing, e-commerce, and one-to-one business are fully implemented. Cool hunting and street fashion are taken-for-granted resources in design and marketing.

The circularity of actual influences is one good reason for the extended interest of management scholars in popular culture, but there is another reason, so well formulated by Wolfgang Iser on the example of the novel: "it is neither an escape from reality nor a substitute for it. Instead, [a novel] reacts to reality, and in doing so interprets it" (Iser, 1989, p. 209). These interpretations may differ from those to be found in management texts, but exactly because of this difference, they may become a source of new insights and a new dialogue.

NOTES

1. "A standing joke about cyberspace is that, in an era of automated teller machines (ATMs) and global banking, *cyberspace is where your money is*" (Bukatman, 1993/2007).
2. I am using this term here to meaning a masterless samurai—which Kumiko in MLO: p. 176 applies to Molly/Sally—to avoid the decisively negative terms hitmen or hitwomen. The purpose of the ronins' actions is rarely to kill; but they do kill if necessary.
3. Gesellschaft mit beschränkter Haftung, the German equivalent of "Ltd."
4. http://en.wikipedia.org/wiki/Situationist_International (accessed March 29, 2011); http://www.nothingness.org/SI (accessed March 29, 2011).
5. The term "synthespian" was coined in 1988 by Jeff Kleiser and Diana Walczak of the Kleiser-Walczak Construction Co. From http://synthespians.net/ (accessed September 9, 2010).
6. A hero of Woody Allen's movie of the same name, and also the name of statistical software. From http://gking.harvard.edu/zelig/ (accessed September 9, 2010).
7. "[T]he most interesting applications turn up on the battlefield or in a gallery" (SC: p. 63).

8. More on locative media can be found in a PowerPoint presentation by Gemma San Cornelio. From www.slideshare.net/gsancornelio/ace-presentation-1488910 (accessed September 9, 2010).
9. "The name of the company would be subtly worked into the patterning around each iris; it would not be readable from the outside, unless someone was extremely close to the wearer (recipient? owner?)" From http://blog.williamgibsonbooks.com/2006/08 (accessed March 29, 2011).
10. Hybridomas are cells that have been engineered to produce a desired antibody in large amounts. From http://en.wikipedia.org/wiki/Hybridoma_Technology (accessed September 9, 2010).
11. Although already in MLO, there is mention of the 51st generation of biochips, which produce something between a ROM personality and a simstim: a fictitious person that can be projected from a small device and serve as a guide and an advisor (MLO: p. 9).
12. From http://en.wikipedia.org/wiki/Playmobil (accessed September 9, 2010).
13. He recently adjusted his dates; before this happens, he now says, there must be robots superior to humans, and they will not be ready until 2050. From www.primitivism.com/superhumanism.htm (accessed September 9, 2010). For enlightening comments on this project, see Hayles (2005/2007).
14. According to Jewish mythology, the letter *aleph* was carved into the head of the golem, and it gave the clay figure life. From http://en.wikipedia.org/wiki/Aleph (accessed September 9, 2010). In *Star Wars*, there is an "aleph-class Starfighter. From http://starwars.wikia.com/wiki/Aleph-class_starfighter (accessed September 9, 2010). According to Gibson's blog: Friday, July 17, 2009: "Aleph" as in the Borges story: the spot under the basement stairs from which all things that have ever existed can be seen simultaneously. From www.williamgibsonbooks.com/blog/2009_07_01_archive.asp (accessed September 9, 2010).
15. From www.technovelgy.com/ct/content.asp?Bnum=112 (accessed September 9, 2010).
16. Lucky Dragon is the first chain to have a nanofax. It plans to fax its logo statuette, but it is the virtual idol, Rei Toei (idoru), that faxes herself throughout the world (ATP: pp. 268–269).
17. From http://en.wikipedia.org/wiki/Internet_cafe (accessed September 9, 2010).

WILLIAM GIBSON'S WORKS CITED IN THE TEXT

NRH: (1981/1986). New Rose Hotel. In *Burning Chrome* (pp. 103–116). New York: Ace Books.
BC: (1982/1986). Burning Chrome. In *Burning Chrome* (pp. 168–191). New York: Ace Books.
JM: (1981/1986). Johnny Mnemonic. In *Burning Chrome* (pp. 1–22). New York: Ace Books.
NR: (1984). *Neuromancer.* London: Victor Gollancz.
CZ: (1986). *Count Zero.* London: Victor Gollancz.
MLO: (1988). *Mona Lisa Overdrive.* London: Victor Gollancz.
VL: (1993). *Virtual Light.* London: Viking.
ID: (1996). *Idoru.* London: Viking.
ATP: (1999). *All Tomorrow's Parties.* New York: Putnam.
PR: (2003). *Pattern Recognition.* New York: Putnam.
SC: (2007). *Spook Country.* New York: Putnam.

REFERENCES

Amazon.com. (2007). Across the Border to Spook Country: An Interview with William Gibson. From www.williamgibsonbooks.com/source/qu/asp (accessed September 9, 2010).

Barley, S. R., and Kunda, G. (2004). *Gurus, Hired Guns and Warm Bodies. Itinerant Experts in a Knowledge Economy.* Princeton, NJ: Princeton University Press.

Baumol, W. J., Litan, R. E., and Schramm, C. J. (2007). *Good Capitalism, Bad Capitalism, and the Economics of Growth and Prosperity.* New Haven, NJ: Yale University Press.

Bergström, O., and Storrie, D. (Eds.). (2003). *Contingent Employment in Europe and the United States.* Cheltenham: Edward Elgar.

Bukatman, S. (1993/2007). Cyberspace. In D. Bell and B. M. Kenedy (Eds.), *The cybercultures reader* (pp. 80–105). London: Routledge.

Clute, J. (2003). Science fiction from 1980 to the present. In E. James and F. Mendlesohn (Eds.), *The Cambridge Companion to Science Fiction* (pp. 64–78). Cambridge, UK: Cambridge University Press.

Czarniawska, B., and Rhodes, C. (2006). Strong plots: Popular culture in management practice and theory. In P. Gagliardi and B. Czarniawska (Eds.), *Management Education and Humanities* (pp. 195–218). Cheltenham, UK: Edward Elgar.

Forty, A. (1986). *Objects of Desire: Design and Society Since 1750.* London: Thames and Hudson.

Gibson, W., and Sterling, B. (1990). *The Difference Engine.* London: Victor Gollancz.

Gustavsson, E., and Czarniawska, B. (2004), Web Woman: The On-Line Construction of Corporate and Gender Images. *Organization, 11*(5), 651–670.

Hayles, N. K. (2005/2007). Computing the Human. In D. Bell and B. M. Kennedy (Eds.), *The Cybercultures Reader* (pp. 557–573). London: Routledge.

Hitchings, H. (2003) Brand-Savvy. *Time Literary Supplement*, 5222, May 2.

Huxley, A. (1924) *Brave New World.* From www.huxley.net/bnw/ (accessed September 9, 2010).

Iser, W. (1989). *Prospecting. From Reader Response to Literary Anthropology.* Baltimore, MD: John Hopkins University Press.

Jenkins, H. (2008). *Convergence Culture: Where Old and New Media Collide.* New York: New York University Press.

Johnson, R. (1986/1987). What Is Culture Studies Anyway? *Social Text, 16*, 38–80.

Kartvedt, S. (1994/1995). Cyberpunk Sage. *Scanorama*, December/January, 54–58.

Kellner, D. (1994). *Media Culture: Culture Studies,Identity and Politics Between the Modern and Postmodern.* London: Routledge.

Klein, N. (2000). *No Logo. Taking Aim at the Brand Bullies.* Toronto: Knopf Canada.

Latour, B. (1992). Where are the missing masses? The sociology of a few mundane artifacts. In W. Bijker and J. Law (Eds.), *Shaping Technology/Building Society: Studies in Sociotechnical Change* (pp. 225–258). Cambridge, MA: MIT Press.

Moravec, H. (1984). Locomotion, vision and intelligence, In M. Brady and R. Paul (Eds.), *Robotics Research 1* (pp. 215–224). Cambridge, MA: MIT Press.

Parker, M., Higgins, M., Lightfoot, G., and Smith, W. (1999). Amazing Tales: Organization Studies as Science Fiction. *Organization, 6*(4), 579–590.

Parker, M., and Rhodes, C. (2008). Images of Organizing in Popular Culture. *Organization, 19*(5), 627–637.

Postman, N. (1985). *Amusing Ourselves to Death. Public Discourse in the Age of Show Business.* New York: Penguin.

Rojek, C. (2001). *Celebrity.* London: Reaktion Books.

San Cornelio, G. (2008, December 4). *Locative Media: Between Art and Entertainment. Towards an Analytical Model.* Paper presented at the International Conference on Advertising in Computer Entertainment Technology, Yokohama, Japan.

Sassen, S. (2001). *The Global City.* Princeton, NJ: Princeton University Press.

Stephenson, N. (1995). *The Diamond Age or, a Young Lady's Illustrated Primer.* New York: Bantam Books.

Stone, A. R. (1992/2007). Will the Real Body Please Stand Up? Boundary Stories about Virtual Cultures. In D. Bell and B. M. Kenedy (Eds.), *The Cybercultures Reader* (pp. 433–455). London: Routledge.

Storrie, D. (2003). Conclusions: Contingent Employment in Europe and the Flexibility-security Trade-off. In O. Bergström and D. Storrie (Eds.), *Contingent Employment in Europe and the United States* (pp. 224–247). Cheltenham: Edward Elgar.

3 Visible, Tradeable Carbon
How Emissions Markets are Constructed

Donald MacKenzie

> Of course it was ambitious to set up a market for something you can't see. . . . (Jacqueline McGlade, Executive Director, European Environment Agency, quoted in *International Herald Tribune* June 19, 2008, p. 1)

Markets in allowances to emit greenhouse gases or in credits earned by not emitting them have emerged in Europe and internationally. [1] Some already exist; others are in construction. Their construction requires that emissions of carbon dioxide (and sometimes also emissions of other greenhouse gases, and CO_2's absorption by the biosphere) be made visible, measurable and fungible, credibly reducing complex physical, chemical and biological processes to identical, interchangeable allowances or credits. If those markets are to shape behavior in the intended fashion, the value of the allowances or credits traded in them and the magnitude of the liabilities that emissions entail also need to be made economically visible. These processes, and some of the difficulties that attend them, are the topic of this chapter.

The chapter describes briefly the route—at the level of 'policy'—that has led to the emergence of carbon emissions markets. It then delves into the conditions of possibility of these markets, by examining two examples in more depth. The examples are how the destruction of one gas in one place is made commensurate with emissions of a different gas in a different place, and how accountants have sought (so far with only limited success) to make 'emission rights' equivalent. Finally, the chapter discusses the political issues that inescapably attend carbon emissions markets: the question of the attitude that should to be taken to them (for example by environmentalists, especially those who conceive of themselves as opponents of 'capitalism'), and the tightly related issue of the process of market design viewed, as it has to be, as politics.

Although the chapter draws upon the 'finitist' perspective sketched briefly below (see Barnes et al.,1996; MacKenzie, 2009), its approach is prompted by the view of economic life suggested by the 'actor-network' theory of Michel Callon and Bruno Latour (for which see, for example, Latour, 2005). In Callon's and Latour's view, the characteristics of an 'actor'—a term which, following semiotics (especially Greimas, 1987), they view as encompassing more than just human beings—are not intrinsic, but are the result of the networks of which the actor is made up and forms part. What we call 'capitalism,' for example, is not an entity with fixed characteristics. 'Que faire contre le capitalisme?' they write 'D'abord évidemment *ne pas y croire*' (Callon and Latour, 1997, p. 67). What is to be done against capitalism? First of all, of course *do not believe in it.*

In Callon's and Latour's view, economic life is 'performed'—framed and formatted—by 'economics at large,' a term that encompasses not just the academic discipline but also economic practices such as accounting and marketing (Callon, 1998, 2007). The characteristics of economic actors and of markets arise from, amongst other things, the 'dispositifs de calcul' (Callon and Muniesa, 2003)—the calculative devices—of which they are made up.

If the characteristics of 'capitalism' are not inherent, they can be changed by changing the calculative devices that constitute it. The markets in greenhouse-gas emissions that are being constructed globally are a set of experiments (Muniesa and Callon, 2007) in the validity of this prediction. Hitherto, greenhouse-gas emissions have been, in economists' familiar terminology, an 'externality.' They are costly in the sense that they will cause widespread economic (and other) damage, but from the viewpoint of the emitter, they bore no monetary cost, and so were economically invisible: they did not figure in emitters' economic calculations. The goal of a carbon market is to make emissions economically visible by giving them a price. In such a market, emissions bear a cost: either a direct cost (because allowances to emit greenhouses gases need to be purchased), or an opportunity cost (because allowances that aren't used to cover emissions can be sold, or because credits can be earned if emissions are reduced below 'business as usual'). A carbon market is thus an attempt to change the construction of capitalism's central economic metric: profit and loss, the 'bottom line.'

The experiments in carbon-market construction have scarcely begun, so the validity of the prediction that capitalism can be 'civilized' (Latour, forthcoming) by changing calculative mechanisms remains undecided. We do not yet know whether the bottom line will be changed to any substantial extent, in particular to an extent sufficient to keep global warming below the threshold (uncertain and fiercely contested, but often taken to be 2°C) beyond which the risk of severe impacts rises sharply (Schellnhuber, 2006).

In consequence, this chapter is necessarily preliminary. The empirical material on which I am drawing is limited. It consists primarily of a set of 30 interviews conducted with 27 people involved with carbon markets (particularly with the European Union Emission Trading System) as market designers, as carbon traders and brokers, as accountants, or as members of nongovernmental organizations (NGOs) seeking to influence the evolution of carbon markets (three key informants were interviewed twice). This interview material is supplemented by analysis of relevant documents such as monitoring reports and contributions to the debate in accountancy touched on below.

The chapter's main aim is to help broaden social-science research on carbon markets, both in terms of its disciplinary base (though their origins lie in economics, carbon markets cannot be understood by the conventional tools of that discipline alone) and in terms of its empirical focus. In that latter respect, I hope to show that it is productive to investigate not just overall questions such as the reasons why policy makers might choose carbon markets rather than other tools to combat global warming, but also the specifics of how carbon markets make (or fail to make) the costs of emissions economically visible. Whether or not carbon markets are environmentally and economically effective depends on such specifics, and the issues involved are various and demand interdisciplinary treatment. One of the two topics examined below—how different gases are made commensurable—is a natural question for the social studies of science and technology; the other—how to find a standard treatment of 'emissions rights'—is a question obviously suitable for researchers in accounting. Although for reasons of space I do not discuss them here, questions for other disciplines can also easily be identified: for example, vastly more needs known about how emission reduction projects in developing countries actually work in practice, a question that raises issues ranging from how verification is conducted to the impact of projects on local communities and local environments. Investigating such issues in genuine depth required the skills of, among others, anthropologists and other area specialists.

Because the specifics of market design matter, I make no apology for the fact that this chapter touches upon matters of apparent detail. The commensurability of gases and the accounting treatment of emission rights are inevitably 'technical' questions, and such technicalities cannot altogether be avoided: the environmental and economic effects of emissions markets can hinge on them. The commensurability of gases, for example, is crucial to how the world's two main existing carbon markets—the European Union Emissions Trading System and the Kyoto Protocol Clean Development Mechanism—interrelate, while there is at least tentative evidence that the accounting treatment of emissions rights affects firms' behaviour in carbon markets. It is precisely issues of this detailed kind that an effective, inter-disciplinary analysis of carbon markets will need to address.

CARBON MARKETS

Carbon markets come in two main species: 'cap-and-trade' and 'baseline-and-credit.'[2] Let me begin with the former. It involves a government or other authority setting a 'cap'—a maximum allowable aggregate total quantity of emissions—and selling or giving the corresponding number of allowances to emitters. The authority then monitors emissions and fines anyone who emits without the requisite allowances. If the monitoring and penalties are stringent enough, aggregate emissions are thus kept down to the level of the cap. The 'trade' aspect of cap-and-trade arises because those for whom reductions are expensive will want to buy allowances rather than incurring disproportionate costs. The requisite supply of allowances is created by the financial incentive thereby provided to those who can make big cuts in emissions relatively cheaply. They can save money by not having to buy allowances, or (if allowances are distributed free) can earn money by selling allowances they don't need. So, as already noted, emissions, which previously had no monetary cost, now have one.

The origins of the idea of controlling emissions via a cap-and-trade scheme can be traced to the work of Nobel Laureate Ronald Coase (1960), but a more proximate source is the University of Toronto economist J. H. Dales, who was the first to put forward the idea in something like full-fledged form (1968a, 1968b).[3] Emissions markets were implemented in relatively minor and sometimes ham-fisted ways in the 1970s and 1980s, mainly in the United States (US) (see, e.g., Hahn, 1989). It was only in the 1990s that the idea became mainstream.

The crucial development was the start of sulphur dioxide trading in the US in 1995 (for which see, especially, Ellerman et al., 2000; Burtraw et al., 2005). It had been known for 20 years or more that damage to the environment and to human health was being caused by sulphur dioxide emissions, notably from coal-fired power stations, which react in the atmosphere to produce 'acid rain' and other acid depositions. Numerous bills were presented to Congress in the 1980s to address the problem, but all failed in the face of opposition from the Reagan administration and from Democrats who represented states that might suffer economically from controls on sulphur dioxide, such as the areas of Appalachia and the midwest in which coal deposits are high in sulphur.

Sulphur trading broke the impasse. It combined a simple, clear goal that environmentalists could embrace (reducing annual sulphur dioxide emissions from power stations in the US by 10 million tons from their 1980 level, a cut of around a half) with a market mechanism attractive to at least some Republicans. The cut was achieved in practice far more cheaply than almost anyone had imagined. Industry lobbyists had claimed it would cost $10 billion a year, while the actual cost was around $1 billion. Allowance prices of $400 a ton were predicted, but in fact prices averaged around $150 or less in the early years of the scheme. The flexibility that trading gave to utilities helped to reduce costs (by around a half compared to having to meet a standard that imposed a uniform maximum emission rate: see Ellerman et al., 2000; Burtraw et al., 2005), but other factors were equally important. 'Scrubbers' to remove sulphur from smokestacks turned out to be cheaper to install and to run than had been anticipated, and rail-freight deregulation sharply reduced the cost of transportation from Wyoming's Powder River Basin, the main source of low-sulphur coal in the US (Ellerman et al., 2000).

That the sulphur dioxide market was, broadly, a success shaped how the Clinton Administration approached the negotiations that led to the 1997

Kyoto Protocol. In the Protocol, the industrialized nations undertook that by Kyoto's 2008–2012 'commitment period,' they would have limited their greenhouse-gas emissions to agreed proportions of their 1990 levels: 93% for the US, 92% for the European Community overall (with varying levels for its member states), and so on.

At the insistence of the US, Kyoto gave its signatories flexibility in how to meet their commitments. The Protocol contains provision for a cap-and-trade market between nation states. States with caps they will exceed can pay others that in the commitment period are emitting less than their caps for their unneeded 'Kyoto units' (quantities of carbon dioxide or their equivalents in other gases: see below). The trading of these units between nation states is only just getting going at the time of writing (September 2009): it is possible it will be quite limited. Similarly limited may be another Kyoto mechanism—'Joint Implementation.' Much more important has been the 'Clean Development Mechanism' (CDM), which is a baseline-and-credit scheme, not cap-and-trade.

The CDM (for which see, for example, Lecocq and Ambrosi, 2007) is a crucial—perhaps *the* crucial—aspect of the Kyoto Protocol (Grubb, 1999), crystallizing the political compromise at the Protocol's heart, between the refusal of developing countries to take on emissions caps and the Clinton Administration's conviction that global emissions could be restrained far more cheaply if the developing world were part of the Kyoto regime. The CDM allows the creation of Kyoto units from projects in developing countries approved by the Executive Board of the CDM (a body established under the United Nations Framework Convention on Climate Change).

To gain approval, it must be shown that a project is 'additional' (that it would not take place without CDM funding) and that it will reduce emissions below the 'baseline' level they would have been at without the project. A developing-world entity, or industrialized-world government, corporation, bank or hedge fund can then earn the difference between emissions with and without the project in the form of a specific type of Kyoto units: 'Certified Emission Reductions' (CERs). A CER is a credit, not a permit or allowance: it doesn't *directly* convey any right to emit. However, some governments are purchasing CERs as a way of meeting their Kyoto caps, and crucially CERs also have monetary value because the European Union permits its member states to issue allowances in the most important cap-and-trade market, the European Union Emissions Trading System (ETS), in exchange for the surrender of CERs (European Parliament, Council, 2004). A credit earned in, for example, China or India can thus be transformed into an allowance to emit in Europe.

As with the CDM, the ETS, launched in January 2005, was shaped by political exigencies.[4] What pushed Europe toward trading rather than its initial preference, harmonized carbon taxes, was in good part an idiosyncratic feature of the political procedures of the European Union. Tax measures require unanimity: a single dissenting country can block them.

Emissions trading, in contrast, counts as an environmental, not a tax matter. That takes it into the terrain of 'qualified majority voting.' No single country can stop such a scheme: doing so takes a coalition of countries sufficiently populous (since voting weights roughly follow population) to form a 'blocking minority.' A plan for a Europe-wide carbon tax had foundered in the early 1990s in the face of vehement opposition from industry and from particular member states (notably the UK), and its advocates knew that if they tried to revive it the unanimity rule meant they were unlikely to succeed. 'We learned our lesson,' one of them told me in interview. Hence the shift in allegiance to trading.

In terms of volume of transactions, the ETS is by far the largest greenhouse-gas market. The scheme has had its difficulties—the over-allocation, violent price fluctuations and windfall profits discussed below—but it saw trades worth $91.9 billion in 2008. The prospect of 'monetizing' CERs via the ETS is the main driver of investment in Clean Development Mechanism projects, which generated CERs worth $6.5 billion in 2008 (Capoor and Ambrosi, 2009, p. 1). The ETS and CDM form the core of the world's currently existing carbon markets, and it is on them that this chapter focuses.

Making Things the Same: Gases

The political decision to create a carbon market such as the CDM or ETS is not the same as constructing such a market. A new commodity—an emission allowance or emission credit—needs brought into being: defined legally and technically, allocated to market participants, made transferable and tradable, and so on. To give a flavor of what is involved, let me concentrate on one issue: the heterogeneity of the means by which the 'sameness'—the fungibility of allowances and credits—necessary for a carbon market is brought into being.[5] Consider, for example, two very different sites: the central-area combined heat and power plant of Edinburgh University, situated 50 meters from my office there, and the refrigerant plant operated by Zhejiang Juhua Co., 6.5 km south of Quzhou City in China's Zhejiang province. How is the activity at one made commensurable with that at the other, so that both can form part of the same market, and CERs at Zhejiang Juhua's plant can be equivalent to the ETS allowances that a European emitter such as Edinburgh University needs?

As its name indicates, the combined heat and power plant in Edinburgh generates electricity (by burning natural gas in a device that resembles a giant car engine), and uses what would otherwise be waste heat to warm up nearby buildings. Because its thermal input capacity is slightly greater than the 20-megawatt (MW) threshold of the European Union Emissions Trading System, this plant became part of the ETS in January 2008. (Most such installations have been part of the scheme since its launch in 2005, but Edinburgh University was exempted from the first phase because of its involvement in an earlier, voluntary UK emissions trading scheme.) The CO_2 emissions from the combined heat and power plant are made visible using a gas corrector meter (the interface of which is shown in Figure 1) on the large pipe that takes gas from the national gas grid into the plant. It is called a 'corrector meter' because it samples temperature and pressure and can thus convert volumes into masses of gas input, which are in turn converted to estimates of CO_2 output using standard multiplication factors.

Zhejiang Juhua Company is involved in something quite different, the manufacture of HCFC-22 (chlorodiflouromethane), which is used mainly as a refrigerant (especially in air conditioners), though also as a foam blower and as a chemical feedstock. The standard process used to produce chlorodiflouromethane involves combining hydrogen fluoride and chloroform, using antimony pentachloride as a catalyst, and even when optimized the process leads to a degree of 'overfluoridation': trifluoromethane, HFC-23, is produced as well.[6] The HFC-23 is, unfortunately, long-lived in the atmosphere and an efficient absorber of infrared radiation; the combination makes it a very potent greenhouse gas.

Figure 3.1 The interface of the gas corrector meter in the input pipe to Edinburgh University's central area combined heat and power plant. Photo courtesy David Somerveil, Estates and Buildings, University of Edinburgh.

Until recently, the Zhejiang Juhua plant's waste gases were discharged into the atmosphere. Now, they are fed into a specialized incineration furnace imported from Japan, in which they are mixed with hydrogen, compressed air and steam, and burned at 1200°C using a high-intensity vortex burner. The HFC-23 is thus converted to hydrogen fluoride, carbon dioxide, and hydrogen chloride. These products pass through a quencher (in which they are cooled rapidly to minimize the formation of dioxins), and the resultant acid solution is either sold or disposed of via a facility for treating fluoric waste (CDM Executive Board, 2007).

For this process to be incorporated into the carbon markets, what needs rendered visible is an absence: a gas that has *not* been emitted, HFC-23. As already noted, for a Clean Development Mechanism project to gain approval it must be shown that it reduces emissions below the 'baseline' level they would have had in its absence, which can be a tricky exercise in establishing a credible counterfactual (Lohmann, 2005): for an introduction to the issues involved, see Michaelowa (2005). In the case of HFC-23 decomposition, however, a straightforward argument has sufficed: without the decomposition process, the HFC-23 would, as already noted, have entered the atmosphere (CDM Executive Board, 2007). However, the amount actually decomposed then needs measured, but in such a way that a connection is kept to the baseline of the HFC-23 that would have been emitted in the absence of the decomposition incinerator. (The quantity of HFC-23 generated is affected by the precise parameters of the HCFC-22 production process, and hence there is a need to reduce the incentive to operate the process in an unoptimized way and generate unnecessary HFC-23 in order to earn credits by destroying it.) So to standard equipment such as flow meters and a gas chromatograph is added a rule: for each ton of HCFC-22 produced, there is a maximum mass of HFC-23 whose decomposition can earn credits.[7]

Crucially, the allowable mass of 'absent' HFC-23 that the rule and the measurement devices have rendered visible is then multiplied by 11,700.[8] By decomposing a ton of HFC-23 in China, one can—via the link between the CDM and ETS—earn allowances to emit 11,700 tons of CO_2 in Europe. Certified Emission Reductions are now a major income stream for China's refrigerant plants and for the Chinese government (which imposes a 65% tax on them, hypothecated for environmental purposes). Indeed, HFC-23 decomposition was originally the biggest single sector of the Clean Development Mechanism, accounting for 67% of the CERs generated in 2005 and 34% of those generated in 2006; it is only gradually being displaced by projects, such as renewable energy, which better fit the scheme's wider 'sustainable development' remit (World Bank, 2007, p. 27). Since the price of CERs is an important determinant of the European carbon price—and thus, for example, a major input into electricity prices—the effects of the commensuration are considerable.

The crucial figure, 11,700, is the product of a calculation of the 'global warming potential' (GWP) of HFC-23 published by the Intergovernmental

Panel on Climate Change (IPCC). Set up in 1988 by the World Meteorological Organization and United Nations Environmental Programme, the IPCC has as its remit the establishment of authoritative scientific knowledge about climate change (see Agrawala, 1998a, 1998b). As the IPCC put it in 1990, GWP is '[a]n index . . . which allows the climate effects of the *emissions* of greenhouse gases to be compared. The GWP depends on the position and strength of the absorption bands of the gas, its lifetime in the atmosphere, its molecular weight and the time period over which the climate effects are of concern' (Houghton et al., 1990, p. 45). Although very similar notions are to be found in the scientific literature of the time (see, e.g., Lashof and Ahuja, 1990), it was the IPCC itself that gave 'global warming potential' its canonical definition:

$$GWP = \frac{\int_0^{TP} a_x[x(t)]dt}{\int_0^{TP} a_r[r(t)]dt}$$

x designates the gas in question (e.g., HFC-23); a_x is an estimate of the effect on the radiation balance at the tropopause (the boundary of the upper and lower atmosphere) of an increase in the amount of gas in the atmosphere, an effect measured in watts per square meter per kilogram; *x(t)* is the mass of the gas that will remain in the atmosphere at time t from l kg released at time zero; and TP is the overall time period in question: in the calculation in the HFC-23 commensuration, it is 100 years. The denominator is the equivalent integral for the reference gas, CO_2.

The expressions in this equation inscribe complex processes. For example, *r(t)* isn't (and obviously couldn't be) determined by releasing a kilogram of carbon dioxide and measuring what happens over a century: it is a mathematical function generated from a standard model (the Bern model: see, e.g., Siegenthaler and Joos, 1992) of the exchange of carbon between the atmosphere, the oceans and the terrestrial biosphere. Likewise, a_x and a_r are in part the products of sophisticated spectroscopic studies, recorded largely in a database managed by the Harvard-Smithsonian Center for Astrophysics. (The database was originally a military project, designed to enhance understanding of absorption of infrared radiation with a view to improving the detection of heat sources: see Taubes, 2004.) But a_x and a_r also assume a scenario that is believed to be helpful in predicting the climatic impact of a gas. In this scenario, temperatures in the stratosphere, which are understood as adjusting relatively quickly to such perturbations, have done so, while temperatures in the lower atmosphere and at the earth's surface (which adjust only slowly) have not.[9] Again, the scenario cannot be observed empirically, so modelling as well as spectroscopy is involved in the determination of a_x and a_r.

In 1990, the IPCC felt able to offer estimates of the GWPs of only 19 gases, not including HFC-23, and it labelled the figures 'preliminary only' (Houghton et al., 1990, p. 59 and table 2.8, p. 60). By 1995–6, the list had expanded to 26 gases and included HFC-23, the GWP of which was estimated as 11,700 (Houghton et al., 1996, table 2.9, p. 121). Both the notion of 'global warming potential' and the IPCC's mid-1990s estimates of GWPs were then inscribed into the Kyoto Protocol, which laid down that they should be used to translate emissions of other greenhouse gases into their equivalents in CO_2 and that the IPCC's mid-1990s estimates should be used until the end of the 2008–2012 commitment period.[10]

The 'exchange rate' of 11,700 used to translate HFC-23 into CO_2 is thus an example of 'black-boxing' in the sense of Callon and Latour (1981) and MacKenzie (1990, p. 26). The GWPs are in no sense simple, self-evident facts about nature. First, we have just had a glimpse of the complexity of the processes by which they are produced. Second, whether GWPs are really an adequate way of capturing the climatic effects of different gases could be and has been challenged (see Shackley and Wynne, 1997; Shine et al., 2005, and the literature cited in the latter): for example, the choice of a 100-year time period is in a sense arbitrary, and very different GWPs can be generated if, for example, 25, 50, or 500 years is used.[11] Indeed, there were suspicions at the time of its introduction that GWP's rise to prominence was precisely because it facilitated the global carbon trading the US government wanted to see introduced (see Shackley and Wynne, 1997).[12] Third, GWP estimates were acknowledged to be subject to significant uncertainties, of the order of +/- 35% (Houghton et al., 1996, pp. 73 and 119). By 2007, for example, the consensus estimate of the global warming potential of HFC-23 had increased from 11,700 to 14,800 (IPCC, 2007, p. 212).

However, neither the criticism nor the uncertainty has spilled over into the carbon market. The GWPs, with their apparent simplicity and the black-box 'possibility of use by policy makers with little further input from scientists' (Shine et al., 2005, p. 297), remain the way in which different gases are made commensurable, and the inscription of the mid-1990s' estimates of GWPs into the Kyoto Protocol means that uncertainties and the changing estimates of GWPs remain inside the black box: a matter for technical specialists, not carbon traders.

This black-boxing is crucial to allowing carbon markets to encompass greenhouse gases other than CO_2: liquidity in such markets would be greatly reduced if the relevant 'exchange rate' between gases had to be negotiated *ad hoc* for each transaction. Note that the black boxing rests upon a 'social' factor: the authority of the IPCC. Although that authority has been challenged by climate change 'sceptics' and 'deniers,' public controversy has focused on the reality, extent of and evidence for anthropogenic climate change, not on matters of 'detail' such as GWPs, debate over which has taken place only in much more limited circles. The IPCC's authority in such detailed matters is thus an essential part of 'making things the same' in carbon markets, by keeping the 'exchange rates' between gases inside the black box and separate from political and economic disputes.

It is perfectly possible, however, that this black boxing may become harder in the future. At the time of the Kyoto Protocol, it is unlikely that

anyone imagined that the figure of 11,700 for the global warming potential
of HFC-23 would determine a flow of funds of the order of $3.5 billion (the
likely total value of credits from HFC-23 decomposition up to 2012: see
Wara, 2007). As negotiations proceed over a successor to Kyoto, however,
the financial consequences of such figures can now be seen. It is possible that
GWPs will remain in practice unchallenged—it would be very hard, given
the diversity of economic interests involved, to get agreement on a measure
other than GWPs, or on anything other than the IPCC's estimates of them
(which are a 'focal point' in game-theoretic terms), so no party to the negotiations may attempt to do so—but it is not a foregone conclusion.

Making Things the Same: 'Emission Rights'

Gases are thus rendered visible and commensurable by a combination of
measurement devices, complex natural science, and the capacity (at least so
far) of the IPCC to keep the estimation of global warming potentials brack-
eted off from carbon-market politics. But practices of many other kinds
are also needed to make 'carbon' fungible, and amongst these accounting
is of particular importance.[13] When they were introduced, the European
allowances that Edinburgh University needs to emit carbon dioxide and
the credits generated by Zhejiang Juhua Company were items that Europe's
(or indeed China's) accountants had not previously encountered. What
kind of items are they? What accounting treatment should they receive?
These questions are significant for the operation of carbon markets, since
accounting makes economic items visible, and whether and how it does so
is consequential.[14]

MacKenzie (2009) argues that a 'finitist' perspective is useful for the
analysis of accounting, especially of accounting classification, and it is
particularly appropriate here. In this perspective, how to classify an item
(not just an accounting item, but an item of any kind) is always implicitly
a choice. Past classifications—which are always finite in number, hence
'finitism'—influence present classifications by analogy ('this item is like
previous items we classified as X, so this should be classified as an X'), but
do not determine them. Of course, classification often does not *feel* like a
choice. Classifiers—bookkeepers, accountants, ornithologists, botanists,
and so on—often, probably normally, come across items that seem familiar
and simply 'see' them as an X ('this *is* an X,' not 'I am classifying this as
an X'). Items that seem to classifiers to be unfamiliar are thus of particular
analytical interest, because they make implicit choice explicit. Instead of
relying on habit and routine, those involved have consciously and explicitly
to decide what classification is appropriate, and the debate that is often
sparked can reveal the contingencies that affect classification.

In the run-up to the launch of the European Union Emissions Trading
System, the International Financial Reporting Interpretations Committee
(IFRIC), a subsidiary body of the International Accounting Standards

Board (IASB), discussed how to apply accounting standards to the new items, which it called 'emission rights,' that were about to come into being. What kind of items were they? For example, were they indeed 'rights'? The IFRIC concluded that they were not: 'an allowance itself does not confer a right to emit. Rather it is the instrument that must be delivered in order to settle the obligation that arises from emissions' (IFRIC, 2004, p. 19).[15]

An allowance was, however, in the IFRIC's view clearly an asset. But what was its nature? Was it an 'intangible asset'—'An identifiable non-monetary asset without physical substance' (IASB, 2005, p. 2227)—and thus within the scope of International Accounting Standard (IAS) 38? Or was it a 'financial instrument'—a 'contract that gives rise to both a financial asset of one entity and a financial liability or equity instrument of another entity' (IASB, 2005, p. 2219)—and thus within the scope of the standard governing such instruments, IAS 39? Some of those who commented on the IFRIC's initial draft argued that an allowance was indeed a financial instrument, but the IFRIC disagreed: though allowances 'have some features that are more commonly found in financial assets than in intangible assets'—such as being 'traded in a ready market'—they were not financial instruments (IFRIC, 2004, p. 21).

An allowance was thus, in the IFRIC's view, an intangible asset, and therefore governed by IAS 38. If governments issued allowances at less than their market value (as noted, most have issued them free-of-charge) the difference was, IFRIC decided, a 'government grant,' and its accounting treatment should therefore follow the relevant standard, IAS 20. Emissions themselves—as noted, previously outside an economic or accounting frame—now had to come within it. The emissions of those governed by cap-and-trade schemes should, said the IFRIC, be treated as giving rise to liabilities that were 'provisions' whose treatment should follow IAS 37 (IFRIC, 2004, p. 7).

The IFRIC's conclusions—crystallized in *IFRIC Interpretation 3: Emission Rights*, issued in December 2004, on the eve of the start of the European Union Emission Trading System—thus made 'emission rights' the same by laying down a homogeneous approach to accounting for them, in which, for example, an allowance received free by an industrial company or bought by an investment bank were both treated in the same way as intangible assets. However, IFRIC 3 encountered strong opposition, with critics arguing that the relationship of IFRIC 3 to the three relevant standards—IAS 20, 37, and 38—would create accounting mismatches, especially in the light of anticipated changes to IAS 20 that would mean that non-repayable government grants have to be recognized when they are received (see Cook, 2009). For example, the fair value of the allowances that a company received free would have to be recognized immediately as income, while the costs of the corresponding emissions would be recognized only gradually as they accumulated. Reflecting the criticism of IFRIC 3, the European Financial Reporting Advisory Group told the European Commission in June 2005 that the interpretation 'will not always result in economic reality being reflected,' and recommended that the Commission not endorse it.[16] The following month, the IASB, while defending IFRIC 3 as 'an appropriate interpretation' of existing accounting standards, acknowledged that it 'creates unsatisfactory measurement and reporting mismatches' and withdrew it.[17]

There was, of course, a 'bottom line' issue underpinning the controversy surrounding IFRIC 3. Corporations generally fear earnings volatility: there is a widespread conviction that investors prefer earnings that rise smoothly to those that fluctuate, even around the same underlying trend. The IFRIC 3 threatened to produce volatility that, in its critics' eyes, would be artificial. For example, the advantage, for corporations, of classifying an 'emission right' as a financial instrument would have been that it would make available the 'hedge accounting' treatment permitted under IAS 39. If allowances could 'be treated as the hedging instrument of a forecast transaction (ie future emissions)' (IFRIC, 2004, p. 20), then allowances and the corresponding emissions would offset each other. If a company received N free allowances and forecasted emissions of N tons of carbon dioxide, and then emitted N tons, then its earnings would at no point be affected. 'Carbon' would thus remain invisible.

The withdrawal of IFRIC 3 means that it remains permissible to treat carbon in this way: as inside an economic frame, but in a sense invisibly so, since no accounting recognition is needed if the above conditions are met. A survey by Deloitte (2007) found that some market participants were doing just that. Others were in effect following IFRIC 3, while others again were doing so partially, treating the provision for the liability created by emissions in a different way.[18] The attempt to make 'emission rights' the same has, in this sense, so far failed.

The partial invisibility of carbon also means that the incorporation of the carbon price into the market's 'calculative mechanisms' (Callon and Muniesa, 2003) is only partial. Although it is impossible to be certain, there is tentative evidence from my interview data of effects of both the accounting visibility of carbon in some firms and its invisibility in others. Consider, for example, the effect of the European Union Emissions Trading System on electricity prices. If allowances are distributed free, one might naïvely think that they should have no effect on the price of electricity. If a generator is given enough allowances to cover its emissions (most generators have actually had to buy some allowances, but let me set that aside), what it charges customers surely shouldn't change? An economist will quickly tell you what's wrong with that argument. As already noted, there's an opportunity cost involved. In a 'perfect market,' a profit-maximizing firm will produce electricity only if the price it receives is greater than what it can earn by not generating electricity and selling its stocks of the required inputs: its coal, its gas, and now its carbon allowances (Point Carbon, 2007, pp 24–25). If its allowances can command a non-zero price, the price of electricity must rise correspondingly.

According to an interviewee in the electricity market, however, it has required accountants to give force to this economists' reasoning. The 'naïve' view prevailed in the industry until explicit valuations of allowances started to be made. The price effect 'should' have been manifest in forward contracts covering supply from January 2005 (the start of the ETS) onwards, but apparently it initially wasn't.[19] The effect began in the UK only once January 2005 was reached, and analysis by the consultancy Point Carbon (2007) suggests it was even slower to appear on the Continent. (Once the effect began, the result in the UK was, for example, an increase in domestic electricity prices in 2005 of around 7%[20]—for example, about £20 on a £300 annual bill—and it is increases of this kind that are the source of the much-criticized 'windfall profits' that electricity generators have made from the Emissions Trading System.)

Carbon has thus been visible for some time in the electricity sector. When, in contrast, carbon is kept invisible in accounting terms effects of three kinds can be anticipated. The first, which is hypothetical (I have no direct evidence on the point), would be to undermine a major desired effect of a carbon market: incentivizing even those companies who have 'enough' allowances to cut their emissions so as to generate income by selling allowances. For this effect to be realized, allowances need to be seen as assets with potential monetary value, not simply as means of complying with regulatory requirements. The second, related effect (of which there is some tentative evidence) is to delay the sale of allowances by those who, even without abatement, have more allowances than they need. The sale of allowances—and also lending allowances for short sale—means that they can no longer be kept invisible. They must be recognized in accounting terms, and, for example, a tax liability may be crystallized. This disincentive may reinforce other reasons for not selling, such as the fact that emission levels will in general be known in advance only approximately and the lack of a culture of proprietary, risk-taking trading in many industrial companies (in contrast to electricity suppliers, which are active traders) that would permit the sale of allowances that probably—but not certainly—will not be needed.

My interview data do not permit me to judge the relative importance of the various reasons for postponing the sale of allowances that are likely to be surplus to requirements, but those interviewees with whom I explored the topic all believed delayed sale to be a real phenomenon in the first phase (January 2005 to December 2007) of the European Emission Trading System. (Behavior seems to have changed in the current phase, which began in January 2008, possibly because the credit crunch has led firms to see allowance sales as a way of raising cash.) Delayed sale was consequential in the first phase because the complex process of setting national allocations for that phase led to over-allocation of allowances. The extent of over-allocation was, however, not clear initially, and the failure of those who were 'long' allowances to bring them to market led to a constriction of supply, which helped market prices to rise to €31/ton (see Figure 2). Curiously, when the extent of over-allocation became clear in the spring of 2006, prices—though plunging dramatically—did not initially fully reflect the fact that allowances no longer had any significant economic value. It took several months for the market price of a phase-one European allowance to fall close to zero (only in 2007 did prices become in effect zero, with allowances towards the end of the year costing less than €0.10/ton). Interviewees suggested that delayed sale by those who were 'long' allowances accounts for this paradoxical behavior of the carbon price. Even though it was clear that allowances were intrinsically close to worthless (because, in aggregate, there were more of them than would be needed), they still commanded a price of several euros, because not enough were brought to market.[21]

The third—again hypothetical—effect of the accounting invisibility of carbon may be to strengthen the hand of managers whose interests lie in protecting market share by not passing on to customers the opportunity cost of allowances that have been allocated free, even when passing on the cost is profit maximizing for their firms. The extent to which firms pass on the opportunity cost is crucial to the environmental effects of a cap-and-trade market—if they pass it on, there is likely to be carbon 'leakage' from the scheme, as imports from outside its boundaries become more attractive—and there is fierce controversy over likely behavior in this respect. Economists tend to predict profit-maximization, cost pass-through and

Figure 3.2 Price history of allowances, phase I of European Union Emission Trading System. Courtesy Point Carbon.

thus leakage, while firms themselves tend to argue that market share will be protected and costs will not be passed through, at least in full. Unfortunately, empirical analysis of the Emissions Trading System so far is too limited to be confident how firms outside the electricity sector have behaved in this respect: see Carbon Trust (2008).

THE POLITICS OF CARBON MARKETS

One could go deeper into the issue of fungibility, of making things the same. A trade, for example, is a legal transaction requiring documentation, and with three bodies (the International Swaps and Derivatives Association, the European Federation of Energy Traders, and the International Emissions Trading Association) competing in this sphere, interviewees reported that it has taken orchestrated action to reduce the differences to a level at which a trade documented in one format can be regarded as similar enough to one documented in another, for example for one to be used to hedge the other. There has also, for instance, been sharp criticism from competitors of the efforts by Barclays Capital, a leading player in the carbon market, to standardize CERs via its SCERFA (Standard CER Forward Agreement). The competitors regard a SCERFA as specific to Barclays, not as a 'standard' entity.

Instead, however, let me consider the question of the attitude to be taken to carbon markets. There is a great deal of suspicion of them, ranging from right-wing distaste for emissions caps to leftwing hostility to an extension of market relations. The efforts at market construction so far have led to some environmental benefits—for example, because of HFC-23's potency, curbing emissions of it is very valuable—but also significant problems. There has, for example, been only modest abatement by Europe's electricity producers (the sharp rise in gas prices in 2005–2006 swamped the carbon-price incentive to switch from coal to gas), while the mechanism discussed above led them, as noted, to make substantial windfall profits.

Similarly, the large sums that can be earned by decomposing HFC-23 also create substantial profits, because the costs of decomposition are modest. A specialized incinerator of the kind needed costs around $4–5 million to install and $20,000 a month to run (McCulloch, 2005, p. 12). Even with China's 65% tax, a large HCFC-22 plant can recoup the installation cost in a few months and go on to earn revenues of well over a million dollars a month. There is debate over just how much the subsidy increases HCFC-22 production: McCulloch (2005) argues that because the cost of HCFC-22 is only a small proportion of the costs of the products in which it is used,[22] a reduction in the price of HCFC-22 will not expand the market for it very much. However, the de facto subsidy may slow the replacement of HCFC-22 by more environmentally friendly refrigerants. (HCFC-22 is an ozone depleter; the use of which as a refrigerant will eventually be phased out under the Montréal Protocol governing such substances, and it is also a greenhouse agent, though not as potent as HFC-23.) Because of fears of this kind, 'new' HCFC-22 production (i.e., over and above 2000–2004 levels) is currently not eligible for CDM credits, but the consequence is that there is no economic incentive not simply to discharge HFC-23 from such new production into the atmosphere rather than decomposing it.

In the light of issues such as these, it is tempting to conclude that carbon markets are inherently flawed means of achieving abatement. As Michel Callon (1998) points out, constructing a market requires an enormous degree of 'cooling' of knowledge, of metrologies, of actors, of identities, and of interests. In a perceptive article, Lohmann applies Callon's analysis to the carbon market and essentially concludes that market construction will indeed fail: 'conditions are not cool enough for the spadework for commercial relations,' and 'an unstoppable fount of complexity' has been uncorked (2005, pp. 211 and 229).

Indeed, much of what I have described is consistent with a bleak, essentialized view of capitalism, as inherently irresponsible and environmentally damaging, rather than Callon and Latour's more optimistic perspective. Yet the conclusion that carbon markets are inherently flawed carries a risk. Abandonment of such markets might well mean no serious international abatement efforts, rather than abatement by other means. If the Emissions Trading System were abandoned, could the European Union find a viable alternative, and how long would it take? The political viability of a harmonized carbon tax, the obvious other route, remains questionable, because of the unanimity required. (It should, however, be noted that the huge government budget deficits caused by the credit crunch have increased interest in some EU member states in carbon taxes.) Similarly, political constraints mean that if international agreement on a replacement for the Kyoto Protocol can be reached, it is likely to include something similar to the Clean Development Mechanism. The CDM is, as noted, a result of the need to secure developing-country participation in abatement efforts in a context in which the developing world was and is unwilling to take on caps: even caps postponed to a later date, given the risk that by then many of the cheaper opportunities for abatement might be exhausted. The reluctance is understandable, given the desire not to allow a problem caused by the industrialized countries to serve as a brake upon development, and it is likely to persist—even in a context in which China, in particular, no longer fits the traditional template of a developing country. Abatement efforts in the developing world are thus likely to continue to require funding from the developed world. Of course, such funding could be achieved by direct government aid—Wara (2007) points out that HFC-23 decomposition could have been achieved far more cheaply via this route than via the CDM—but that again raises the question of whether governments would in practice make the requisite large transfers of resources.[23]

To conclude that carbon markets must fail may also be unduly pessimistic, in that it would miss the extent to which carbon markets hitherto have been experimental, in the case of phase 1 of the European Union Emissions Trading System, quite explicitly so: interviewees involved in establishing it reported the many compromises that had to be made to get it up and running, such as the fact that it was possible to challenge only the most egregiously over-generous national allocations of allowances. While existing carbon markets unquestionably have major flaws, those flaws are increasingly becoming manifest, and ways of remedying them are available. Thus, windfall profits within the European scheme could be eliminated by moving from free allocation to full auctioning (Dales's original proposal), and it appears as if this will now happen from 2013 on, at least in the electricity sector (although the European Commission's proposals for auctioning have been watered down somewhat in the face of fierce pressure from countries such as Poland in which electricity generation is heavily dependent on coal).

Can carbon markets be improved? One example of a successful intervention is of particular interest from the viewpoint of this paper, because it involves making things *not* the same. NGOs, especially the World Wildlife Fund, have sought to create a separate category of 'gold standard' CERs, covering only renewable energy and energy conservation projects and excluding industrial gas projects such as HFC-23 decomposition.[24] The gold standard is a form of cooling in Callon's sense (as with the CDM as a whole, there is a formal methodology, automated tools, a role for auditors, and so on), and there are 'bottom-line' effects. Although from the viewpoint of the Kyoto Protocol or of monetisability via the European Emissions Trading System, an ordinary and a gold standard CER are identical, my interviewees reported the market price of the latter to be around 10–20% higher. (They suggest that the cause of the higher price is that those who are buying CERs not just for compliance but to achieve 'carbon neutrality' or other forms of offsetting fear reputational risk if it is discovered that 'neutrality' is being achieved via industrial gas projects such as HFC-23.) 'Multiple monies' have emerged in the carbon market, as a result of intervention by activists.

The intervention by the World Wildlife Fund and other NGOs was informal: it did not alter the formal procedures of the CDM. However, NGOs are also seeking to practice a politics of market design in a more formal sense, seeking to alter rules and procedures. That, indeed, is precisely the course of action that Callon and Latour's perspective implies. If markets are plural—Callon's best-known work is titled *The Laws of the Markets* (Callon, 1998)—and 'capitalism' has no unalterable essence, then this may indeed be productive. Such efforts are too recent and too limited to know whether they will be successful. However, it is worth noting that changes in market design of a kind that seem potentially achievable could be consequential.

Take the underlying issue of a carbon market versus a carbon tax. Many environmental activists prefer the latter, as do some economists such as Nordhaus (2007), who argues that the classic analysis by Weitzman (1974) of the conditions that influence the relative efficiency of 'quantity-based' instruments (such as a cap-and-trade scheme) and 'price-based' instruments (such as a carbon tax) suggests, given the specific cost-benefit features of combating global warming, the superior efficiency of a carbon tax. Intriguingly, however, a cap-and-trade market, with full auctioning rather than free allocation, can be equivalent to an optimally set tax. In both, polluters pay, either by having to buy permits or by paying the carbon tax. Under admittedly 'idealized conditions' (Hepburn, 2006, p. 229) they pay the same amounts, and the environmental outcomes are the same. Thus, if the relationship between emission levels and the costs of achieving those levels is known with certainty, either a cap-and-trade market or a correctly set tax can achieve a required level of abatement, and the necessary tax rate will be the same as the allowance price.

Of course, the relationship between levels of abatement and their costs is not known with certainty, and for that and other reasons the full equivalence between auctioned permits and a tax does not pertain in the real world. However, economists' analyses suggest ways of designing a carbon market that might make it and a tax more closely equivalent in practice. These include rules facilitating the 'banking' of permits for future use and the 'borrowing' of permits from future years, regulated perhaps by an adjustable requirement for firms to hold a certain amount of permits in reserve, analogous to the adjustable reserves that banks are required to hold (Newell et al., 2005). At the time of writing (October 2009), it seems to be mainly the possibility of banking permits for future use that is keeping the phase-two European carbon price from collapsing—as the phase-one price did—in the face of low net demand for permits (the current problem is not over-allocation but the sharp falls in industrial activity caused by the recession).

Precisely because of the similarity of auctioning to a carbon tax, emissions markets seem almost always initially to involve free allocation, because this reduces lobbying against them and political opposition. However, once a market is well-established, as the European Union Emissions Trading System now is, shifting to auctioning becomes easier (especially in the case of the ETS since the 'economic experiment' of its Phase I made publicly visible the problems that free allocation leads to). As early as October 2007 Sweden announced that it was ending free allocation of allowances to its electricity and heat sectors,[25] and, as noted above, in the third phase of the ETS, from 2013 onwards, auctioning will be much more prevalent, at least in sectors such as electricity that cannot easily move production outside of the European Union.

The effort to shift the ETS to auctioning is 'politics' of a classic, recognizable kind, involving governments, the policy makers of a supranational body, nation-state representatives, fierce industry and nation-state lobbying against auctioning, and so on. Not all the politics of carbon markets, however, fit that recognizable template. Neither the IPCC nor the IASB see themselves as political bodies, and indeed it is of particular importance that the former not be seen as political, despite the efforts of its critics to paint it as such. Yet they are arguably locales of 'sub-politics' in Beck's sense: politics 'outside and beyond the representative institutions of the political system of nation-states' (Beck, 1996, p. 18; see Holzer and Sørensen, 2003). For example, the IFRIC and now the IASB (which at the time of writing is examining the accounting treatment of emission rights) have to contend with pressure that has had the effect of blocking efforts to 'make things the same' in carbon markets. In the case of the IPCC, the key 'subpolitical' matter is, paradoxically, preserving the boundary between 'science' and 'politics,' since that boundary is precisely what is needed to facilitate political action, because it matters that action can be seen as based upon 'sound science.'

The subpolitics of carbon markets may seem esoteric, and it is certainly not simple, but it is important. Clearly, such markets are only one tool for combating global warming, and other tools are also important: direct regulation, carbon taxes (where these are feasible), greatly increased public expenditure on research and development and on necessary infrastructure (for example, the electricity grid changes needed to make increased renewables production more attractive economically), the removal of the many subsidies for fossil-fuel extraction and use, and so on (see, for example, Lohmann, 2006; Prins and Rayner, 2007). Nevertheless, making carbon markets more effective is crucial, and the esoteric nature of their subpolitics means that researchers have a particularly salient role to play in bringing to light matters of apparent detail that in fact play critical roles in this respect.

It is this author's hope that this chapter will encourage the work of this kind that is so badly needed. The existing and planned experiments in changing capitalism's bottom line are heterogeneous, widely diffused worldwide, and involve many aspects—scientific, technological, political, accounting, sociological, anthropological, geographical—beyond economics as narrowly conceived. The experiments need 'witnesses' (Shapin and Schaffer, 1985), and those witnesses must be multiple: lay as well as professional, from many countries, and if they are academics from many disciplines.[26] Carbon markets need to become part of a process of 'social learning' (q.v. Williams, Stewart and Slack, 2005), in which institutions to mitigate climate change are created, evaluated and reshaped.[27] Such multiple witnessing and social learning needs to concern not just the overall features of carbon markets but the crucial 'nuts and bolts' of their construction, questions such as how different carbon sources and sinks are commensurated, how allowances are treated in accounting terms, and many other such matters that I have been unable to discuss for space reasons. If this chapter helps recruit others to take part in this multiple witnessing and social learning, then it will have achieved its goal.

NOTES

1. This chapter is a revised and updated version of an article that appeared in *Accounting, Organizations and Society* 34(3/4), April–May 2009.The research was supported by the United Kingdom (UK) Economic and Social Research Council (RES-051-27-0062) and by the Nuffield Foundation (NCF/35037).
2. This chapter concentrates on regulatory markets, largely setting aside the 'voluntary' market, in which, for example, firms choose to 'offset' their emissions, even though they are under no compulsion to do so.
3. The history of emissions trading is treated in more detail in MacKenzie (2009).
4. On the emergence of the ETS, see, e.g., Zapfel and Vainio (2002), Christiansen and Wettestad (2003), Damro and Méndez (2003), Cass (2005), Wettestad (2005), Skærseth and Wettestad (2008), and Braun (2009).
5. On commensuration in the SO_2 market, see Levin and Espeland (2002).
6. 'HFC-23' and 'HCFC-22' are not standard chemical formulae, but instances of a code, widely used in the refrigerant business, for identifying haloalkanes. The standard formula for trifluoromethane is CHF_3, but 'HFC-23' is how it is referred to in carbon markets.
7. The mass of HCFC-22 produced (which is determined by weighing shipping containers and storage tanks) determines the 'eligible quantity' of HFC-23: the quantity for the incineration of which credits can be earned. For each ton of HCFC-22 produced by the standard antimony pentachloride process, the eligible quantity of HFC-23 is 0.0137 tons, corresponding to the lowest recorded emission level from a process optimized to minimize HFC-23 production (see McCulloch, 2005, p. 11). The mass of gas fed into the incinerator is determined from the readings of a flow meter, and the concentration of HFC-23 in it is determined by gas chromatography of periodic samples. (A correction for leakage is also applied.) The product of mass of gas (in tonnes) and HFC-23 concentration, up to the maximum given by the eligible quantity, is, as noted in the text, then multiplied by 11,700 to give the quantity of Certified Emission Reductions earned (SGS United Kingdom Ltd., 2007).
8. I'm grateful to Thomas Grammig and to members of the audience of a talk I gave at the University of Oxford for sparking my interest in how gas equivalents are brought into being.
9. 'The long-term forcing is . . . more accurately represented by that acting after the stratosphere has returned to a state of global-mean radiative equilibrium. Studies with simple models show that the climate response, that is, the surface temperature change, is proportional to the radiative forcing when the radiative forcing is defined in this way . . . Importantly, the proportionality constant is found to be the same for a wide range of forcing mechanisms' (Pinnock et al., 1995, p, 23227).
10. See article 5, paragraph 3 of the Kyoto Protocol, the text of which is from http://unfccc.int/resource/docs/convkp/kpeng.html (accessed March 24, 2006).
11. Among other criticisms is 'the fact that, despite its name, the global *warming* potential does not purport to represent the impact of gas emissions on temperature. The GWP uses the time-integrated radiative forcing and this does not give a unique indication of the effect of pulse emissions on temperature, because of large differences in the time constants of the various greenhouse gases. Although a strong greenhouse gas with a short lifetime could have the same GWP as a weaker greenhouse gas with a longer lifetime, identical (in mass terms) pulse emissions of the two gases could cause a different tempera-

ture change at a given time. Economists have also criticised the GWP concept for not being based on an analysis of damages caused by the emissions' (Shine et al., 2005, p. 282).

12. It should, however, be noted that GWP had a predecessor in the role of the 'ozone depletion potential' (a measure of the relative extent to which different halocarbons damage the ozone layer: see, e.g., Wuebbles, 1981) in the framing of the 1987 Montréal Protocol, which does not involve emissions trading.

13. I am deeply grateful to Allan Cook, who served as Co-ordinator for the International Financial Reporting Interpretations Committee at the end of the period in question for his help in the research underpinning this section. Cook (2009) is his own account of these events. For broader legal debate over the nature of carbon credits and allowances, see Wemaere and Streck (2005).

14. The issue of devising appropriate frameworks for making carbon emissions visible in other ways, for example in corporate accounts, has received considerable attention: see, for example, the work of Fred Wellington and his colleagues at the World Resources Institute (such as Lash and Wellington, 2007) and the Prince's Charities (2007). How to account for emissions allowances, however, has received much less attention: see Cook (2009) and Casamento (2005).

15. 'It therefore follows that a participant in a cap and trade scheme does not consume the economic benefits of an allowance as a result of its emissions. Rather a participant realises the benefits of that allowance by surrendering it to settle the obligation that arises from producing emissions (or by selling it to another entity). Therefore, the IFRIC observed that amortisation, which is the systematic allocation of the cost of an asset to reflect the consumption of the economic benefits of that asset over its useful life, is incompatible with the way the benefits of the allowances are realised. Although the IFRIC agreed that this observation pointed to precluding amortisation, it agreed with those respondents who highlighted that in some cases such a requirement could be inconsistent with the requirements of IAS [International Accounting Standard] 38. The IFRIC therefore decided not to proceed with its proposal . . . that allowances should not be amortised. Nonetheless, for most allowances traded in an active market, no amortisation will be required, because the residual value will be the same as cost and hence the depreciable amount will be zero' (IFRIC, 2004, pp. 22–23).

16. Letter from Stig Enevoldsen to Alexander Schaub, May 6, 2005. From http://www.iasplus.com/interps/ifric003.htm (accessed June 11, 2007).

17. International Accounting Standards Board, IASB withdraws IFRIC Interpretation on Emission Rights.,From http://www.iasplus.com/interps/ifric003.htm (accessed June 11, 2007).

18. Deloitte (2007) does not estimate the relative prevalence of the three forms of accounting treatment. Those in the third category 'recognise a provision on the following bases:
    - To the extent that the entity holds a sufficient number of allowances, the provision should be recognized based on the carrying value of those allowances (i.e., the cost to the entity of extinguishing their obligation)
    - To the extent that the entity does not hold a sufficient number of allowances, the provision should be recognized based on the market value of emission rights required to cover the shortfall; and
    - The penalty that the entity will incur if it is unable to obtain allowances to meet their obligations under the scheme, and it is anticipated that the penalty will be incurred (note that the obligation to deliver allowances must still be fulfilled)' (Deloitte, 2007, p. 3).

19. This is an interviewee's assertion. Unfortunately, I do not have access to the price data needed to test it quantitatively.
20. Calculation by Karsten Neuhoff, quoted on BBC Radio 4, 'File on Four,' June 5, 2007. Controversy developed across Europe about these 'windfall profits.' In the UK, for example, the energy regulator Ofgem called for the windfall profits of the UK's electricity generators in the 2008–2012 phase of the Emission Trading System—which Ofgem estimates at £9 billion—to be used to help customers in fuel poverty (Crooks, 2007). In Germany, the Bundeskartellamt (Federal Cartel Office) charged electricity generator RWE with behaving illegally by incorporating in the price it charged industrial consumers the market value of permits it had received free. The case was settled out of court in September 2007, with RWE continuing to defend its pricing but agreeing that in 2009–2012 it would hold annual auctions of quantities of power almost equivalent to its annual sales to German industry (46,000 GWh in total over the four years) and transfer to the purchasers, free of charge, the corresponding carbon allowances if it had received these at no cost (RWE AG, 2007).
21. One interviewee, at a hedge fund, reported making a considerable amount of money by taking a short position in allowances in this period.
22. An air conditioning unit retailing at $500–$1,000 needs less than a kilogram of HCFC-22, which costs around $1–$2 (McCulloch, 2005, p. 7).
23. For an intriguing suggestion of a means of achieving north-south transfers at a sufficient level to make a significant impact on developing countries' needs to adapt to climate change, see Müller and Hepburn (2006).
24. See http://www.cdmgoldstandard.org, (accessed January 17, 2008).
25. Announcement of Environment Minister Anders Calgren, reported by news service Point Carbon: From www.pointcarbon.com (October 11, 2007).
26. I owe this way of formulating the matter to Andrew Barry.
27. There is of course a trade-off between the need to evaluate and improve a market's design and the need for rules that are stable over reasonably long time periods. The European Union's trade-off seems reasonable—an explicitly experimental three-year initial phase, then a five-year second phase, followed by a third phase that is likely to last eight years (2013–2020).

REFERENCES

Agrawala, S. (1998a). Context and Early Origins of the Intergovernmental Panel on Climate Change. *Climatic Change, 39,* 605–620.

———. (1998b). Structural and Process History of the Intergovernmental Panel on Climate Change. *Climatic Change, 39,*621–642.

Barnes, B., Bloor, D., and Henry, J. (1996). *Scientific Knowledge: A Sociological Analysis.* London: Athlone and Chicago: Chicago University Press.

Beck, U. (1996). World Risk Society as Cosmopolitan Society? Ecological Questions in a Framework of Manufactured Uncertainties. *Theory, Culture and Society, 13*(4):1–32.

Braun, M. (2009). The Evolution of Emissions Trading in the European Union: The Role of Policy Networks, Knowledge and Policy Entrepreneurs. *Accounting, Organizations and Society, 34,* 469–487.

Burtraw, D., Evans, D. A., Krupnick, A., Palmer, K., and Toth, R. (2005). Economics of Pollution Trading for SO_2 and NO_x. *Annual Review of Environmental Resources, 30* 253–289.

Callon, M. (Ed.). (1998). *The Laws of the Markets.* Oxford: Blackwell.

———. (2007). What does it mean to say that economics is performative? In D. MacKenzie, F. Muniesa, and L. Siu (Eds.), *Do economists make markets? On the performativity of economics* (pp. 311–357). Princeton NJ: Princeton University Press.

Callon, M., and Latour, B. (1981). Unscrewing the big leviathan: How actors macro-structure reality and how sociologists help them to do so. In K. Knorr Cetina and A. V. Cicourel (Eds.), *Advances in social theory and methodology: Toward an integration of micro- and macro-sociologies* (pp. 277–303). Boston: Routledge and Kegan Paul.

———. (1997). 'Tu ne calculeras pas!' Ou comment symétriser le don et le capital. *Revue du MAUSS, 9*(1), 45–70.

Callon, M., and Muniesa, F. (2003). Les marchés économiques comme dispositifs collectifs de calcul. *Réseaux, 21*(122), 189–233.

Capoor, K., and Ambrosi, P. (2009). *State and Trends of the Carbon Market 2009.* Washington, DC: World Bank.

Carbon Trust. (2008). EU ETS Impacts on Profitability and Trade: A Sector by Sector Analysis. London: Carbon Trust.

Casamento, R. (2005). Accounting for and taxation of emission allowances and credits. In D. Freestone and C. Streck (Eds.), *Legal aspects of implementing the Kyoto Protocol mechanisms: Making Kyoto work* (pp. 55–70). Oxford: Oxford University Press.

Cass, L. (2005). Norm Entrapment and Preference Change: The Evolution of the European Union Position on International Emissions Trading. *Global Environmental Politics, 5*(2), 38–60.

CDM Executive Board. (2007). Project 0868: No. 2 HFC-23 Decomposition Project of Zhejiang Juhua Co., Ltd, P.R. China. From http://cdm.unfccc.int/Project, (accessed June 11, 2007).

Christiansen, A. C., and Wettestad, J. (2003). The EU as a Frontrunner on Greenhouse Gas Emissions Trading: How did it Happen and will the EU Succeed? *Climate Policy, 3*, 3–18.

Coase, R. H. (1960). The Problem of Social Cost. *Journal of Law & Economics, 3*, 1–44.

Cook, A. (2009). Emission Rights: From Costless Activity to Market Operations. *Accounting, Organizations and Society, 34*, 465–468.

Crooks, E. (2007). Watchdog Wants £9bn Windfall Electricity Profits Clawed Back. *Financial Times*, January 17, 1.

Dales, J. H. (1968a). Land, Water, and Ownership. *Canadian Journal of Economics, 1*, 791–804.

———. (1968b). *Pollution, Property and Prices: An Essay in Policy-Making and Economics.* Toronto: University of Toronto Press.

Damro, C., and Luaces Méndez, P. (2003). Emissions Trading at Kyoto: From EU Resistance to Union Innovation. *Environmental Politics, 12*(2), 71–94.

Deloitte LLP. (2007). Accounting for Emission Rights. From www.deloitte.com/dtt/cda/doc/content/us_er_Accounting%20ForEmission%20Rights_0220_2007.pdf (accessed July 31 2007).

Ellerman, A. D., Schmalensee, R., Bailey, E. M., Joskow, P. L., and Montero J.-P. (2000). *Markets for Clean Air: The U.S. Acid Rain Program.* Cambridge: Cambridge University Press.

European Parliament, Council. (2004). Directive 2004/101/EC of the European Parliament and of the Council. *Official Journal of the European Union, 338*, 18–23.

Greimas, A. J. (1987). *On Meaning: Selected Writings in Semiotic Theory.* London: Pinter.

Grubb, M. (1999). *The Kyoto Protocol: A Guide and Assessment.* London: Royal Institute of International Affairs.

Hahn, R. W. (1989). Economic Prescription for Environmental problems: How the Patient Followed the Doctor's Orders. *Journal of Economic Perspectives,* 3(2), 95–114.

Hepburn, C. (2006). Regulation by Prices, Quantities, or Both: A Review of Instrument Choice. *Oxford Review of Economic Policy,* 22, 226–247.

Holzer, B., and Sørensen M. P. (2003). Rethinking Subpolitics: Beyond the 'Iron Cage' of Modern Politics. *Theory, Culture and Society* 20(2), 79–102.

Houghton, J. T., Jenkins G. J., and Ephraums J. J. (Eds.). (1990). *Climate Change: The IPCC Scientific Assessment.* Cambridge: Cambridge University Press.

Houghton, J. T., Meira Filho L. G., Callander B. A., Harris N., Kattenberg A., and Maskell K. (Eds.). (1996). *Climate Change 1995: The Science of Climate Change.* Cambridge: Cambridge University Press.

IASB (International Accounting Standards Board). (2005). *International Financial Reporting Standards (IFRSs) 2005.* London: IASB.

IFRIC (International Financial Reporting Interpretations Committee). (2004). IFRIC Interpretation 3: Emission Rights. London: International Accounting Standards Board.

Intergovernmental Panel on Climate Change. (2007). Climate Change 2007: The Physical Science Basis. From http://ipcc-wg1.ucar.edu/wg1/wg1-report.html, (accessed August 31, 2007).

Kanter, J. (2008). Europe's Carbon Market Holds Lessons for the U.S. *International Herald Tribune,* June 19, 1.

Lash, J., and Wellington, F. (2007). Competitive Advantage on a Warming Planet. *Harvard Business Review,* 85(3), 95–102.

Lashof, D. A., and Ahuja, D. R. (1990). Relative Contributions of Greenhouse Gas Emissions to Global Warming. *Nature, 344,* 529–531.

Latour, B. (2005). *Reassembling the Social: An Introduction to Actor-Network Theory.* Oxford: Oxford University Press.

———. (Forthcoming). Résumé d'une enquête sur les modes d'existence, ou Bref éloge de la civilisation qui vient. Unpublished typescript.

Lecocq, F., and Ambrosi P. (2007). The Clean Development Mechanism: History, Status, and Prospects. *Review of Environmental Economics and Policy,* 1, 34–151.

Levin, P., and Espeland W. N. (2002). Pollution futures: Commensuration, commodification, and the market for air. In A. J. Hoffman and M. J. Ventresca (Eds.), *Organizations, policy, and the natural environment: institutional and strategic perspectives* (pp. 119–147). Stanford, CA: Stanford University Press.

Lohmann, L. (2005). Marketing and Making Carbon Dumps: Commodification, Calculation and Counterfactuals in Climate Change Mitigation. *Science as Culture,* 14, 203–235.

———. (2006). Carbon Trading: A Critical Conversation on Climate Change, Privatisation and Power. *Development Dialogue,* (48) ,4–359.

MacKenzie, D. (1990). *Inventing Accuracy: A Historical Sociology of Nuclear Missile Guidance.* Cambridge, MA: MIT Press.

———. (2009). *Material Markets: How Economic Agents are Constructed.* Oxford: Clarendon.

McCulloch, A. (2005). Incineration of HFC-23 Waste Streams for Abatement of Emissions from HCFC-22 Production: A Review of Scientific, Technical and Economic Aspects. Comberbach, England: Marbury Technical Consulting. From http://cdm.unfccc.int/methodologies/Background_240305.pdf (accessed October 11, 2007).

Michaelowa, A. (2005). Determination of baselines and additionality for the CDM: A crucial element of credibility of the climate regime. In F. Yamin (Ed.), *Climate change and carbon markets: A handbook of emission reduction mechanisms* (pp. 289–304). London: Earthscan.

Müller, B., and Hepburn C. (2006). IATAL: An Outline Proposal for an International Air Travel Adaptation Levy. Oxford: Oxford Institute for Energy Studies.

Muniesa, F., and Callon M. (2007). Economic experiments and the construction of markets. In D. MacKenzie, F. Muniesa, and L. Siu (Eds.), *Do economists make markets? On the performativity of economics* (pp. 163–189). Princeton, NJ: Princeton University Press.

Newell, R., Pizer W., and Zhang J. (2005). Managing Permit Markets to Stabilize Prices. *Environmental and Resource Economics, 31,* 133–157.

Nordhaus, W. D. (2007). To Tax or Not to Tax: Alternative Approaches to Slowing Global Warming. *Review of Environmental Economics and Policy, 1,* 26–44.

Pinnock, S., Hurley, M. D., Shine, K. P., Wallington T. J., and Smyth T. J. (1995). Radiative Forcing of Climate by Hydrochlorofluorocarbons and Hydrofluorocarbons. *Journal of Geophysical Research, 100,* 23227–23238.

Point Carbon. (2007). Carbon 2007: A New Climate for Carbon Trading. Oslo: Point Carbon.

Prins, G., and Rayner, S. (2007). Time to Ditch Kyoto. *Nature, 449,* 973–975.

RWE AG. 2007. RWE erzielt Einigung mit Bundeskartellamt in CO_2-Verfahren." Essen: RWE AG, September 27. From http://www.rwe.com, (accessed September 28, 2007).

Schellnhuber, H. J. (Ed.). (2006). *Avoiding Dangerous Climate Change.* Cambridge: Cambridge University Press.

SGS United Kingdom Ltd. (2007). Verification and Certification Report for HFC23 Decomposition Project of Zhejiang Juhua Co., Ltd, P. R. China. From http://cdm.unfccc.int/Usermanagement (accessed May 11, 2007).

Shackley, S., and Wynne B. (1997). Global Warming Potentials: Ambiguity or Precision as an Aid to Policy? *Climate Research, 8*(2), 89–106.

Shapin, S., and Schaffer, S. (1985). *Leviathan and the Air-Pump: Hobbes, Boyle, and the Experimental Life.* Princeton, NJ: Princeton University Press.

Shine, K. P., Fuglestvedt, J. S., Hailemariam, K., and Stuber, N. (2005). Alternatives to the Global Warming Potential for Comparing Climate Impacts of Emissions of Greenhouse Gases. *Climatic Change, 68,* 281–302.

Siegenthaler, U., and Joos, F. (1992). Use of a Simple Model for Studying Oceanic Tracer Distributions and the Global Carbon Cycle. *Tellus, 44B,*186–207.

Skærseth, J. B., and Wettestad, J. (2008). *EU Emissions Trading: Initiation, Decision-Making and Implementation.* Aldershot, Hants: Ashgate.

Taubes, G. (2004). An interview with Dr. Laurence Rothman. From http://www.in-cities.com/papers/LaurenceRothman.html, (accessed May 31, 2007).

The Prince's Charities. (2007). Accounting for Sustainability. London: the Prince's Charities.

Wara, M. (2007). Is the Global Carbon Market Working? *Nature, 445,* 595–596.

Weitzman, M. L. (1974). Prices vs. Quantities. *Review of Economic Studies, 41,* 477–491.

Wemaere, M., and Streck, C. (2005). Legal ownership and nature of Kyoto units and EU allowances. In D. Freestone and C. Streck (Eds.), *Legal aspects of implementing the Kyoto Protocol mechanisms: Making Kyoto work* (pp. 35–53). Oxford: Oxford University Press.

Wettestad, J. (2005). The Making of the 2003 EU Emissions Directive: An Ultra-Quick Process due to Entrepreneurial Proficiency? *Global Environmental Politics, 5,* 1–23.

Williams, R., Stewart, J., and Slack, R. (2005). *Social Learning in Technological Innovation: Experimenting with Information and Communication Technologies.* Cheltenham: Elgar.

World Bank. (2007). State and Trends of the Carbon Market 2007. Washington, DC: World Bank.

Wuebbles, D. J. (1981). The Relative Efficiency of a Number of Halocarbons for Destroying Stratospheric Ozone. Livermore, CA: Lawrence Livermore National Laboratory report UCID-18924.

Zapfel, P., and Vainio, M. (2002). Pathways to European Greenhouse Gas Emissions Trading History and Misconceptions. From http://ssrn.com/abstract=342924 (accessed September 19, 2006).

Part II

Imagining Technologies and Technologies of Imagination

4 Imagining Technology in Organizational Knowledge

Entities, Webs, and Mangles

Susan V. Scott and Wanda J. Orlikowski

INTRODUCTION

The majority of research about representation in the academy focuses on the natural sciences and, in particular, laboratory studies (see Latour and Woolgar, 1986; Lynch, 1991). However, the notion that certain epistemic possibilities are bound up with the way that things are represented in/to the world extends to all fields of scholarship. Images are laden with scripted meanings and make visible what scholars assume about the world and how they believe people engage with it. Henderson, in a study about engineers, observes

> ... visual representations shape the structure of the work, who may participate in the work, and the final products of design engineering. They are a component of the social organization of collective cognition and the locus for practice-situated and practice-generated knowledge. (1991, p. 44)

The process of knowledge generation is thus charged with interests and values. As Haraway observes (1988, p. 583)

> There is no unmediated photograph or passive *camera obscura* in scientific accounts of bodies and machines; there are only highly specific visual possibilities, each with a wonderfully detailed, active, partial way of organizing worlds. (1988, p. 583)

The rhetorical gift for appearing like "a conquering gaze from nowhere" is a talent of the dominant (Haraway, 1991, p. 188–189; see also Walsham (1995) on the field of information systems). Particular forms of representation acquire epistemological weight and become intertwined with institutional politics, material configurations, and structures of legitimacy. As Lynch and Woolgar note, "[t]he organization, sense, value, and adequacy of any representation is reflexive to the settings in which it is constituted and used" (1988, p. 109).

Our discussion builds on the principle that neither theory nor methods are axiomatically neutral; the assumptions underpinning approaches to research not only direct our analytical gaze but also give us (in)sight into some things and not others (Morgan, 1983). We concur with the position that "representations and objects are inextricably interconnected; that objects can only be 'known' through representation" (Lynch and Woolgar, 1988, p. 111). It follows that if the majority of literature on work, technology, and organizations manifests primarily around a few dominant images then this limits a key knowledge resource that in turn shapes how we think about and act with business. Morgan (1986) connects the metaphors and ideas underlying organization with action, noting that images provide "frameworks for action"—or in other words, *imagin-action*. He suggests the maxim: "we organize as we imaginize; and it is always possible to imaginize in many different ways" (1986, p. 343). We draw upon his construct of imaginization to explore the implications of two images underlying the dominant methodological positions taken with regard to technology in the management literature.

As a caveat, we should note that we are not interested in creating a hierarchy of genres of research. Our analysis is designed to treat the images that we identify symmetrically, and the spirit of our critique is the identification of a palette of approaches each of which holds its own particular quality. However, we recognize, as Haraway notes that "an optics is a politics of positioning," (1988, p. 586) and that different genres of research are so penetrated by theory that they may be irreconcilable (Lynch and Woolgar, 1988). Thus, the aim of our discussion is not so much to debate or dialogue differences, but an invitation to be generative; for colleagues to reflect on the images within their practices and to consider potential transferences between images and positions. Through this crafting of resemblances, we move away from seeing research practice as the product of technical steps and relationships and focus instead on the potentiality of imaginative motion.

In this chapter, we explore the interrelationship between our images of technology in organizing and the production of organizational knowledge about such technologies. Our discussion is based on a detailed review of the management literature over the past decade (Orlikowski and Scott, 2008). We found that the published articles can be characterized in multiple ways, depending on purpose, point of view, modes of inquiry, forms of articulation, and methods of analysis. We focus here on how technology is made visible in these articles, highlighting the distinctive images of technology that are inscribed in contemporary organizational knowledge. We then consider the influence of these conceptualizations on specific research practices by considering the work currently being done by different scholars in the area of social media. Drawing on this analysis, we suggest that a (re) imaginization of technology in organizing may be warranted so as make visible the multiple, emergent, and dynamic sociomaterial (re)configurations that constitute contemporary organization practices (Law and Urry, 2004; Suchman, 2007). Such alternative imagin-action will require moving beyond entrenched views of technology and organizations as separate phenomena and towards images that make visible the ontological fusion of technology and work in organizing.

IMAGINING TECHNOLOGY IN MANAGEMENT RESEARCH

Our analysis of the management literature finds that considerations of technology are largely absent from the work of most organizational scholars (Orlikowski and Scott, 2008). Specifically, we selected four leading US-based academic journals that publish management research—*The Academy of Management Journal* (AMJ), *The Academy of Management Review* (AMR), *Administrative Science Quarterly* (ASQ), and *Organization Science* (OS)—and analyzed all the research articles published from January 1997 to December 2006. For each article, we examined the title, keywords, abstract, and body to assess whether and how the role and influence of technology in organizations was acknowledged and/or investigated. We found that over the past decade of management research published in four journals, over 95% of the 2,027 articles do not consider technology at all in their examining and theorizing of organizations.

Technology is quite simply 'missing in action' in most accounts of organizational life. This is an interesting and important paradox given the empirical presence of technology in contemporary organizations, industries and economies (Dewett and Jones, 2001; Zammuto et al., 2007). Morgan (1986) has noted that thinking about images of organization highlights how knowledge production is a creative process that participates in the performance of business. In this case, it appears that much of the business being performed by organizational researchers and the practitioners they interact with is devoid of technology. Given the increasing dependence on technology in contemporary business, such a lack of imagination and consideration in the production of organizational knowledge renders materiality, as Barad cogently noted, inconsequential in scientific practice "Language matters. Discourse matters. Culture matters. But there is an important sense in which the only thing that does not seem to matter anymore is matter" (2003, p. 801).

Of the 5% of published management research articles that did consider materiality in organizations, we identified two dominant ways of imagining and performing technology in research—entities and webs. We consider how each of these images has constituted organizational knowledge about technology to date.

IMAGINING TECHNOLOGY AS ENTITIES

Ontologically, an *entity* approach reflects a commitment to a world of discrete objects that have some inherent and relatively stable characteristics.

This is a focus on individual actors and things that are seen to be independent and linked through unidirectional causal relationships. Such an approach is realist in its assumptions about the world: there is a common external reality "out there," having a fixed, definite, and identifiable structure. Technology here is imagined as a largely exogenous and relatively autonomous driver of organizational change, having more or less deterministic impacts on various human and organizational outcomes.

Methodologically, an entity approach imagines technology in terms of machines, devices, tools, or techniques, but this concreteness is not carried through epistemologically, where the espoused realism of material objects is reduced methodologically to abstract measurements and general relationships. Research studies tend to operationalize and "objectively" measure technology through such metrics as the number of units installed, the amount of monies spent on technology, or perceptions of tools scored on numeric scales of "usability" and "value." This approach draws principally on the methods of the natural sciences, where law-like regularities among entities are sought.

Researchers' pursuit of abstractions stems from their interest in comparability, generalizability, and predictability. Following a positivistic approach to social science, and a variance logic (Mohr, 1982), in particular, scholars adopting an entity approach seek to produce organizational knowledge that goes beyond the specific technologies and particular contexts investigated and applies to a broad range of organizations and types of technologies. As a result, the more abstract the conceptualizations of technology and organizational characteristics, the more generalizable researchers believe their explanations and predictions can be. The view of knowledge evident in an entity approach is the traditional image of scientific representations as corresponding to or reflecting reality: science as the mirror of the world (Rorty, 1979).

IMAGINING TECHNOLOGY AS WEBS

In contrast to an entity approach, imagining technology as part of a *web* represents an ontological commitment to mutual dependence, where actors and technologies are seen to be related through a reciprocal and dynamic process of interaction, leading over time to co-evolved complex systems or networks. Kling describes a web model of technology as "conceiv[ing] of a computer system as an ensemble of equipment, applications, and techniques with identifiable information-processing features" and as "view[ing] information systems as complex social objects constrained by their context, infrastructure, and history" (1991, p. 358).

A web approach tends to adopt an interpretative approach; emphasis is placed on the embedded and dynamic meanings, interests, and activities that are seen to produce the web of technological relations over time (Kling,

1991; Markus and Robey, 1988). Such an approach tends, more or less, towards constructivism in its assumptions about the world: reality cannot be understood independently of the human actors who construct and make sense of it. Instead, there is a focus on situated and intersubjective meanings and actions. Structures and relationships are understood to be embedded and emergent, and as such, seen to be indeterminate.

Methodologically, a web approach imagines technology in terms of the processes through which it is designed and used in particular contexts. Researchers tend to draw on a process logic (Mohr, 1982), typically engaging in detailed field studies or ethnographic accounts of technological development and change in order to understand the meaning, role, and consequences of technology. As a result, scholars eschew unidirectional models of technological change, arguing that any examination of a technology's ramifications across a range of settings, occupations, or organizations will reveal that single or invariant relationships do not apply (Barley, 1988).

Having briefly described the two dominant ways of imaging technology in organizational knowledge, we turn now to a consideration of their implications for action, specifically in this case, implications for how scholars conceptualize and study empirical phenomena.

IMAGINING SOCIAL MEDIA IN RESEARCH PRACTICE

The images of technology that we use are conceptual metaphors for methodological practice and help us to abstract particular approaches to studying technology into genres of scholarly research. In this section we consider how these conceptual-metaphors shape imagin-action in scholarly practice. We view research as at heart "a creative process where new images and ideas can create new actions" (Morgan, 1986, p. 343). So, when an innovation presents interesting contemporary research opportunities, how does it come to be framed by the images of research practice that we have outlined above? What are the consequences for the data that are gathered, for what counts as evidence, and the nature of findings that can be claimed based on such evidence? As indicated above, we draw upon a series of examples from research on social media to illustrate our analysis of methodological practice in use to study technology in organizations.

Social media are designed to support computer-mediated and Internet-based peer-to-peer interaction, performing a variety of purposes such as exchanging perspectives (e.g., British Broadcasting Corporation (BBC) Talking Point), entertainment (e.g., YouTube), product review (e.g., Epinions), evaluating travel experiences (e.g., TripAdvisor), and social networking (e.g., Facebook). In practice, most social media Web sites serve multiple functions including a transaction environment and feedback process. While the primary focus of social interaction within online auctions is transaction based (e.g., eBay), we include them within our broad definition of social media in recognition of their emergence as peer-to-peer applications composed largely of user-generated content.

The literature on representation in scientific practice suggests that there is a "serial relation" between representational products (Amann and Knorr-Cetina, 1988). Scholarly practice tends to build upon previous genres of discourse that condition the methods used to identify and investigate research questions. Innovations in social media have attracted researchers from a number of subfields within management, including management economics, media studies, and marketing. In each case, scholars have drawn on the methodological traditions that have developed and become established within their disciplines over time and applied these to the study of social media. Thus, management economists typically employ quantitative discrete factor analyses and game theoretic approaches, media studies researchers tend to use qualitative methods such as those designed for virtual ethnographies of online communities, and marketing scholars appropriate aspects of both quantitative and qualitative approaches, adapting these to their particular interests. We note that there are always exceptions to any broad characterization of research trajectories (including the one performed here). However, in our review of the research on social media in management studies, we observe a notable thematic shift in interest across these subfields, from online auctions, virtual communities, to behavioral factors, respectively.

Following the progressive representation logic, one could argue that this has had consequences for the way that social media has been framed within existing images of research practice. To explore this proposition more closely, we focus on a series of examples drawn from the current management literature on social media. Not surprisingly, we find that the same two dominant images in use within this literature as in the broader management literatures—images of entities and webs. After considering research examples from each of the subfields of management economics, media studies, and marketing in turn, we will suggest an alternative imagining of social media in organizations, which may open up possibilities for new forms of imagin-action in this emerging domain.

Social Media as Online Auctions: A View from Management Economics

We begin by examining online auctions where the core scholarship resonates with the entity imagery. The most well-known and extensively studied online auction is eBay (see Resnick and Zeckhauser, 2002). eBay is an electronic marketplace with over 50 million registered users. Founded in 1995, the Web site describes the marketplace as a community:

> . . . made up of individual buyers and sellers who come to the site to do more than just buy or sell-they have fun, shop around, and get to know

each other, for example, by chatting on the eBay discussion boards. Through the discussion boards, members meet and get to know each other, discuss topics of mutual interest, and help each other to learn all about eBay. These discussion boards are public forums that encourage open communication between users. eBay becomes a part of members' lifestyles. Many members have created second businesses, or left day jobs altogether, by selling items on eBay. For hundreds of thousands of others, eBay is the place to share a passion for items that are special. (http://pages.ebay.co.uk/aboutebay/community.html, May 16, 2008)

Economists have been drawn to the study of auctions because these offer an opportunity to study the influence of different market designs on economic behavior and outcomes. More specifically, auctions offer researchers an environment in which to understand how the availability of different types of information shape individual decisions (see Coyle 2007, pp. 149–150). This has been taken forward in scholarship about online marketplaces, for example, examining classic economic themes such as moral hazard in the use of pseudonyms by buyers and sellers (see Friedman and Resnick, 2001), as well as using game theory to study online feedback mechanisms and electronic word-of-mouth (see MacDonald and Slawson, 2002; Dellarocas, 2003; Goldsmith 2006).

Game theoretic approaches represent a distinctive, theory-driven analysis of interactions involving various mechanisms (e.g., tit-for-tat, Nash equilibrium, calculation of payoffs, reputation effects, Stackelberg type, Stackelberg action). Technology is a central aspect of these interactions in online marketplaces but is treated here as an independent variable in the hypotheses posited and tested. Key research questions focus on how these mechanisms affect the behaviour of participants, the extent to which mechanisms can be manipulated, ways to optimize particular market designs, and how communities can protect themselves from potential abuse (Dellarocas, 2003, p. 1409). Data for testing the hypotheses derive mostly from surveys and laboratory experiments with either actual or pseudo-users, where various parameters are manipulated and responses are measured statistically. Inscribed in this approach is the assumption that designers can precisely control and monitor the operation of social media though automated feedback mechanisms.

The tools that management economics methods, such as game theory, bring to bear are useful for developing complex conceptual models of social media, but the role of technology in these models while sometimes substantive remains largely instrumental. Technology is a discrete entity with stable and knowable properties that performs predictably over time and context. While there is some recognition that this is a limited image of technology, the proposed way forward maintains a stylized view of human action as separated from context. For example, Dellarocas calls for "precise modeling, not only of the technological components of [these] systems, but also of the human users," (2003, p. 1421) a proposal that will necessarily reproduce an instrumental perspective.

Coyle argues that even though game theory is often criticized for its theoretical abstractions and lack of attention to the social context of choices, it is

> . . . in the nature of using models that they simplify away from this kind of detail. Game theory is a profoundly important and useful technique. It extends the fundamental methodology of economics to any aspect of human society. (2007, p. 247)

We recognize the value of scholarship within the image of entities but return to our theme of serial representations in order to highlight the tendency within any genre of scientific practice to self-reproduce. For example, consider this call for further research that embraces multi-disciplinary innovation but uses resources that share kinship through their discrete view of work, technology, and organization:

More collaboration is needed in this promising direction between both computer scientists, who better understand the new possibilities offered by technology, and management scientists, who better understand the tools for evaluating the potential impact of these new systems. (Dellarocas, 2003, p. 1421)

Social Media as Virtual Communities: A View from Media Studies

We turn now to scholarship in media studies to consider how social media innovations are framed by researchers' practices in this subfield. In 1999, Silverstone urged us to study media in Isaiah Berlin's terms "as part of 'the general texture of experience' . . . as social and cultural as well as political and economic dimensions of the modern world" (Silverstone, 1999, p. 2). While his motivation was to acknowledge the ubiquitous and pervasive influence of media, Silverstone recognized that the two primary discourses on media were rooted in history and sociology:

> Sociologists have long been concerned with the nature and quality of such a dimension of social life, in its possibility and in its continuity. Historians too, at least in Berlin's view, cannot escape their dependence on it for their work, like all those in the human sciences, in turn depends upon their capacity to reflect upon and understand the other. (1999, p. 2)

The major research publications on media studies are patterned by both of these reference disciplines with detailed descriptions of the emergence of social media and discussions of the implications of a participation culture and "hypersociality" (see Levy, 1997; Jenkins, 2000; Surowiecki, 2005). It is notable that methodological practices being undertaken in this subfield draw predominantly on prior art from studies of virtual communities (see Hine, 2005; Howard, 2002; Lindlof and Shatzer, 1998; Rheingold, 1993; Wellman et al., 1996;). The ethnographic principles that permeate this approach predispose researchers in media studies towards a focus on culture and a particular interest in a number of recurring themes, for example, the identification of social structures, motivations and modes of participation, the development of (digital) identity, and the authenticity of (virtual) social relationships.

The data focused on in these studies are predominantly online texts with an emphasis on the micro-interactions constituting the virtual communities over time. Although the availability of online data is often plentiful, the method of analysis usually centers deliberately on a small, descriptively rich subset, which is then placed alongside journal or field notes compiled by the researcher during the period of observation. These collections of multiple textual data are then treated to a deep interpretive and discursive analysis to reveal insights into the meanings and processes of the virtual communities in question.

Although ethnography is a holistic research method founded on the principle that phenomena should be studied in context and cannot be understood independently or in isolation, the attention to technological details in virtual community research is often relatively limited. Ethnography's traditional concern with social structures and cultural practices within communities tends to designate technology as one of many socially constructed artifacts drawn upon by social actors. In this regard, these research practices tend to reproduce a view of technology that resonates with the web imagery.

Social Media as Behavioral Factors: A View from Marketing

We now move on to the third body of research that has been conducted on social media by scholars in the field of marketing. It is difficult to categorize work on technology in this literature because to a large extent it remains relatively under-theorized. When marketing research on social media does consider technology, a significant cadre of it adopts images that hover between those of entities and webs.

For example, in research within the tourism sector, technological progress is regarded as "going hand in hand" (Buhalis and Law, 2008, p. 609) with business transformation. The image of technology is presented as something that drives change, empowers consumers, offers tools, and evolves over time. Technology is presented as a radicalizing force "out there" marking the vanguard of progress and a factor upon which the future of marketing organizations is dependent. There is a growing body of literature focusing on what has been labeled by some as "e-Tourism" (see Buhalis, 2003), which examines the extent to which the travel sector is dependent upon technology for future growth and revenue enhancement. However, the role of technology in developing and mediating the web of resources and services available to customers and businesses engaged in the process of travel is not explored; it is simply assumed to be given and unproblematic.

In this stream of research, behavioral factors influencing transaction execution, product development and service delivery are rendered into statistical variables. For example, consumer behavior regarding online travel Web sites is examined through such measures as demographics, lifestyle characteristics, brand awareness, attitudes towards online security, satisfaction with prior online experiences, etc. These choices would seem to place marketing research practice within the image of entities. However, there is also a general recognition that the context of decision-making and interpretation of subjective phenomena such as Web site reputation and brand loyalty necessitate a broader methodological approach. For this reason, there is widespread use in this subfield of qualitative methods such as focus groups, personal interviews and market-oriented ethnography or "netnography" (Kozinets, 2002).

While the marketing literature is hampered by a conceptually weak notion of technology, it is ironic that we also find a methodological pluralism characterizing the different kinds of research practice currently being used to study social media. This suggests an interest to render the research available for "imagin-action" by practitioners. In other words, by using multiple approaches, researchers in this domain allow those wishing to use their work and make it thinkable in business terms to switch among images until they find one that they can connect with. We would argue that this transference between images holds considerable potential for exploring phenomena from multiple perspectives and affording a range of "imagin-actions" in the world.

We explore new possibilities for imagin-action in this domain by considering how social media might be framed by alternative images of technology.

ALTERNATIVE IMAGININGS OF SOCIAL MEDIA IN RESEARCH PRACTICE

As indicated above, the standard images of entities and webs in research practice blind us to key dimensions that may be relevant to the study of social media. Entities put context, change, and relational issues out of the frame, while webs tend to focus our attention on local events and emergent relations. The configuration of social media resists both approaches: discrete entities rendered via statistics do not provide substantive insight into the matters of taste, aspiration, and compulsion that imbue engagement with social media; ethnographic data delve into issues of identity and social organization but rarely fuse these with detailed analysis of how choices are conditioned by the performance of material agency.

Technologically charged innovations such as social media not only challenge practitioner preconceptions about how to create and manage organizational knowledge, they also disturb the neatness of our scholarly methodological practices challenging us to reframe them. For the purposes of this discussion, we focus on three key issues raised by the study of social media: first, the glocal traceability of social media collectives; second,, the mash of social media with routine sense-making practices; finally, the multiple, inter-dependent quality of the dynamic social and technical relationships through which they are constituted.

When initiating the study of a phenomenon, we seek to understand how it may be bounded by history, geography, membership, organizational forms, and governance arrangements. In a regrettably cursory nod to history and geography, we briefly note that social media are a relatively recent development, and participation is for the most part a preoccupation in the industrialized north. This enables us to draw attention to the stickier latter points. While virtual communities may be formed and maintained over time by those who invest social capital in them, social media are often sustained by a 'purpose-full' collective whose participation may be temporary. Social media are more thoroughly *glocal* (Sveningsson and Alvesson, 2003) than many virtual communities because their participants tend to come and go as strangers. This makes the research questions of virtual ethnography that are typically framed around "life online" and "second selves"— and its analytical commitment to "what is online?"—problematic. That is, while their virtual status and accessibility disembed social media from geographic "place," their *use* is certainly placed in the context of multiple locales and embedded practices.

This mash of social media with routine sense-making practices may help explain the pluralism in methods used within the marketing literature. Identifying statistical patterns in population data is useful to practitioner audiences, if these can be understood in terms of customer segments, buying habits, perceptions of quality/reputation, and demand for products/services. While participants leave traces of their intentions embedded in click stream data and usage patterns, the transformation of their social media experience into organizational knowledge remains embodied and embedded. We would argue that this is where alternative images of technology can be particularly useful, especially those that support interest in understanding the fusion between the multiple forms of embedded and embodied agency entailed in social media.

This brings us to the final point in our discussion, which centers on understanding the texture of multiple agencies referred to above and their constitutive interdependency with materiality to create what may be labeled sociomateriality (Suchman, 2007). Both the images of entities and webs assume a separation of humans (organizations) and materiality (technology). Attempting to overcome such an ontological separation, Pickering (1993, 1995) draws on Actor Network Theory (Callon, 1986; Latour, 1987) to develop an image and approach to studying science and technology whereby technology and humans are seen to be so mangled in practice that they cannot be distinguished. This image of a *mangle* represents an emergent genre of research that challenges deeply taken-for-granted assumptions that technology and organizations should be conceptualized as discrete entities or as interacting webs. In contrast, it advances the view that there is an inherent inseparability between the technical and the social in practice.

Pickering argues that human and material agency are constitutively related or in his terms "reciprocally and emergently intertwined" (1995, p. 15). He proposes the metaphor of tuning (as in tuning a radio) to articulate the process through which human and material agencies mutually adapt over time. He sees this process as an ongoing "dialectic of resistance and accommodation" through which human actors attempt to shape material agency to align with certain intentions over time. This way of imagining technology in organizations reflects a focus on the sociomateriality of work, where the material and the human are entangled in ongoing organizational practices (Jones, 1998).

A methodology guided by the image of a mangle would combine multiple types of data to give a sense of saturated practice characterized by a fusion of social and technical agencies that show interdependencies in performance. Research design would focus on moments of interest in which algorithmic agency shapes practice and vice versa. For example, reconfiguring the performance of online ratings calculations or the influence of an influx of user-generated content on those ratings processes as qualitative material and calculation form a continuum constituting what Callon and Muniesa (2005) have labeled "qualculation". Our attention would be drawn to how such qualculation shapes sense-making routines and the political consequences of mutual manipulations. Such a fresh image may inspire and generate a deeper theorization of technology, work, and organization. This theoretical turn needs to be capable of conveying the distinctive multiple, interdependent quality of the dynamic social and technical relationships through which phenomenon like social media are constituted.

CONCLUSION

Our discussion has focused on the connections between images of technology in organizing and the production of organizational knowledge about such technologies. Our starting point was a review of the research on technology and organizations published in prominent management journals over the past decade. Examining the ways in which technology had been imagined and conceptualized in this extended body of scholarship over time, we found a surprising paucity of attention being paid to technology in this work; notably, only 5% of the published articles considered or conceived of technology in any way.

This leads directly to the paradox, that while technology seems to be everywhere in the world of organizational practice, it is conspicuously absent from the world of organizational knowledge. As scholars, this leaves us sadly lacking in rich images with which to revitalize our thinking and theorizing, and for practitioners, it renders them bereft of innovative ideas with which to reconceive and reorganize their technological practices. Morgan observes:

> "Images and metaphors are not only interpretive constructs or ways of seeing; they also provide frameworks for action. Their use creates insights that often allow us to act in ways that we may not have thought possible before." (1986, p. 343)

From such a perspective, the vacuum of imagery about technology in the management literature is more than an oversight in research agenda; it is a creative deficit in a core area of organizational self-knowledge. The significance of this is reinforced when we consider that spending on technology constitutes the largest category of investment for many organizations (Dewett and Jones, 2001), representing billions in the annual corporate budgets of global firms. Whether a start-up enterprise, mid-sized manufacturing firm, local government, regional nongovernmental organization (NGO), or global pharmaceutical corporation, it is hard to conceive of the operations and activities of any contemporary organization that do not, to some degree, depend critically on multiple technologies.

Of the research work that does conceptualize technology in organizing, we found that two predominant images—entities and webs—have been inscribed into organizational knowledge over time. Drawing on research into the emerging phenomenon of social media, we examined the methodological research practices underpinning this scholarship. We found the dominant images of entities and webs much in evidence, and considered the way that these precondition and direct scholars' analytical gaze. Using examples from social media research in three subfields—managerial economics, media studies, and marketing—we discussed their conceptual entailments with respect to this phenomenon. We found that the limited visual palette in use is not without consequences.

In their book, *Images of Strategy*, Cummings and Wilson (2003) maintain that any one image may let us down, and that when faced with complexity, we need to either juxtapose one image with another (referring, for example, to arraying images on Google Earth alongside maps of a place and handwritten directions from a friend) or refresh our thinking by switching images altogether. In this spirit, we proposed the imaginative possibilities entailed in the notion of the mangle advanced by Pickering (1995), suggesting that this image may help to generate additional perspectives that conceive and theorize the ontological fusion of technology and work in organizations. We believe that reconsidering the dominant images of technology along these lines (of sight) may help to render the presence of and make possible the inquiry into multiple, emergent, dynamic, and complex sociomaterialities that constitute contemporary organizational practices and organizational knowledge.

REFERENCES

Amann, K., and Knorr Cetina, K. (1988). The Fixation of (Visual) Evidence. *Human Studies*, 11, 133–169.

Barad, K. (2003). Posthumanist Performativity: Toward an Understanding of How Matter Comes to Matter. *Signs*, 28(3), 801–831.

Barley, S. R. (1988). Technology, Power, and the Social Organization of Work. *Research in the Sociology of Organizations*, 6,:33–80.

Buhalis, D. (2003). *e-Tourism: Information Technology for Strategic Tourism Management*. Cambridge, England: Pearson (Financial Times/Prentice-Hall).

Buhalis, D., and Law. R. (2008). Progress in Information Technology and Tourism Management: 20 Years on and 10 Years After the Internet—The State of eTourism Research. *Tourism Management*, 29, 609–623.

Callon, M. (1986). Some elements of a sociology of translations: domestication of the scallops and the fishermen in St Brieuc Bay. In J. Law (Ed.), *Power, action, and belief: A new sociology of knowledge* (pp. 196–229). London: Routledge.

———., and Muniesa, F. (2005). Economic Markets as Calculative Collective Devices. *Organization Studies*, 26(8) 1229–1250.

Coyle, D. (2007). *The Soulful Science: What Economists Really Do and Why It Matters*. Princeton, NJ: Princeton University Press.

Cummings, S., and Wilson, D. (2003). *Images of Strategy*. Oxford, England: Blackwell.

Dellarocas, C. 2003. "The Digitization of Word of Mouth: Promise and Challenges of Online Feedback Mechanisms," *Management Science*, 49(10), 1407–1424.

Dewett, T., and Jones, G. R. (2001). The Role of Information Technology in the Organization: A Review, Model, and Assessment. *Journal of Management*, 27(3), 313–346.

eBay. *About eBay, Commumity*. http://pages.ebay.co.uk/aboutebay/community.html (retrieved March 30, 2011).

Friedman, E., and Resnick, P. (2001). The Social Cost of Cheap Pseudonymns. *Journal of Economic Management Strategy*, 10(1), 173–199.

Goldsmith, R. E. (2006). Electronic word-of-mouth. In M. Khosrow-Pour (Ed.), *Encyclopedia of e-commerce, e-government and mobile commerce* (pp. 408–412). Hershey, PA: Idea Group Publishing.

Haraway, D. (1988). Situated Knowledges: The Science Question in Feminism and the Privilege of Partial Perspective. *Feminist Studies*, 14(3), 575–599.

———. (1991). *Simians, Cyborgs, and Women: The Reinvention of Nature*. London: Free Association Books.

Henderson, K. (1991). Flexible Sketches and Inflexible Data Bases. *Science, Technology, and Human Values*, 16(4), 448–473.

Hine, C. (2005). Virtual methods and the sociology of cyber-social-scientific knowledge. In C. Hine (Ed.), *Virtual Methods: Issues in Social Research on the Internet* (pp. 1–13). New York: Berg.

Howard, P. N. (2002). Network Ethnography and the Hypermedia Organization: New Media, New Organizations, New Methods. *New Media and Society, 4*(4), 550–574.

Jenkins, H. (2000). *Convergence Culture: Where Old and New Media Collide.* New York: New York University Press.

Jones, M. R. (1998). Information Systems and the Double Mangle: Steering a Course Between the Scylla of Embedded Structure and the Charybdis of Material Agency. In T. Larsen,L. Levine, and J. I. DeGross (Eds.), *Information systems: Current issues and future challenges* (pp. 287–302). Laxenburg, Austria: IFIP Press.

Kling, R. (1991). Computerization and Social Transformations. *Science, Technology, and Human Values, 16*(3), 342–367.

Kozinets, R. V. (2002). The Field Behind the Screen: Using Netnography for Marketing Research in Online Communities. *Journal of Marketing Research, 39*(1), 61–72.

Latour, B. (1987). *Science in Action.* Boston: Harvard University Press.

———., and Woolgar, S. (1986). *Laboratory Life: The Construction of Scientific Facts* (2nd ed.). Princeton, NJ: Princeton University Press.

Law, J., and Urry, J. (2004). Enacting the Social. *Economy and Society, 33*(3), 390–410.

Levy, P. (1997). *Collective Intelligence: Mankind's Emerging World in Cyberspace.* Cambridge: Perseus.

Lindlof, T. R., and Shatzer, M. J. (1998). Media Ethnography in Virtual Space: Strategies, Limits, and Possibilities. *Journal of Broadcasting and Electronic Media, 42*(2), 170–189.

Lynch, M. (1991). Method: Measurement—Ordinary and scientific measurement as methodological phenomena. In G. Button (Ed.), *Ethnomethodology and the human sciences* (pp. 77–108). Cambridge, UK: Cambridge University Press.

———., and Woolgar, S. (1988). Introduction: Sociological Orientations to Representational Practice in Science. *Human Studies, 11*, 99–116.

MacDonald, C. G., and Slawson, V. C., Jr. (2002). Reputation in an Internet Auction Market. *Economic Inquiry, 40*(3), 633–650.

Markus, M. L., and Robey, D. (1988). Information Technology and Organizational Change: Causal Structure in Theory and Research. *Management Science, 34*(5), 583–598.

Mohr, L. B. (1982). *Explaining Organizational Behavior.* San Francisco, CA: Jossey-Bass.

Morgan, G. (Ed.). (1983). *Beyond Method: Strategies for Social Research.* Thousand Oaks, CA: Sage Publications.

———. (Ed.). (1986). *Images of Organization.* Thousand Oaks, CA: Sage Publications.

Orlikowski, W. J., and Scott. S. V. (2008). "Sociomateriality: Challenging the Separation of Technology, Work and Organization," *Annals of the Academy of Management, 2*(1), 433–474.

Pickering, A. (1993). The Mangle of Practice: Agency and Emergence in the Sociology of Science. *American Journal of Sociology. 99*(3), 559–589.

———. (1995). *The Mangle of Practice: Time, Agency and Science.* Chicago, IL: University of Chicago Press.

Resnick, P., and Zeckhauser, R. (2002). Trust among strangers in Internet transactions: Empirical analysis of eBay's reputation system. In M. R. Baye, (Ed.), *The economics of the Internet and e-commerce: Advances in applied microeconomics* (p. 11). Greenwich, CT: JAI Press.

Rheingold, H. (1993). *The Virtual Community: Homesteading on the Electronic Frontier.* Reading, MA: Addison-Wesley.

Rorty, R. (1979). *Philosophy and the Mirror of Nature*. Princeton, NJ: Princeton University Press.

Silverstone, R. (1999). *Why Study the Media?* Thousand Oaks, CA: Sage.

Suchman, L. A. (2007). *Human-Machine Reconfigurations: Plans and Situated Actions*. Cambridge, England: Cambridge University Press.

Surowiecki, J. (2005). *The Wisdom of Crowds: Why the Many Are Smarter Than the Few*. Grand Rapids, MI: Abacus.

Sveningsson, S., and Alvession, M. (2003). Managing Managerial Identities: Organizational Fragmentation, Discourse and Identity Struggle. *Human Relations*, 56(10), 1163–1193.

Walsham, G. (1995). The Emergence of Interpretivism in IS Research. *Information Systems Research*, 6(4), 376–394.

Wellman, B., Salaff, J., Dimitrova, D., Garton, L., Gulia, M., and Haythornthwaite, C. (1996). Computer Networks as Social Networks: Collaborative Work, Telework, and Virtual Community. *Annual Review of Sociology*, 22, 213–238.

Zammuto, R. F., Griffith, T. L., Majchrzak, A., Dougherty, D. J. and Faraj, S. (2007). Information Technology and the Changing Fabric of Organization. *Organization Science*, 18(5), 749–762.

5 Process Flowcharts
Malleable Visual Mediators of ERP Implementation

Joanne Locke and Alan Lowe

INTRODUCTION

This chapter engages with Enterprise Resource Planning (ERP) systems in an empirical setting. Our interest is in ERP implementation and the visual objects, the flowcharts that are deployed to help with this task. Flowcharts are a well-established tool from the pre-computer era dating back to around the early1920s[1]. The rhetoric surrounding their acceptance in a variety of settings includes their ability to capture important aspects of yet-to-be-created and complex real systems and to communicate them effectively to a wide variety of audiences (Boczko, 2007; Colter, 1984). The symbols for writing a flowchart have been standarized and disseminated by the national standards body of the United Kingdom (UK) British Standards Institution (BSI) and the International Organization for Standardization (ISO)[2].

Bloomfield and Vurdubakis (1997a) examine how particular "inscription devices" are used to construct visions of the objects and processes 'that they purport to render visible' (p. 639). These authors take a strongly discursive line in order to emphasize

> . . . the way visions of organization (articulated through vocabularies of efficiency, effectiveness, the centrality of information in management, management by objectives, etc.) are translated into . . . specific organizations of vision. (Bloomfield and Vurdubakis, 1997a, p. 639)

Our aim in this chapter is to further demonstrate the centrality of these artifacts and trace their function as representations, inscriptions, and boundary objects (Carlile, 2002, 2004; Gal et al., 2004; Star and Greisemer, 1989). Boundary objects play a part in facilitating communication among different groups of people and, in this case, the ERP technology. They are translation devices in the rather direct sense that they act to make the technology understandable to the people and facilitate the conversion of, at times idiosyncratic, business processes and practices into the technology. In Actor Network Theory (ANT), objects such as the process flowcharts we describe play an active role in mediating the interface between people and technology and work to engage or enroll people into complex assemblages of human and technology objects—socio-technical systems (Latour, 1987, 1996, 2005; Law, 1997, 2002). Process flowcharts are a visualization technique (Henderson, 1991; see also Gal et al., 2004), which, at the research site, acted as a boundary object to draw the nascent users in the case company into an engagement with the new ERP. The flowcharts help to create the ERP.

Our aim is to illuminate the struggle needed to map the adopting organization's processes to the ERP and the ERP's modules into the organization. We report on some of the events and disputes that take place during a time of implementation when the ERP is not configured and is still 'unknowable.' The nature of the technology as obscure and unknowable makes it difficult for people to engage with the system as it is assembled in the organization (Ciborra et al., 2001; Dechow and Mouritsen, 2005; Quattrone and Hopper, 2005; Scott and Wagner, 2003; Walsham, 1993). We focus attention in our discussion of the case material on the role of process flowcharts.

The next section of the chapter discusses the literature on representations as boundary objects as the basis for our conceptualization of our fieldwork. Following that we provide a brief description of how process flowcharts broadly of the type adopted in the case company are presented in the literature. We then report how the flowcharts were deployed in our case organization and provide a particular emphasis on evidence of the users' responses to the construction of the flowcharts and the processes around objectifying their work practices. The discussion section considers how, with effort, the standard technique presented in the literature can become malleable and dynamic, the focus of translation and action: a boundary object. A final section provides brief concluding comments.

OBJECTS AND THE NEGOTIATION OF INTRA-ORGANIZATIONAL BOUNDARIES

There has been considerable interest in concepts developed in the Sociology of Translation and ANT to help in the theorizing of information communication technology (ICT) systems (Angerou et al., 2004; Hanseth, Aanestad and Berg, 2004; Knorr Cetina and Bruegger, 2002; Scott and Wagner, 2003). In the accounting literature (Briers and Chua, 2001; Dechow and Mouritsen, 2005; Lowe, 2001a; Lowe and Koh, 2007; Quattrone and Hopper, 2005), these concepts have invariably been deployed to help conceptualize aspects of information systems and their impact on organization.

A number of writers have incorporated the idea of boundary objects (Briers and Chua, 2003; Carlile, 2002, 2004; Dechow and Mouritsen, 2005; Locke and Lowe, 2007a) into their explanations of ICT systems in organizational settings. Several categories of boundary objects exist (see Table

5.1), many of which have representational or visual characteristics. Inscriptions and images play an important role as boundary objects. Dechow and Mouritsen (2005) talk about SAP's use of business objects depicted in graphics called event-driven process chain 'EPC' diagrams as a way of permitting SAP to "'black box' the technology so that the control implications were not clear" (p. 704). We theorize the role of process flow diagrams as representational technology as a way of opening the black boxes of ERP technology and business process, if only to a limited extent.

THE ROLE OF REPRESENTATION

Representation enables economy and mobility through aggregation and simplification. The mobility of representation helps us to understand why paper and increasingly electronic records are so essential to organizations and organizing. These characteristics of inscription and representation are what Latour describes as providing "immutable mobiles."

> . . . inscriptions are mobile, flat, reproducible, still and of varying scales, they can be reshuffled and recombined. (Latour, 1994, p. 45)

It is through mobility that remote control is made possible. Inscriptions of events that are remote in space and time can be instantly collated in paper or electronic form to produce representations that are amenable to action. Displacement provides a critical influence by enabling inscriptions from many remote locations to be brought together. Displacement brings remote events near while, also, keeping them at a remove through the intervening representations. The power of representation enables those at the center to control remote events.

> . . . displacement [operates in such a way that] . . . representation is always a substitution for or re-presentation of the event and never the event itself." (Cooper, 1992, p. 257; see also Bloomfield, 1995; Bloomfield and Vurdubakis, 1997b; Latour, 1994; Law, 1996)

Remote control and displacement are insufficient to achieve this creation of organizational "reality" alone. It is the quality of abbreviation that underlies representation (Cooper, 1992; see also Bloomfield, 1995; Bloomfield and Vurdubakis, 1997b; Latour, 1994; Law, 1996; Zuboff, 1988). Abbreviation simplifies the complex and reduces the big into the small . . . the compact or "complete" picture. The "real thing" is reduced into the model so that as much as is needed is condensed into as little as is needed so as to enable ease of perception and action. Through abbreviation, inscriptions and representation are made compact, versatile, and transportable. This is a central feature of the practices of representation, such as the process flowcharts we examine later, as it is to accounting practice (Robson, 1992, 1994; Lowe, 2001b).

BOUNDARY OBJECTS: REPRESENTATION AND VISUALIZATION

The concept of 'boundary objects' has a significant history in the sociology and social study of science literature. Star and Griesemer (1989) adopt the concept to enable them to make sense of the more general process of translation (Callon, 1986; Latour, 1987). The incorporation of 'boundary objects' enables Star and Griesemer to provide a more structured framework within which they describe the broader translation process. These authors use the 'boundary object' concept to provide receptacles into which they are able to categorize different objects and practices that are

> ... plastic enough to adapt to local needs ... yet robust enough to maintain a common identity ... weakly structured in common use, and become strongly structured in individual site use. These objects may be abstract or concrete. **They have different meanings in different social worlds but their structure is common enough to make them ... recognisable.** (Star and Griesemer, 1989, p. 393, emphasis added)

Table 5.1   Boundary Objects Types

Repositories	These contain ordered collections of objects that are indexed in a standardized fashion. Examples of repositories include libraries and museums. The repository has the advantage of being modular and standardized in some way.
Ideal type	These objects include diagrams and representations. Ideal types arise as a result of abstraction. Star and Griesemer argue that they "result in the deletion of local contingencies from the common object and have the advantage of adaptability (Ibid, p 410).
Coincident boundaries	Star and Griesemer describe these as common objects that have the same boundaries but different internal contents. Star and Griesemer argue that such devices enable "different means of aggregating data ... result[ing] ... in different sites and with different perspectives ... conducted autonomously while cooperating parties share a common referent [and the] ... resolution of different goals (Ibid, p 411).
Standardized forms	These are boundary objects devised as methods of common communication across dispersed work groups. Star and Griesemer associate this last type of object with Latour's 'immutable mobiles' – but this seems an unreasonable assertion. In fact there might be a closer fit between 'immutable mobiles' and the ideal type. At the very least there is some confusion here since 'immutable mobiles' certainly exhibit aspects of both ideal types and standardized forms.

Source: adapted from Star and Griesemer, 1989, p. 410–411.

The next section provides a brief description of how flowcharts are presented in the literature. We will return in the case section to examine the implications and trials and tribulations associated with the insinuation of the technology into the practices of the ERP user group.

PROCESS FLOWCHARTS AS A VISUAL COMMUNICATION TECHNIQUE

One of the features of flowcharts commonly reflected in normative descriptions of their use is their ability to assist communication (Hurt, 2007, p. 78) and "develop a common understanding about a system . . ." (Boczko, 2007, p. 296). "Flowcharts tend to provide people with a common language or reference point when dealing with a project or process" (Clemson University, 2008, p. 1). There is an obvious link here in the language these authors use with that used to describe boundary objects (Star and Greisemer, 1989; see also Carlile, 2002, 2004; Gal et al., 2004). The value in the boundary object is in encouraging or enabling communication across boundaries. In our examination of the part played by flowcharts in ERP implementation it is this socio-technical contribution that we are interested in revealing.

The process flowchart can perhaps, best be seen as a standardized form (see Table 5.1), which acts in a way that overcomes the user's uncertainties about the new system. We will describe later how such boundary objects are not constructed without considerable effort. The ability of the object to standardize is necessarily also a potential barrier to its use. Though these objects can play a role in translating among disparate groups they also tend to be somewhat foreign to, or beyond the experience of, at least some of those groups. We describe in the case section of the chapter some of the work undertaken among the user group which clearly shows the difficulty of deploying such objects without risking damage to communication among different members of the 'community.'

Our research, following Star and Greisemer and others, seeks to focus on what makes these representational practices work. The interpretation of the work of boundary objects that we adopt is one that leaves room for equivocality in the construction of shared meaning and of cooperative activity rather than control (see also Lowe and Locke, 2008). In this context we are happy to report the idiosyncratic nature of the simple representational practices such as the flowcharts that are at the center of our research story on ERP implementation.

"A flowchart is a work of art" declares Farina (1970, p. 25). Within the boundaries of the accepted flowcharting symbols and standards, it is a creative activity (Farina, 1970, p. 25). It is not to be expected that two people considering the same problem or process will represent it in a flowchart in the same way (Farina, 1970, p. 25; Hurt, 2007, p. 78). More recent 'textbook' definitions of flowcharts are perhaps more circumspect than Farina (1970) but nevertheless emphasize their representational and visual characteristics:

> A flowchart is essentially a picture—a map of a process, a flow or a system. More precisely it is a diagrammatic representation of a system, a computer program or a document flow . . . . (Boczko, 2007, p. 296)

> A flowchart is defined as a pictorial representation describing a process being studied or even used to plan stages of a project. (Clemson University, 2008, p. 1)[3]

These descriptions of the nature and process of creating flowcharts stand in some contrast to the presentation of flowcharting as a rational, reductionist, instrumental technique for capturing, analyzing, and designing processes and systems. The 'textbook' literature typically does not reflected on the often controversial setting in which flowcharts are drawn upon to create a 'common understanding' and reduce the messy complexity of systems such as ERPs to their structural components for easier packaging and digestion. In our case study we observe not only this 'textbook' approach applied in a frantic and complex setting but also its adaptation and use as a channel through which to create momentum to leave key users of an emerging ERP system no choice but to engage with it at the level of their day-to-day activity, for many of them, for the first time.

The specific technique the 'key users' were required to use to document their practices was a process flowchart. Ungan (2006) defines a process using the American Production and Inventory Control Society's 1995 dictionary entry as "a planned series of actions or operations . . . that advance a material or procedure from one stage of completion to another" (p. 401). A process flowchart is designed to document the sequence of the actions or operations using standard symbols and structures. Colter (1984) identifies this type of documentation as pre-dating the first generation of 'computer-based analysis approaches' (p. 55). There is no one definitive style for a process flowchart—variations have developed and are applied differently in specific contexts. Some have specialized symbols for transportation, storage, and other specific operations (see Appendix 1, which includes annotations for symbols for process flowcharts) and some include a multi-column structure so that the person, functional area, or other 'mechanism' responsible for each operation or activity is reflected in the documentation. Generally the flowcharts represent the sequence of activities as beginning at the top of the diagram and moving downwards. The person or function may be represented in columns horizontally ('swim lane' style) or vertically. More recent evaluation reflects the fact that despite their antediluvian 'pre-computer' classification, they are still widely used in business process re-engineering (Ungan, 2006) as well as in the implementation of ERP software. Ungan attributes this to their perceived usefulness in designing or re-designing processes as well as the requirement to flowchart all business processes in ISO 9001:2000 (p. 401; Babicz, 2000).

In our interpretations of the efforts of our case company to implement ERP we see the process flowchart technology as a critical device. While process flowcharts have standard forms and symbols, they are malleable enough to scale up or down or apply at different levels of detail and use different software to implement. The flowchart is an approach to visualizing processes within a company so it may also become the object that enables users to articulate their business practices in a form that is tractable to the ERP software vendor's people, both programmers and consultants.

VISUALIZING THE ERP THROUGH THE USE OF PROCESS FLOWCHARTS

The section presents excerpts of interactions taken from two internal "user group" meetings, the process flowcharts at the center of debate, descriptions of a flowchart workshop, and the researchers' interpretation of the outcome of the deployment of the flowcharting technique. The two internal meetings lasted about one hour each and were two of seven internal meetings that were held prior to the more formal Steering Committee meetings, which involved representatives of the software vendor in addition to the key managers and users from within Pukekoe[4]. Our research included three other internal meetings, four steering group meetings, and in excess of 20 interviews. The ERP implementation process took place over approximately six months, extending from January through June, though delays in programming led to 'go-live' slipping to the end of July.

The internal meetings began to be held on a more formal and regular basis as the project 'go-live' approached. The process flowcharts were particularly contentious in the second and fourth of these internal meetings. Our focus is on the use of this representational informational technology (IT) to translate (Latour, 1987; Star and Griesemer, 1989) among the different user groups within the organization, the software vendor, and the ERP software.

Of the meetings we refer to, the earlier one took place in late April and the later meeting in mid-May. Though both meetings had several agenda items, we focus attention on the central role played by the use of process flow diagrams. The project leader was the senior IT employee (of only two) in the company. As he worked with the software vendor to configure the ERP, the need to relate the business processes of the company to the 'techno-logic' of the ERP (Dechow and Mouritsen, 2005) became pressing. The software vendor's process for implementing the system hinged on a series of 'conference room pilots,' which were partial but 'realistic' mock-up test runs of the system that also served as training for Pukekoe's key users. Through all this process there was significant pressure on the project leader to get the processes right and get the key users actively engaging with the new system.

At the earlier meeting, it was apparent that views differed markedly on the new system. Some were still quite ignorant of the system and were quite prepared to acknowledge this. It was clear to the researchers that the project was vital to the organization. Having embarked on the implementation, at the point these meetings were held, there was no going back. Successful implementation was the only outcome that would ensure the survival of the organization. The ERP was a very significant investment in time and money that the company could not afford to have go badly without a large negative impact on customer relations. Pukekoe had a handful of very significant customers who accounted for approximately 80% of the revenue stream who could quickly change suppliers if they were not completely satisfied. They were also within a few months of their highest volume sales and production season.

After the announcement of the revised 'go-live' date, the project leader outlined the significant implementation activities and deadlines. The meeting remained in information dissemination mode for some 20 minutes. At this point he turned the attention of those present to the question of documenting business processes and, in particular, the use of process flowcharts. These were to be a central artifact in the assimilation of the ERP software into the organization. The role of the flowcharts could be seen from differing perspectives. The view proffered by the project leader who was an IT specialist was essentially to see the charts as a necessary bridge to link the ERP system with the business processes existing within Pukekoe. They were conceptualized as a tool that would enable the main business processes in each area to be expressed in a form that could be enacted through in the conference room pilots scheduled for June and July. It was intended that the flowcharts would act to consolidate the limited training experiences with the new system with the individual's work practices and then inform the configuration of the 'conference room pilot' episodes, which were to ensure the system worked at least in model form prior to 'go-live.'

The choreographed 'pilot' episodes serve a number of purposes. As a formal element of the system implementation process, they enable the software vendor to check company specific modifications, or 'mods', against actual transactional data. They also provide an element of the formal 'training' of client company people, enabling a degree of realism in interacting with aspects of and/or subroutines within the software package. In a less formal sense, these scripted events provide a good opportunity for the vendor's staff to demonstrate their proficiency and mastery of the software, while client staff perform as the appreciative audience. The substance of the internal meeting hinged largely on the activities that were deemed necessary in order that a script could be written and performed during each of the planned 'conference room pilots.' Clearly these pilot episodes are also at work as boundary objects, bringing together internal staff with differing perspectives based on their functional expertise, and the software vendor staff who have markedly different specialist expertise and the ERP technology itself. The choreographed performances that these pilot episodes represent also play a part in the construction of shared meanings and mutual understandings. A consideration of these artifacts is beyond this chapter because of space constraints. They are relevant to our story because they provide the immediacy behind the requirement to fabricate the process flowcharts. The charts come to form the key processual ingredient in the planned pilot tests.

At this meeting there was clearly a good deal of positive sentiment toward the new system, but many of the key users had only had a single, brief familiarization session with it and had not had access since to explore it any further. Much of the discussion emphasized the uncertainties in the process and the amount of work to be done prior to 'go-live.' The chair, after about 30 minutes of discussion, turned the attention of the meeting to the issue of flowcharting of business processes. A blank of the process flowchart the users were being asked to complete is shown in Figure 5.1. The symbols they were provided with to learn and use were only the essential ones compared to the broad range recommended in the business literature (see Appendix 1). They were required, however to use a multi-column format and to note where a step in the process relates to a menu item in the ERP system. The guidance was to cut and paste the symbols where they were required and complete the process description at a 'high level.'

Figure 5.1 Process flowchart template.

The second meeting we report on took place in May, two weeks later, and there had been no progress with the flowcharts. The meeting began with an extensive discussion of the tasks remaining to be done, rounded out by the comment:

> . . . what I have done is I've taken all of the systems documentations, the project plan that we had last month and other lists and things that have come up and I've put them into a spreadsheet which I haven't really finished . . . But what I have done is listed everything that . . . you guys need to be responsible for making happen and the time it is meant to be done by . . . There might be some things that have been missed off our list so I would like you to come back to me . . . so we can make sure that we do all the things that are dependant on other things (Project Leader).

At this point a light-hearted comment was made by the Stores Manager who jokingly referred to the prospect of heavy overtime payments, which the group did not expect and knew would not be forthcoming. This comment and the reaction to it around the table indicates the informality of the meeting at this point. The Project Leader came back in to list a number of other issues and then made the following comment in regard to making progress on the documenting and flowcharting of business processes.

> . . . I would suggest that your first point of call there is . . . [to] try and work out what the flow is to do that initial job . . . here is one for example . . . price book maintenance. Now you probably think off the top of your head I can do a process flow diagram for that, fair enough. Okay but when you actually get to the system and log in, go through and find where say price book maintenance, or whatever, fits into your programmes . . . then you're able to piece together the data entry requirements and [the ERP system] screens you need to go through. You will probably get faults, you might have areas that you can identify are still . . . to do . . . What I am saying is I can assist everybody to do their flow diagrams . . . because when we do conference room pilot that's what we are going to be following (Project Leader).
>
> . . . [don't] we need a procedure to do that? (Product Manager—in a slightly confused tone).
>
> Yea but its only at a high level . . . like the examples . . . you do this that and this that and that's how you complete the task (Project Leader).

There followed an intense discussion over what seemed to be a considerable degree of concern at the ability of people to follow the model the Project Leader had tried to explain, in the previous meeting and earlier in this meeting. A number of users showed a degree on uncertainty and anxiety about just what was going to be a reasonable flow diagram, or for that matter what was meant by 'high level.'

I am thinking for [this] process . . . I would rather you actually tried to develop your stuff as much as you can and then come to me with issues rather than coming up front when I sit down with you and fill in a blank page, because then it's going to make you go and have a look at the system and try and work it out and you will learn a lot more that way (Project Leader).

(many people begin talking at once in response to the above comment)

It will be like training ourselves! (Production Manager—some consternation in this response).

It will be like . . . yea (mumbling with many voices)
   . . . something like changing a price, if I was you [I'd] load up [the ERP software] . . . you'll get a menu you will be able find basically how to do that and when you open the selected item you will be able to see what you do and you might have some questions and that's fine . . . but don't come in and get me to show you . . .because all you are doing is wasting time and you are not taking any responsibility (Project Leader).

So what you are actually saying is that we need to try to do this ourselves (Operations Manager).

That's exactly what I am saying and you come and ask me when you need to. That's what I am saying (Project Leader).
   The thing here, what you are saying for example I've got here Raise the purchase order so. . . by 22nd May are you expecting me to know how to raise the purchase order . . . and done these flowcharts (Stores and Distribution Manager).

I'd say you should have an 80% idea of how to do that job (Project Leader).
And these are really flowcharts? (Stores and Distribution Manager).

Many people began talking at once at this point. The comments above from the various users illustrate a typical reaction. There was a general concern and nervousness at this point in the meeting as a number of users strove to express their anxieties. They are being asked to understand a yet-to-be created system well enough to document how their business process relates to it and express that in an unfamiliar flowchart. The Project Leader sees it as an opportunity to get the users to engage with the system and resists attempts to rely on him to make the flowchart problem go away. He made a further attempt to make his point and clarify what he wanted.

   . . . all you are doing is listing are the steps that you go through. [pause]
   . . . it should only take like five to ten minutes to do, to know what you want to do . . .
(Interrupted . . . followed by three or four people speaking together).

Some agitation again at this point. People are shifting in their seats and trying to get an opportunity to speak. The Stores and Distribution Manager breaks in with the following remark directed at the Project Leader:

> You see you've sat and dealt with each aspect of [ERP system] for weeks on end, some of us have come in for a couple of hours! (Stores and Distribution Manager).

> I know and that's what I am saying. I am saying lets think about . . . (Project Leader).
>   (two or three people talking over each other)

> . . . but I must be working blind . . . I think . . . be honest [when] you don't even know where you are going, you are going to be wasting a lot of your time just trying to find the things [against the alternative where we'd bring it to you] then you could . . . have done it (Production Manager).

> But when you get into the (ERP) system, when you are sitting there and looking at it won't you think oh . . . yea you do it like this (Operations Manager).

> There is [sic] quite a lot of steps to it . . . I want you to try that . . . basically (Project Leader).

> (many people talking at once in response to the above comments)

In spite of further attempts by the Project Leader to again try to clarify, as precisely as possible, what he wanted and why he thought it should be doable the meeting was becoming more and more restless. People were talking to one another, and others were trying to gain the attention of the group to speak.

The group continued to focus on this item for a further 30 minutes. There was intense discussion and significant contributions from around the table. It became clear that many of the users present were quite anxious about this exercise and felt they lacked the knowledge of the new software and also of what was required on the process flowchart technique. They wanted more certainty and fewer unknowns. Effectively they seemed to lack confidence in their ability to cope with what seemed to them a rather abstract activity. This is a problem with flowcharts. It is perhaps common for those familiar with the representational approach of flowcharts to downplay the difficulty of applying them. For those used to carrying out their day to day activities without giving their actions a 'second thought' the concept of distilling their work practices into such an abstract form of representation was clearly threatening.

At this stage in the meeting, the Operations Manager made a number of attempts to resolve the conflicting views of how to make progress. He suggested a compromise to what had been suggested to make the process more circumscribed by suggesting a time limit on how long the users should try to work out the interrelation between the ERP software and the business practices they were responsible for. He supported the Project Leader by arguing that

> . . . the only way to do these flowcharts is to fumble your way through it, to find out how to work it, and if you can't do that in three or four hours and you still don't feel confident because after three or four hours opening up [ERP system]. I am sure a lot of you will gain a lot more confidence on your own . . .

But added that after this period of time it would be reasonable to seek help

> . . . you just go through it for four hours and then if you really have a problem with that for four hours in one day or three hours, then you got to see [Project Leader].

Each of these contributions had the effect of reducing the atmosphere of conflict between the project team and the users but the issue remained unresolved. A number of the users were still expressing discomfort over the uncertainty of the tasks that they were faced with in different ways.

> Shouldn't we be given the flowchart to follow just for that? (Sales User)

> . . . so how are we trying understand something we've got to be right ourselves . . . if we don't understand it. (Operations User)

> . . . the idea is to go through each part like entering a factory order. So you sit in front of your machine, switch it on [ERP system], and then you navigate your way through [the process of] entering a factory order. (Project Leader)

> So when you have a flowchart and show me how to do that. (Operations User)

> No you can't . . . (Operations Manager) (Over talking again)

The Operations Manager and, indeed, a number of the users, are a little exasperated here. Further discussion ensues that again ends unresolved. Then the Project Leader tries again to make clear why it is important for the users themselves to document their work practices:

> Because we've got to look . . . to use that as a basic process for training, because remember every company is different and they do things

differently. So what we are doing is we are saying here's how we are going to do it on the new system and then when we do our conference pilot . . . the system meets our needs and works for us, we are going to follow the flow that we are saying that we are going to use.

Production and purchase reorder forecasting is suggested as an example and the purchasing manager responds in the following way:

> So use the forecasting as an example. I genuinely don't have a clue how [ERP system] does the forecasting, even though we sat there and did that thing [training] for a couple of hours, I genuinely don't have a clue how it works, so how can I . . . (Purchasing Manager)
>
> (over talking)

The Project Leader takes this example up by suggesting that this is a good example of how problems might be resolved by working through what the steps on the previous system would have been and trying to locate them within the new software.

> But then you might get to the blockage and say I don't know how to do that so I have opened up [ERP system] and so okay, what is in here now . . . you go to [ERP system], you open it up . . . [get] the forecast and you will be able to find this. You will go there and say forecast maintenance, and you load that up and then you will say okay it looks like I need to load further data . . .

The discussion then focused for a time on the problems of a lack of knowledge of the ERP software. A lack of 'familiarisation' as the Operations Manager put it. But again, after a few minutes, it was clear that this was not reducing the tension between contributing to the creation of the new system and the need to gain a first-hand knowledge of it, too.

> You know I do agree with what you are saying that you will familiarise yourself with it but ideally we should probably have some sort of manual . . . I know we are going to find this is what's going to help design the manual . . . but then we should have some sort of instruction there to help us with this. (Stores and Distribution Manager)
>
> There is a manual as well, the manual details . . . (Project Leader)
>
> (Interruption by the Stores and Distribution Manager)
>
> I looked at that manual in there, and it . . . is huge . . . just for the inventory side of it. I thought I would print this and then I got to 90 pages so I cancelled it, before it printed out a ream of paper.

(Some giggling and over talking here)

. . . but to be honest I think we've only had a quick snapshot, this is it and then on to the next thing and we ended up having quite in depth discussions about processes and . . . didn't get a lot of hands on practice.

Calm was restored for a while as the group discussed with more care what was to be done or required in order to be ready for conference room pilot. It was established, clearly to the relief of a number of users, that it was expected that they would still be learning to move between the flowcharts and the ERP software at this stage. Similarly, they were not expected to have everything sorted in relation to the ERP software at the first conference room pilot but to be sufficiently familiar with the business process that the software vendor staff should be able to interpret any gaps between the flowcharts and the software.

At this point the Operations Manager came back in, perhaps conscious that it was largely his people who seemed to be expressing their discomfort with the flowcharting exercise.

Is it a quick shortcut . . . just as an option . . . is there anyway that [Software Vendor] or somebody can be employed to do that process flow as our business rules ???

To do that for each area and come back here and say to [Key User], just check this over, this is how we see the business flow of what you do here, just check it through, amend it, and then make our way and develop the flow and that will also detail where we interact with [ERP system] as well, so you have got one person over the next two or three weeks that we are paying to develop these areas, rather than all these people trying to 'fuffle' their way through it.

[we could get] . . . something that is a little bit generic but that can then be developed after conference room pilot

The intervention was surprising given the discussion so far. One problem with such an approach would be that even more of the business process would be ceded to the software vendor with the likely outcome that the system would remain remote to the users and foreign to their day to day activities. It was also at odds with the purpose the Project Leader had outlined—to get the users to work with the new system.

The Project Leader found himself in a difficult situation. He had trouble making his points without interruption, and the meeting was beginning to feel as if it was getting out of control. As we have documented above, the meeting had degenerated at times to the point in which several people were talking at once, and there was clearly a good deal of misunderstanding about what the users were being asked to do and why. People were talking about different things without realizing it. These are key points in the meeting where meaning is being created within the group. But while it's clear there are different interpretations being expressed, it's less clear how these different understandings will, or can, be reconciled. The project Leader tries to correct this with the following statement:

> (over talking) . . . there's no point in getting some generic stuff . . . all I said that [is needed is] one page [on the] process right through.
>
> . . . it's those individual menus and whereabouts in [ERP system] . . .
>
> (Over talking)
>
> . . . and write that on the process on that side of it but . . . um the actual finding out what does this file do and what does it mean and all that sort of stuff, and there's no way we are going to be able to document that alright. That's all the learning process that we have to go through.
>
> I know we are not documenting it but when we are . . . going to go in and do a price change. (Stores and Distribution Manager)
>
> I mean look, we've got a big opportunity here to develop these process things and learn ourselves and we . . . are going then [to go] through a conference room pilot . . . things there will crystallise very quickly. (Project Leader)
>
> (Over talking)
>
> I'm actually surprised that we have been asked to do this . . . I'm surprised that [ERP Vendor] don't have a flowchart for putting in purchase orders or for doing any of these steps. (Sales User)

Further confusion was revealed in the following remarks from the Purchasing Manager and responses from the Project Leader.

> So what if we haven't, so what if we haven't changed purchase orders, why can't they give us a flowchart to say this is what you put in [data entry] (Purchasing Manager).
>
> What you documented is not what you are putting in [data entry]. It's basically what other steps that you need to do to get a purchase order created. (Project Leader)
>
> So if we had more training . . . (Purchasing Manager).
>
> (over talking)
>
> What do you want to do? How do you want to do this? Because if people are struggling with this now they are going to . . . I know you are

going to put it off, its too hard, its not going to happen in time, we're going to go to this meeting next week and nothing is going to happen because I've asked you to start it.

. . . yea we can do an example, I mean I am happy enough to have a workshop next week where we can run through three or four examples, early next week or something if that will help. . . . What's wrong with say blocking out two hours one day next week between Monday and Wednesday, and try navigating your way through it and then come back . . . On Wednesday we will go into the training room and everyone has the same chance . . . (Project Leader)

After some more anxious discussion, it was resolved that this would be the strategy. The key users committed to taking the time to explore the system for a couple of hours before Wednesday, and the Project Leader would run a workshop to go over the process flowcharts again. One of the researchers attended the workshop. It was largely a non-event. The majority of users had either failed to find the time or had sorted their process flowchart. Figure 2 shows a completed process flowchart.

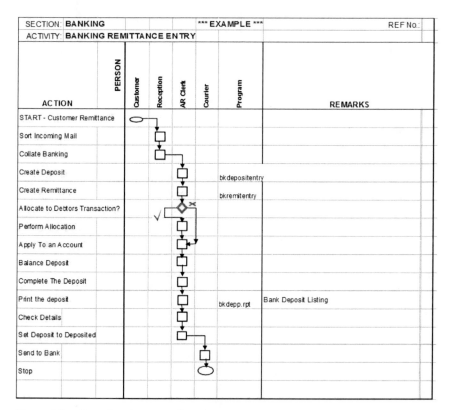

Figure 5.2   Completed process flowchart.

Without having made the effort, the complaints of the more vocal users were less justified, especially as the number of staff successfully completing their flowcharts increased. One of the users, who was vocal in the meeting we reported above, had to justify in the next internal users meeting why he had not been on the system and produced his flowchart. The explanation went

> I was going to do one yesterday between 3 and 5 and you took the[ERP System] down so . . .

> [laugh] and you could have gotten away with that [excuse] (Project Leader)

> Honest, honest. . . No, I haven't . . . sorry. . . .We didn't know that [ERP System] was going to be taken down so we couldn't get into it so. We need it going for an hour and going for 2 hours . . .
> [The flowchart is] top priority, I'm sorry about that.

The process flowcharts were completed for setting up the conference room pilots and as the testing revealed weaknesses in the flowcharts or the need to change the configuration of the system, the fabrication of the flowcharts and the system converged to an (at least temporary) expression of how the system was understood by Pukekoe's users and the software vendor staff.

The flowcharts could be seen as simply a 'flash point' for dissent as the pressure of coping with the implementation grew. On the other hand, we argue that the widely used visual technique achieved interessement in the case situation. The standardized form of the flowchart is familiar to the IT people in Pukekoe and the software vendor. It is also simple enough to be understood by those other employees who need to. Flowcharting is unfamiliar to them, but it is less overwhelming than the ERP system that they are surprised to find they are to be partly responsible for bringing into existence in their company.

What the exchanges in the meeting show is how much work is required to reach a point at which people, with the best of motivations, can be drawn in to co-operate in the creation of a dialogue. This dialogue is needed in order to fashion an integrated system for the organization. In the case company, it was primarily this exchange in this meeting that enabled the user group to accept the role of the process flowcharts as artifacts, 'standardised forms,' that play a crucial role in the construction of common understandings (Star and Griesemer, 1989). The flowcharts become "strongly structured in individual site use," they capture knowledge of existing practices that are important in the present situation of an ERP implementation prior to 'go-live.' They also become artifacts that remain and can be used to pass knowledge to and enroll future employees and future software vendors who may wish to modify or replace the system. They also act as a medium through which two-way exchanges between disparate social groups, in this case the ERP people and the users within Pukekoe, can take place.

DISCUSSION

We have described in this chapter an excerpt from the implementation of an ERP. In the process of the construction of the ERP and its entry into the everyday activities of the organization, we have highlighted the role of a specific boundary object. The object we describe is distinguished by its ability to represent visually many different aspects of mundane business processes. It is able to do this in a consistent and 'logical' manner, in part, as a result of its simplicity and ability to represent and abbreviate (Zuboff, 1988).

In the context we studied, the managers we observed spent much of their time constructing inscriptions and providing representations of their organization to the ERP vendor's staff. Other groups are similarly, intimately linked to material worlds through their practice (Knorr Cetina, 1999; Knorr Cetina and Bruegger, 2002). The process flow diagrams we describe, are based on a principle of economy, or abbreviation ". . . in which the affairs of the world are made pliable, wieldable and therefore amenable to human use through technologies of representation" (Cooper, 1992, p. 257).

Process flowcharts have been around for at least 40 years in various forms. They have become one of the staple accoutrements of a number of professional groups, including management consultants and software vendors and are commonly associated with the identification and transfer of best practice. The exchange of best practice across organizations has been heralded by both populist management literature and much of the academic literature for many years (Boubekri, 2001; Bradford et al., 2001; Palaniswamy and Frank, 2000). The ICT technologies, and ERP in particular, play a central role in this transmission and institutionalization of these 'best practices' (Avital and Vandenbosch, 2000; Francalanci, 2001; see also Orlikowski, 2002). We have not made claims about the identification of best practice. In this chapter our aim is to shed light on the surprisingly important role of mundane techniques, such as process flowcharts, that are used in the organizational change process.

In the case we report process flowcharts are the technology of choice that, not without effort, act as the translation device to facilitate communication across functional and organizational boundaries. The flowchart techniques, which are anything but new, are central to the insinuation of the ERP into the adopting company. They provide a mechanism and a visualization medium (Henderson, 1991; see also Gal et al., 2004), which makes is possible for the user group at Pukekoe to represent their business processes to the consultants and programmers from the ERP vendor.

We regard flowcharts as an excellent example of a boundary object, one which is "weakly structured in common use" but becomes more specific and idiosyncratic as it is constructed by an individual in a specific context. The boundary object becomes strongly structured in individual site use (see Figures 5.1 and 5.2 for simple illustrations from the case company). Flowcharts are

> ... plastic enough to adapt to local needs ... yet robust enough to maintain a common identity" such that they remain recognizable to people outside the organization including the ERP vendor's consultants and programmers. Flowcharts are an example of an abstract visualization, a boundary object that is highly malleable. The chart while appearing to be a highly specific tool is nevertheless open to considerable flexibility. While their structure and visual appearance is 'common[ly] recognizable' they remain open to different interpretations by programmers and ERP users who inhabit 'different social worlds.' (Star and Griesemer, 1989, p. 393)

The accounts we present from the internal user group meetings, at the case site, indicate that boundary objects are often not easily deployed but require significant effort to be expended (see also Carlile, 2002, 2004). There is also evidence here that even ostensibly simple technologies such as flowcharts can take a great deal of work and negotiation in order for them to become accepted among a group of people even within a single organization. The flowcharts like other elements of the implementation act to enroll and mobilize; if successfully, they strengthen the technology in the specific setting. These techniques are in common use by ERP vendors and other consultants but in order for them to work in a given situation they must be insinuated into the implementing organization, even if only temporarily, in such a way as to form a close and intimate assemblage consisting of the boundary objects and the people (Carlile, 2004; Law, 1996, 2002; Latour, 2005).

The ERP systems, with their tendency to formalization and standardization, can be naturally perceived as a threat to users. The objective of an ERP, at least in part, is to increase certainty by establishing standard procedures that increase the predictability of work tasks (Adler and Borys, 1996; see also Courpasson and Reed, 2004; Gouldner, 1954; Hodgson, 2004; Räisänen and Linde, 2004). The use of representational devices as boundary objects is identified here and elsewhere (Dechow and Mouritsen, 2005) as a means of inscribing user knowledge into the ERP as it is configured and at the same time draws the key users into an engagement with the still unsettled system.

CONCLUSION

We see our research as responding to the call made by Bloomfield and Vurdubakis to shift our attention 'away from the "products" of representational practices and towards how they work' (1997a, p. 664). The boundary object concept provides a way of interrogating the use of representational devices in intra- and inter-organizational settings.

Our research describes a rather more modest situation where flowcharts, acting as boundary objects, function to enrol key members of the ERP user group in the organization. We do not see these flowcharting techniques predominantly as 'technologies of control' but as offering a framework sufficiently robust to provide common ground among the users, the project manager, the ERP software and the ERP vendor's staff. Bloomfield and Vurdubakis also argue that

> Enframing. . . is best understood as a form of social performance. It is . . . **an essential means for the institution of an authoritative representation and the exclusion of competing alternatives** (1997a, p. 664, emphasis added).

While we accept that there is scope for the exercise of power relations and that any claims of the objectivity or truth of such representations are problematic, we regard the role of boundary objects as much less pervasive in their impact. Rather than displacing one vision of organization with another, they draw actors into a program of action while allowing them to retain a degree of autonomy. Boundary objects enable a common purpose to be attained by being plastic enough to adapt to local needs without the need for actors to rigidly accept a unified organizational vision.

Flowcharts played a critical role in the assimilation and acceptance of an ERP into the company we describe, but they do this only in association, as part of an assemblage. The meetings we describe are typified by somewhat frantic exchanges as the user group tries to come to terms with the concept and its ability to use it to codify their day-to-day practice. In part this difficulty may be to do with the abstract nature of the flowchart compared to the richness of their work lives. What is lost in the use of such boundary objects is difficult to assess. In order to construct these flowcharts, experience and subjective choices are made to abstract from the detail a depiction; the individual's impression. Our case and the literature suggest that though flowcharts as a device may appear to be a technology of logic, once performed they are also a work of art (Farina, 1970). The flowchart is a work of art not just as a visual representation but also because it is not completely generalizable but tends to the idiosyncratic in any specific application.

For the purposes of our argument, this idiosyncratic nature is not a flaw. Our story is about the role of flowcharts as a standardized form, a boundary object which provides a vehicle that supports communication (Star and Griesemer, 1989; Carlile, 2002, 2004; Gal et al., 2004). The way this works is not by producing some perfect representation of business practice that maps somehow directly into ERP software, but the ability of the objects to translate, even very small processes, in a way which brings the users into proximity with the ERP software. This gives the users a way to increase their awareness and familiarity of what is a vastly complex and inherently unknowable technology (Dechow and Mouritsen, 2005; Locke and Lowe, 2007b).

APPENDIX 1: FLOWCHART SYMBOLS

Symbol	Symbol Name (Alternate Shape Name)	Symbol Description
	Terminator (Terminal Point, Oval)	Terminators show the start and stop points in a process. When used as a Start symbol, terminators depict a trigger action that sets the process flow into motion.
	Process	Show a Process or action step. This is the most common symbol in both process flowcharts and business process maps.
	Predefined Process (Subroutine)	A Predefined Process symbol is a marker for another process step or series of process flow steps that are formally defined elsewhere. This shape commonly depicts sub-processes (or subroutines in programming flowcharts). If the sub-process is considered "known" but not actually defined in a process procedure, work instruction, or some other process flowchart or documentation, then it is best not to use this symbol since it implies a formally defined process.
	Alternate Process	As the shape name suggests, this flowchart symbol is used when the process flow step is an alternate to the normal process step. Flow lines into an alternate process flow step are typically dashed.
	Decision	Indicates a question or branch in the process flow. Typically, a Decision flowchart shape is used when there are 2 options (Yes/No, No/No-Go, etc.)
	Data(I/O)	The Data flowchart shape indicates inputs to and outputs from a process. As such, the shape is more often referred to as an I/O shape than a Data shape.
	Document	Pretty self explanatory - the Document flowchart shape any process flow step that produces a document.
	Multi-Document	Same as Document, except, well, multiple documents. This shape is not as commonly used as the Document flowchart shape, even when multiple documents are implied.
	Preparation	As the names states, any process step that is a Preparation process flow step, such as a set-up operation.
	Display	Indicates a process flow step where information is displayed to a person (e.g., PC user, machine operator).

(continued)

Symbol	Symbol Name (Alternate Shape Name)	Symbol Description
	Manual Input	Manual Input flowchart shapes show process flow steps where the operator/ user is prompted for information that must be manually input into a system.
	Manual Operation	Manual Operations flowchart shapes show which process steps are not automated. In data processing flowcharts, this data flow shape indicates a looping operation along with a loop limit symbol (which is not supported by Microsoft Office, but a Manual Operation symbol rotated 180° will do the trick.)
	Card	This is the companion to the punched tape flowchart shapes. This shapes is seldom used.
	Punched Tape	If you're very good at stretching all the life out of a machine, you may still have use for the Punched Tape symbol - used for input into old computers and CNC machines.
	Connector (Inspection)	Process Flowchart: In process flowcharts, this symbol is typically small and is used as a Connector to show a jump from one point in the process flow to another. Connectors are usually labeled with capital letters (A, B, AA) to show matching jump points. They are handy for avoiding flow lines that cross other shapes and flow lines. They are also handy for jumping to and from a sub-processes defined in a separate area than the main flowchart.Business Process Map: In process maps, this symbol is full sized and shows an Inspection point in the process flow.[Just to confuse things further, some people will use a circle to indicate an operation and a square to indicate an inspection. That's why it's important to include a symbol key in the flowchart.]
	Off-Page Connector	Off-Page Connector shows continuation of a process flowchart onto another page. When using them in conjunction with Connectors, it's best to differentiate the labels, e.g. use numbers for Off-Page Connectors and capital letters for Connectors. In actual practice, most flowcharts just use the Connect shape for both on-page and off-page references.
	Or	The logical Or symbol shows when a process diverges - usually for more than 2 branches. When using this symbol, it is important to label the out-going flow lines to indicate the criteria to follow each branch.
	Summing Junction	The logical Summing Junction flowchart shape is shows when multiple branches converge into a single process. The merge symbol is more common for this use, though. This symbol and the Or symbol are really more relevant in data processing flow diagrams than in process flowcharts.

(continued)

Symbol	Symbol Name (Alternate Shape Name)	Symbol Description
	Collate	The Collate flowchart shape indicates a process step that requires organizing data, information, or materials according into a standard format or arrangement.
	Sort	Indicates the sorting of data, information, materials into some pre-defined order.
	Merge (Storage)	Process Flowchart: In process flowcharts, this symbol shows the merging of multiple processes or information into one.Business Process Map: In process mapping, this symbol is commonly indicates storage of raw materials.
	Extract (Measurement)	Process Flowchart: In my personal experience, I have only seen the Extract flowchart shape indicates a Measurement, with a capital 'M' inside the symbol.Business Process Map: Often indicates storage of finished goods.
	Delay	The Delay flowchart symbol depicts any waiting period that is part of a process. Delay shapes are common in process mapping.
	Stored Data	A general Data Storage flowchart shape used for any process step that stores data (as opposed to the more specific shapes to follow next in this table).
	Magnetic Disk (Database)	The most universally recognizable symbol for a data storage location, this flowchart shape depicts a database.
	Direct Access Storage	Direct Access Storage is a fancy way of saying Hard Drive.
	Internal Storage	Used in programming flowcharts to mean information stored in memory, as opposed to on a file.
	Sequential Access Storage (Magnetic Tape)	Although it looks like a 'Q', the symbol is supposed to look like a reel of tape.

Source: Hebb (2007) http://www.breezetree.com/article-excel-flowchart-shapes.htm

NOTES

1. See www.wikipedia.org and http://www.webster.edu/~woolflm/gilbreth. html. According to Wikipedia "the flow process chart, was introduced by Frank Gilbreth to members of ASME in 1921 as the presentation "Process Charts—First Steps in Finding the One Best Way."

2. ISO 5807:1985 (http://www.iso.org/iso/iso_catalogue/catalogue_tc/
catalogue_detail.htm?csnumber=11955) and BSI 4058:1987 (http://www.
bsi-global.com/en/About-BSI/).
3. See also Hurt (2007, p. 77); Romney and Steinbart (2006, p. 70).
4. The real name of the company and software are not used to protect their confi-
dentiality. We would like to thank the company and the participants for allowing us to observe the implementation and the additional time they gave us for
interviews even though they were already working overtime and weekends.

REFERENCES

Adler, P. S., and Borys, B. (1996). Two Types of Bureaucracy: Enabling and Coer-
cive. *Administrative Science Quarterly, 41*, 61–90.
Angerou, C., Ciborra, C. U., and Land, F. (Eds.). (2004). *The Social Study of Infor-
mation and Communication Technology: Innovation, Actors and Contexts.*
Oxford: Oxford University Press.
Avital, M., and Vandenbosch, B. (2000). SAP Implementation at Metalica: An Organi-
zational Drama in Two Acts. *Journal of Information Technology, 15*(3), 183–194.
Babicz, G. (2000). Give Your process the Right Flow. *Quality, 39*, 34–36.
Bloomfield, B. P. (1995). Power, Machines and Social Relations: Delegating to Information Technology in the National Health Service. *Organization, 2*, 489–518.
Bloomfield, B. P., and Vurdubakis, T. (1997a). Visions of Organization and Organizations of Vision: The Representational Practices of Information Systems
Development. *Accounting, Organizations and Society, 22*, 639–668.
———. (1997b). Paper Traces: Inscribing Organisations and Information Technology. In B. P. Bloomfield, R. Coombs, D. Knights, and D. Littler (Eds.), *Information technology and Organisations; Strategies, Networks and Integration* (pp.
85–111). Oxford: Oxford University Press.
Boczko, T. (2007). *Corporate Accounting Information Systems.* London: Financial Times/Prentice Hall.
Boubekri, N. (2001). Technology Enablers for Supply Chain Management. *Integrated Manufacturing Systems, 12*, 394.
Bradford, M., Mayfield, T., and Toney, C. (2001). Does ERP Fit in a LEAN World?
Strategic Finance, 82, 28–34.
Briers, M., and Chua, W. F. (2001). The Role of Actor-Networks and Boundary
Objects in Management Accounting Change: A Field Study of an Implementation
of Activity-Based Costing. *Accounting, Organizations and Society, 26*, 237–269.
Callon, M. (1986). Some elements of a sociology of translation: Domestication of
the scallops and the fishermen of St Brieuc Bay. In J. Law, Power (Ed.), *Action
and belief: A new sociology of knowledge?* (pp. 196–233). London: Routledge
and Kegan Paul.
Carlile, P.R. (2002). A Pragmatic Vew of Knowledge and Boundaries: Boundary
Objects in New Product Development. *Organisation Science, 13*, 442–455.
———. (2004). Transferring, Translating, and Transforming: An Integrative
Framework for Managing Knowledge Across Boundaries. *Organisation Science, 15*, 555–568.
Ciborra, C. U., Braa, K., Cordella, A., Dahlbom, B., Failla, A., Hanseth, O.,
Hepsø, V., Ljungberg, J., Monteiro, E., and Simon, K. A. (2001). *From Con-
trol to Drift: The Dynamics of Corporate Information Infrastructures.* Oxford:
Oxford University Press.
Clemson University. (2008). Tutorial notes MG303. Retrieved 10th November 2008,
from http://www.garmento.org/mg303/CLEMSON%20FLOW%20CHART.htm.

Colter, M. A. (1984). A Comparative Examination of Systems Analysis Techniques. *MIS Quarterly, 8,* 51–66.

Cooper, R. (1992). Formal organization as representation: Remote control, displacement and abbreviation. In M. Reed and M. Hughes (Eds.), *Rethinking Organization: New Directions in Organization Theory and Analysis* (pp. 254–272). London: Sage.

Courpasson, D., and Reed, M. (2004). Introduction: Bureaucracy in the Age of Enterprise. *Organization, 11,* 5–12.

Dechow, N., and Mouritsen, J. (2005). Enterprise Resource Planning Systems, Management Control and the Quest for Integration. *Accounting, Organizations and Society, 30,* 691–733.

Farina, M. V. (1970). *Flowcharting.* Englewood Cliffs: Hemel Hempstead: Prentice-Hall.

Francalanci, C. (2001). Predicting the Implementation Effort of ERP Projects: Empirical Evidence on SAP/R3. *Journal of Information Technology, 16,* 33–48.

Gal, U., Yoo, Y., and Boland, R. J., Jr. (2004). The Dynamics of Boundary Objects, Social Infrastructures and Social Identities. Sprouts: Working Papers on Information Environments, Systems and Organizations, vol. 4, pp. 193–206.

Gouldner, A. (1954). *Patterns of Industrial Bureaucracy.* New York: Free Press.

Hanseth, O., Aanestad, M., and Berg, M. (2004). *Actor-Network Theory and Information Systems,* vol. 17. Bradford, England: Emerald Group.

Hebb, N. (2007). *Flowchart Symbols Defined: Flowchart Symbols and Their Meanings. How to Create Flowcharts in Excel Series*: Sherwood, OR: Breeze-Tree Software.

Henderson, K. (1991). Flexible Sketches and Inflexible Data-Bases: Visual Communication, Conscription Devices and Boundary Objects in Design Engineering Science, *Technology and Human Values, 16,* 448–473.

Hodgson, D. E. (2004). Project Work: The Legacy of Bureaucratic Control in the Post-Bureaucratic Organization. *Organization, 11,* 81–100.

Hurt, R. (2007). *Accounting Information Systems: Basic Concepts and Current Issues.* New York: McGraw Hill Irwin.

Knorr Cetina, K. D. (1999). *Epistemic Cultures.* Cambridge, MA: Harvard University Press.

Knorr Cetina, K. D., and Bruegger, U. (2002). Global Microstructures: The Virtual Societies of Financial Markets. *American Journal of Sociology, 107*(4), 905–950.

Latour, B. (1987). *Science in Action: How to Follow Scientists and Engineers Through Society.* Cambridge, MA: Harvard University Press.

———. (1994). On Technical Mediation—Philosophy, Sociology, Genealogy. *Common Knowledge, 3,* 29–64.

———. (1996). *Aramis: Or the Love of Technology.* Brighton: Harvester Wheatsheaf.

———. (2005). *Reassembling the Social: An Introduction to Actor-Network-Theory.* Oxford: Oxford University Press.

Law, J. (1996). Organizing accountabilities: Ontology and the mode of accounting. In R. Munroe and J. Mouritsen (Eds.), *Accountability: Power, ethos and the technologies of managing* (pp. 283–306). London: International Thompson Business Press.

———. (1997). Traduction/Trahison: Notes on ANT. Centre for Social Theory and Technology (CSTT). From http://www.keele.ac.uk/depts/stt/staff/jl/pubs-JL2.htm. (accessed 20 January 1998)

———. (2002). Objects and Spaces. *Theory Culture and Society, 19(5/6),* 91–105.

Locke, J., and Lowe, A. (2007a). Researching XBRL as a socio-technical object. In R. Debreceny, M. Piechocki, and C. Felden (Eds.), *New Dimensions of Business Reporting and XBRL* (pp. 19–56). Wiesbaden: DUV-Verlag, Springer.

———. (2007b). A Biography: Fabrications in the life of an ERP package. *Organization, 14*(6), 793–814.

Lowe, A. (2001a). Casemix Accounting Systems and Medical Coding: Organisational Actors Balanced on "Leaky Black Boxes." *Journal of Organizational Change Management, 14,* 79–100.

———. (2001b). Action at a Distance: Accounting Inscriptions and the Reporting of Episodes of Clinical Care. *Accounting Forum, 25,* 31–55.

Lowe, A., and Koh, B. (2007). Accounting as Representation: Some Evidence on the Disputation of Boundaries Between Production and Accounting. *Critical Perspectives on Accounting, 18,* 952–974.

Lowe, A., and Locke, J. (2008). Enterprise Resource Planning and the Post Bureaucratic Organization: "Formalization" as Trust in the System Versus "Solidarity" as Trust in Individuals. *Information Technology and People, 21*(4), 375–400.

Orlikowski, W. J. (2002). Knowing in Practice: Enacting a Collective Capability in Distributed Organizing. *Organization Science, 13,* 249–273.

Palaniswamy, R., and Frank, T. (2000). Enhancing Manufacturing Performance with ERP Systems. *Information Systems Management, 17,* 43–55.

Quattrone, P., and Hopper, T. (2005). A 'Time-Space Odyssey': Management Control Systems in Two Multinational Organisations. *Accounting, Organizations and Society, 30,* 735–764.

Räisänen, C., and Linde, A. (2004). Technologizing Discourse to Standardize Projects in Multi-Project Organizations: Hegemony by Consensus. *Organization, 11,* 101–121.

Robson, K. (1992). Accounting Numbers as "Inscription"; Action at a Distance and the Development of Accounting. *Accounting, Organizations and Society, 17,* 685–708.

———. (1994). Inflation Accounting and Action at a Distance: The Sandilands Espisode. *Accounting, Organizations and Society, 19*(1), 45–82.

Romney, M. B., and Steinbart, P. J. (2006). *Accounting Information Systems.* Upper Saddle River, NJ: Pearson Education.

Scott, S. V., and Wagner, E. L. (2003). Networks, Negotiations, and New Times: The implementation of Enterprise Resource Planning into an Academic Administration. *Information and Organization, 13,* 285–313.

Star, S. L., and Griesemer, J. R. (1989). Institutional Ecology, 'Translations' and Boundary Objects: Amateurs and Professionals in Berkeley's Museum of Vertebrate Zoology. *Social Studies of Science, 19,* 387–420.

Ungan, M. (2006). Towards a better understanding of process documentation. *The TQM Magazine, 18*(4), 400–409.

Walsham, G. (1993). *Interpreting Information Systems in Organisations.* Chichester, UK: John Wiley and Sons.

Zuboff, S. (1988). *In the Age of the Smart Machine: The Future of Work and Power.* New York: Basic Books.

Part III

Publicity

Brand, Icons and Humor

6 Style and Strategy
Snapshot Aesthetics in Brand Culture

Jonathan E. Schroeder

Style and strategy inhabit different domains. Style generally remains the province of the humanities, whereas strategy occupies important positions within the applied social sciences, management in particular. Yet style forms a foundational element of strategic communication. Style helps organizations tell stories within recognizable genres. Style associates strategy with high culture. Style performs the brand. To provide a distinctive interdisciplinary perspective on strategy, I turn to particular styles as illustrative examples of how style intersects with organizational communication and informs strategy.

Visual images constitute much corporate communication about products and services, economic performance, and organizational identity. Moreover, pictures of people—models, celebrity endorsers, spokespersons, "average" consumers, managers and employees—make up a large part of organizational imagery on Web sites, in annual reports, brochures, podcasts, and marketing communication (Borgerson and Schroeder, 2005; Campbell et al., 2009; Guthey and Jackson, 2005). This chapter analyzes the use of snapshots or snapshot-like imagery as a valuable strategic resource for organizational communication. A key aspect of the snapshot style is *authenticity*—snapshot-like images often appear beyond the artificially constructed world of typical corporate communication. This visual quality can be harnessed to promote organizations as authentic, to invoke the "average consumer" as a credible product endorser, and to demonstrate how the brand might fit in with the regular consumer's or employee's lifestyle. I argue that the *snapshot aesthetic* embodies the experience economy by showing consumers in the midst of seemingly real, sometimes exciting, but often mundane experiences. In this way, we can think about snapshot aesthetics as an important visual aspect of documenting, marketing, and understanding experience and an exemplary strategic style.

Snapshot aesthetics illuminates important connections between style and strategy. Style represents a technology of glamour (Thrift, 2008). Focusing on style helps articulate and highlight organizational construction and strategic deployment of icons, codes, and representational conventions across a range of actors—including fine art, advertising, corporate reportage, fashion photography, Web design, popular photography, and film. I discuss the role of snapshot aesthetics in contemporary brand communication and trace a brief visual genealogy of the snapshot, encompassing historical precedents in Dutch genre art, photographic genres such as street photography and reportage, and contemporary uses of the snapshots, such as paparazzi photography and photoblogs. The *staged spontaneity* of the snapshot offers a powerful and flexible stylistic tool that forms a basis of the image economy.

INTRODUCTORY CASE STUDY: YVES SAINT LAURENT

Figure 6.1   Yves Saint Laurent advertisement, 2008.

The iconic French fashion house Yves Saint Laurent's (YSL's) 2008/2009 brand campaign features odd images of models barely recognizable as luxury advertising. For example, one ad shows a man draped over an industrial railing in a nondescript staircase. His unkempt hair covers his eyes. He leans over the railing, almost appearing as if falling down, or walking off balance. His leg sticks out from his body in a strange way. The photograph itself is harshly lit, with strong shadows, far from the typical sumptuous studio portrait that YSL usually employs. Why has YSL chosen this snapshot-like image for their visual brand strategy? What strategic role does this style play in contemporary marketing communication? An investigation into style and strategy offers some answers. By harnessing style as a strategic aesthetic, organizations build upon cultural references to produce meaning and value.

THE BRAND CULTURE PERSPECTIVE

A brand culture perspective (Schroeder, 2008a, 2008b; Schroeder and Salzer-Mörling, 2006) reveals how branding has opened up to include cultural, sociological, and theoretical enquiry that both complements and complicates economic and managerial analysis of corporate strategy. If brands exist as cultural, ideological, and aesthetic objects, then researchers require tools developed to understand culture, ideology, and aesthetics, in conjunction with more typical branding concepts, such as equity, strategy, and value. This approach to brand culture encompasses Doug Holt's cultural branding model (Holt, 2004); research within this tradition often focuses on the cultural building blocks of value for particular brand campaigns.

In my research, I have argued for an art historical imagination within communication, branding, and consumer research, one that reveals how stylistic conventions—or common patterns of portraying objects, people, or identities—work alongside rhetorical processes in ways that often elude management studies. Whereas I readily acknowledge a multitude of issues within organizational communication and strategy, I focus on style, drawing upon interdisciplinary theory to investigate strategic communication. Moreover, I am particularly interested in how photographic style—encompassing still, video, digital, film, and consumer-generated imagery—works as a branding and communicative tool. This chapter introduces several new theoretical concepts, including snapshot aesthetics—the growing use of snapshot-like imagery in strategic communication—that provide productive directions for research that takes style as an important, if often overlooked, category of organizational communication.

In the following, I discuss the role of snapshot aesthetics in contemporary brand communication and trace a brief visual genealogy of the snapshot, encompassing historical precedents in Dutch genre art, photographic genres such as street photography and reportage, and contemporary uses of the snapshots, such as paparazzi photography and photoblogs. I then present a wider view of the relationships between style and strategy. The snapshot aesthetic concept offers researchers a host of questions to pursue. What associations do snapshot aesthetics help consumers build? Many luxury goods draw on snapshot aesthetics; will this erode their brand image? Should companies utilize consumer-generated imagery that draws upon snapshot aesthetics? And will this transform the advertising industry? What are the cultural connections of the snapshot, and how might these work within visual communication? What is the visual genealogy of snapshot aesthetics? Is it a fad that may soon fade away? Does snapshot aesthetics relate to new media forms such as Twitter, an audio analog of the snapshot, with quickly composed tweets acting as verbal snapshots of everyday life? In short, what is the relationship between the snapshot style and strategy?

SNAPSHOT AESTHETICS: CONSTRUCT DEFINITION AND CONCEPTUAL OVERVIEW

The snapshot, a straightforward, generally unposed photograph of everyday life, has emerged as an important style in contemporary strategic communication. Many recent advertisements, annual reports, and Web sites portray models in classic snapshot poses—out of focus, eyes closed, poorly framed—in contrast to more traditional and historical patterns of formal studio shots or highly posed tableaux. Companies such as American Apparel, Apple, Coca-Cola, IKEA, and Renault-Nissan deploy snapshot-like images in their print, television, and Internet communications. These snapshots often appear less formal, more everyday, or "real"—more "authentic." "Intentional" snapshots are often characterized by disruptions in formal photographic traditions—off lighting, poor focus, blurred images, awkward poses, harsh shadows, or other deviations from formal photographic practice.

For example, Dr. Martens original boots feature prominently in their new advertising campaign–"presented in a contemporary fashion context." Model Daisy Lowe stars in the campaign, appearing in various edgy poses, pairing her Dr. Martens boots with a patent trench coat, leggings, and shorts. As Ian Tan, a Dr. Martens manager, refers to the ads: "The brand has long been associated with punk and grunge. Instead of narrowing it down to a subculture, think of Dr. Martens as a piece of fashion which you can mix and match for self-expression." (from Dr. Martens Singapore Web site http://www.drmartens.sg/, accessed November 29, 2009). In a film produced about the campaign, Daisy Lowe reports, "The thing about this shoot is that it's not stylized at all" (from YouTube video "Dr. Martens and Daisy Lowe," accessed March 15, 2009).

Figure 6.2   Dr. Martens Web site, 2010.

As sophisticated consumers, we should know that, of course, the campaign *is* stylized—and the YouTube video of the shoot reveals how much effort went into to making it appear 'not stylized.' Listen as Lowe enthuses about the products and the shoot—that the making of this print and television campaign was filmed for Dr. Martens makes its' staged spontaneity all the more apparent. The snapshot aesthetics harnessed by Dr. Martens via their use of Daisy Lowe—a so-called 'rock n roll heiress'—revolves around an insouciant, unstaged quality of the images. They don't *appear* staged, yet they are. How does this work? To find some answers, we turn to image producers—photographers and editors—for insights into this strategic style.

Internationally celebrated fashion photographer Terry Richardson has emerged as one of the most successful 'snapshot' photographers. He shot Daisy Lowe for the cover of *i-D* fashion magazine and currently works with Jimmy Choo in a widely publicized campaign for their high-profile shoes. Richardson explains "Ninety percent of the images I've ever taken have been done with a small camera. You don't have to focus it or do a light reading. You can't fuck up. And because you don't have full control over it, they allow for accident. [. . .] Those cameras aren't invasive. It's less formal" (quoted in Braddock, 2002, p. 161). *Vogue* magazine editor Robin Derrick agrees "Snap cameras, rather than elaborate technical cameras, put the emphasis back on the photographer as auteur, rather than as technician.

[. . .] With point-and-shoot cameras, what becomes interesting is what you point it at" (quoted in Braddock, 2002, p 161). The snapshot, along with its close relatives paparazzi photography, reality television, and photoblogs, represents a particularly influential style that many well known photographers have embraced.

For example, the Marc Jacobs brand has productively employed snapshots by well known German photographer Jürgen Teller in a consistent campaign that has attracted wide attention. The *New York Times* discussed the images in an article about fashion photography: "An astonishing array of people have appeared in the ads, generally doing not much—lying in the grass, kicking up their heels, teasing a squirrel. [These ads] serve an authentic record of the distractions and tastes of the moment . . ." (Horyn, 2008, p. 1). By "not doing much" the ads visually emphasize the celebrities and semi-celebrities that form the core of the Marc Jacobs lifestyle brand. The authenticity of these images—they appear not constructed—contributes to their appeal, both as a photograph and as an ad—and they circulate widely on the Internet, in blogs and fashion forums. Further connections show how a style accumulates particular signature characteristics—Daisy Lowe was hired by Marc Jacobs as their new 'face' for 2009. Thus, the style of Marc Jacobs' communication provides the basis for a successful, long running branding campaign, attracting interest outside the confines of strategic communication.

SNAPSHOT AESTHETICS AS A STRATEGIC RESOURCE: STAGED SPONTANEITY AS STYLE

I contend that snapshot aesthetics—an increasingly prominent style of strategic imagery—by accelerating photography's apparent realism, provides an important strategic resource for corporate communication. In this way, in brand communication that deploys snapshots, or images that appear as snapshots, several strategic goals might be met. First, these photographs appear *authentic,* as if they are beyond the artificially constructed world of typical promotional photography. Authenticity has been argued as a key component of consumer interaction with brands. Thus, an authentic-looking image may support authentic brands by appearing honest, sincere, and unstaged.

As Colin Decker, creative director of popular online broadcaster Current TV explains, the coveted 18- to 34-year-old demographic "does not respond positively to something overly produced and (that is) a hard sell" (quoted in Mills, 2006). Snapshot aesthetics may work against an overly produced, hard sell appearance. Photography curators Susan Kismaric and Eva Respini, in discussing fashion photography, place snapshot aesthetics and authenticity into a wider cultural context: "two of the dominant narrative modes in fashion photography of the last decade are the influence of the cinema and the snapshot. Both of these strategies create storylines and interrupted narratives, which imbue the images with dramatic complexity and an aura of personal intimacy and authenticity" (Kismaric and Respini, 2008, 30.) Thus, *style supports strategy*—in this case, the visual style of the snapshot provides synergy with the strategic (and aesthetic) goal of authenticity.

Second, snapshot aesthetics supports a *casual* image of brands, particularly consumer lifestyle brands. Many brands appeal to less formal consumption—from family dinners to online financial management. Popular fashion firms, in particular, court casual images for their brands and subbrands. Moreover, as the casual clothing market has grown in recent years, fueled by "dress-down Fridays," expanded demand for men's clothing in between suits and blue jeans, and haute couture designers' turn toward basic, everyday clothing in their secondary lines—casual wear such as jeans and T-shirts—the aesthetic regime of the snapshot has developed into a potent marketing tool. Well-known examples include Burberry, Diesel, and Sisley—each deploy snapshot-like photographs in high-profile branding campaigns for their everyday clothing lines. Benetton has elevated the snapshot, along with journalistic imagery, to style icon in its long-running, often criticized, and widely imitated United Colors of Benetton campaign (e.g., Borgerson et al., 2009). Thus, fashion and design companies offering casual product lines often rely on snapshot-like imagery in the ads, catalogs, and on Web sites, to show their products intended use, signal their casual style and visually link the brand to authentic experience. This imagery also serves to distance the brand from corporate control—associating instead with consumer co-creation (see Schroeder, 2010).

In this way, photographic style helps articulate market segmentation strategy. For example, Italian designer Giorgio Armani's Collezioni clothing—his most expensive ready-to-wear collection—generally appears in classically composed black-and-white promotional images, whereas the Armani Jeans line—a more recent, entry-level brand—usually features snapshot-like images of sexualized bodies. Likewise, Burberry's successful rebranding from conservative classic to contemporary cool seemed to have benefited greatly from snapshot-like photographs, featuring the likes of supermodels Kate Moss and Stella Tennant (Schroeder, 2006). Of course, the Burberry rebranding effort encompassed many other strategic initiatives, but I contend that for consumers, their iconic early 2000s black-and-white photographic ad campaign remains the most visible and persuasive rebranding device.

Snapshot aesthetics provide a *visual frame* for marketing images—a "here and now," contemporary look, by (seeming to) capture a moment, offering a fresh, unposed look. Snapshots often appear rushed, carelessly composed, taken almost by chance, thus revealing subjects unposed, "natural" (e.g., Batchen, 2008; Nickel, 1998). As advertising photographer John Spinks explains "The style is basically a recontextualisation of documentary practice. The equipment is rudimentary, but the lie is far more sophisticated, it appears to be verité but it's not. It can be set up and contrived and as much of a fantasy as more technical shoots. A lot of the work is in the edit" (quoted in Braddock, 2002, p. 162.) Snapshots within strategic brand communication invoke a *realist* effect that supports a range of brand associations. I argue that this realist aspect of snapshot aesthetics underlines the fashion element of many products—up-to-date, hip, and cool—distinguishing them from classic, boring, or yesterday's goods. In this way, the snapshot look may help to accelerate fashion cycles and trends.

Figure 6.3 Mercedes-Benz "Boomers" advertisement, 2003.

Snapshot aesthetics further blurs the line between strategic marketing communication and popular photography. Advertising excels in appropriating or borrowing cultural codes and styles—snapshot aesthetics draws on the codes and conventions of popular, home photography, but transforms the humble snapshot into a powerful strategic tool. Furthermore, many snapshot ads appear as if produced by average consumers. Snapshot aesthetics also has important connections to Twitter, blogging, and viral marketing campaigns. With the rising popularity of Web sites that allow users to post their own photographs and videos, such as Collected Visions, Facebook, Flickr, fotolog.com, MySpace, and YouTube, as well as Google and Yahoo image and video search engines, the snapshot enjoys higher circulation than ever (see Cohen, 2005; Currie and Long, 2006; Smith, 2001).

As marketing scholars John Deighton and Leora Kornfeld point out, the "new marketplace rewards more participatory, more sincere, and less directive marketing styles than the old" (Deighton and Kornfeld, 2009, p. 4). Snapshot aesthetics offers a way in to *participatory* (consumer-generated images), *sincere* and *less directive* (more ambiguous and flexible, perhaps) strategic style.

Furthermore, many consumers happily create their own ads, which are often in the snapshot or documentary style. Web sites such as Current TV and YouTube offer consumers a forum to try their hand at brand communication—and occasionally successful specimens are snapped up by brand

Figure 6.4   Ray-Ban Web site, 2007.

managers for more conventional broadcast. In 2007 Ray-Ban, for example, successfully re-introduced their iconic Wayfarer sunglasses with 24 hours of consumer-generated images projected in New York's Times Square and followed up with consumer-generated videos, viewable on their Web site. Many companies sponsor consumer-generated ads, including Converse, MasterCard, and Sony (Petrecca, 2006).

Snapshot aesthetics signals a step away from corporate control and staging, in that snapshots appear to let consumers take charge and assume central importance as both subjects and producers of strategic imagery. These images seem to contain less artifice, as they appear consumer focused. For example, *Teen Vogue* magazine recently staged a snapshot contest that offered 'real girls' a chance to appear on the *Teen Vogue* blog. A recent 'girl of the week' shows a stylish 16 year old, with her own fashion blog, who aspires to be a Hollywood actress. She appears in a snapshot-like pose that mimics the magazine's fashion spreads. By opening up their blog to 'real consumers' and showing them in snapshots, *Teen Vogue* both empowers young fashionistas and benefits from their work for the brand (e.g., Zwick et al., 2008).

A BRIEF VISUAL GENEALOGY OF SNAPSHOT AESTHETICS

One difficulty in apprehending snapshot aesthetics as an intentional style—as well as a strategic resource—lies in its apparent realism. I argue that this aspect of snapshot aesthetics underlies and supports its contemporary uses as 'authentic' (looking) communication. Realism, as an important artistic movement, often eludes traditional discourses of style: "the commonplace notion that Realism is a 'styleless' or transparent style, a mere simulacrum or mirror image of visual reality, is another barrier to its understanding as an historical and stylistic phenomenon" (Nochlin, 1971, p. 14). In other words, realistic-looking snapshots often seem to have no style at all, as Daisy Lowe perceptively noted in her discussion about her Dr. Martens ads.

For example, one of my bright Chinese students reacted poorly to the 2008/2009 YSL campaign. She thought its downbeat, snapshot-like images didn't work well with the brand's upscale, luxury image. I realized that her eye "missed" the aesthetics of the ads—she didn't realize that this style represents—at least to some viewers—a link to the world of high culture, photography museums, and realist art. The historical connection, and part of the strategic rationale, escaped her. On the other hand, a French colleague who has done extensive work on YSL immediately connected this campaign to legendary photographer Helmut Newton's iconic work for the brand over several decades (see Lagerfeld and Newton, 2007). She saw clear links—a strategic consistency—between contemporary campaigns and hallmark Newton images from the 1970s and 1980s, including his legendary photograph of "le smoking"—the women's suit that helped define Yves Saint Laurent's strategic style. Thus, a central part of realizing the potential strategic power of style rests in understanding its cultural background.

Styles have meaningful histories. Style forms a fundamental core of art history: "style itself can be a system of signs used to embrace meaning, whatever the art or medium. Every work of art and architecture has a meaning—an iconography—and a set of characteristics special to it" (West, 1996, p. 826). To understand how certain styles "work"—including within strategic communication—we must understand their cultural history, as these offer clues to contemporary connections and uses.

Histories must begin somewhere, even if that starting point appears arbitrary. For my work on snapshot aesthetics, I start with the Dutch genre art of the Golden Age, a period that most art historians agree signaled a new era in Western painting. For the first time, ordinary people began to appear in oil paintings, formerly the province of kings and queens, holy figures, and mythical characters. I then jump to Impressionism, the 19th-century art movement that focused on fleeting qualities of light, outdoor scenes, and picnics in the park. Other important antecedents of contemporary snapshot aesthetics include the photographic genres of amateur photography, reportage, street photography, and film styles neo-realism and documentary that largely emerged during the 20th century (see Cotton, 2004; Mora, 2007; Schroeder and Zwick, 2004; Scott, 2007).

GOLDEN AGE DUTCH ART

Many photographic conventions, including advertising photography, can be traced to Dutch art of the Golden Age, a period that art historians consider crucial in the history of Western art. Frans Hals, Jan Vermeer, and many other Dutch artists portrayed regular people in scenes of everyday life, playing music, reading, cleaning, or just sitting around. These *genre* paintings represent a clear cultural antecedent to contemporary snapshot aesthetics. One recurrent theme was reading letters—a typical painting showed a young women intently gazing at a precious letter from one who was away. Countless art historians have contemplated the deeper symbolic connections of these images, invoking themes of literacy, adultery, alienation, and subjective worlds to discuss these enigmatic paintings.

Dutch art often appears to show simple scenes, without the trappings of Renaissance or Byzantine art. In other words, meanings seem readily apparent—the subjects of the paintings are often easily recognizable. However, as historian Simon Schama points out, Dutch art quivers with visual signification: "Dutch art invites the cultural historian to probe below the surface of appearances. By illuminating an interior world as much as illustrating an exterior one, it moves back and forth between morals and matter,

Figure 6.5   Johannes Vermeer, *The Love Letter*, ca. 1669, Rijksmuseum, Amsterdam. Reproduced with permission.

between the durable and the ephemeral, the concrete and the imaginary [. . .]" (Schama, 1988, p. 10). Comparisons with brand communication are apt—for it too, seems to exist in the moment, an ephemeral visual form the merely illustrates product or lifestyle images.

There are many potential connections between Dutch art and contemporary snapshot aesthetics. Much like advertising, Dutch art offers a window and a mirror to society. Cultural and economic resonances include a flowering of consumer culture, exemplified by a growing international economy that celebrating wealth, a concern for cleanliness and keeping a nice house, and economic speculation, such as the famous tulip bulb craze

(Schama, 1988). The Dutch art market that emerged during the 1600s is highly reminiscent of today's image culture. Dutch homes collected scores of paintings for their homes, much the way contemporary consumers generate photographs that fill albums, frames, and refrigerator doors. Finally, we celebrate "Golden Ages"–our representational system picks and chooses referents—we rarely see links to the tarnished years before the Dutch Golden Age or of Greek society in the early 1920s. There are also specific visual referents between Dutch art and current visual forms, especially advertising photography (Schroeder, 2002). More speculatively, we might consider the homepage's roots in the elaborate, spotless, and fascinating Dutch interiors, painted hundreds of years ago.

Golden Age Dutch art shows a world constructed, posed, groomed, and carefully represented to portray a vision of the secular good life. Like contemporary snapshot aesthetics, Dutch paintings portray consumer lifestyles, filled with friends, lovers, consumer goods, and entertainment. Dutch art is often seen in moral terms—the images provide instructions in how to live a good, pious life. One might say that contemporary advertising delivers instructions in how to live a good, prosperous life. The style of Dutch art profoundly influenced painting, and in turn, advertising. Dutch art relied on a realist style; the domestic scenes were mostly painted without classical or mythical iconography (e.g., Lloyd, 2004). Dutch art showed recognizable people in realistic settings. I suggest that this realistic style has exerted a profound influence upon the way photography was received as a technology for "accurately" representing the world. The interior genre scenes of Dutch art encapsulate a way of seeing and representing the world; a world in which interior space signifies privacy, seclusion, withdrawal, and escape. Many Dutch paintings are of interiors and present a vision of single-family home, a women's domestic space, and a way of life that included orderliness, possession, and display. These kind of scenes fill contemporary marketing communication—now called the *slice of life,* that reify the everyday, the vernacular, the lost moment—an entire range of consumer experience.

TWENTIETH-CENTURY PHOTOGRAPHY

Snapshot aesthetics offers the most closely related artistic genre to the contemporary use of snapshot photography. In the mid-20th century, photographers, equipped with high-quality, portable cameras, began to photograph and exhibit everyday life—in the streets, on the road, in private settings, and developed a realist style:

> In the mid-1960s, the idea of a "snapshot aesthetic" began to gain currency in art photography circles. Photographers like Lee Friedlander and Garry Winogrand prowled the streets of New York with handheld

cameras, producing images that seemed random, accidental, and caught on the fly. (Fineman, 2004)

Friedlander, for example, became known for his photographs taken from moving vehicles. One of his aesthetic contributions rests on showing how the world looks when traveling in a car. Winogrand, too, shot pictures on the move, in his lifelong attempt to show what things looked like when photographed.

Particularly in the United States, snapshot, street, or documentary-style photography exerted profound influence on aesthetic and social questions about the role photography could play in culture and was embraced by leading museums and curators, such as the Museum of Modern Art in New York, propelled by its influential photography curator, John Szarkowski (Mora, 2007). Often associated with documentary photography, this style seemed separate from the commercial world of advertising and fashion photography. Ironic, perhaps, that the style lends itself so well to strategic aims.

STYLE AND STRATEGY: FURTHER DIRECTIONS

Snapshot aesthetics represents only one style that exerts influence upon contemporary strategy. Although style often is underestimated as mere surface, I assume style is core to understanding how visual communication works. Within marketing research, a few scholars have begun to articulate and document visual rhetoric and its associated styles. In particular, the landscape of strategic communication has undergone a visual turn, in a profound stylistic change. This change reflects a basic transformation in how people are addressed by strategic communication, largely centering on the triumph of the visual over the verbal: "the changes observed in advertising style reflect substantive changes in the consumers to which these ads were directed, and that these stylistic changes were necessary if such advertising was to continue to be effective" (McQuarrie and Phillips, 2008, p 95). Thus, connections between style and strategy go deep.

In the following, I introduce further examples of style and strategy. I veer away from the snapshot into historical notions of classical architecture, on the one hand, and cutting-edge appropriations of fetishism, on the other, to sketch the variegated domain of style and strategy. Architecture represents a powerful cultural and stylistic code, drawing upon history, materiality, and signification, whereas fetishism turns inward toward psychology, anthropology, and magic to produce its strategic effects. Together, these exemplars of style provide insights into the cultural codes of strategic communication, as they represent disparate ends of the style spectrum, and reveal how style performs distinctive work for organizations and appeals to diverse market segments and audiences.

CLASSICAL STYLE AND THE FINANCIAL INDUSTRY

A *visual genealogy* of contemporary communication strategies in the banking industry revealed the staying power of classical architecture for transmitting certain key values about banks and building brand images for global financial institutions. I studied bank Web sites, financial institution's brand campaigns, credit card advertising, and investment firm annual reports and found the classical language of architecture remains, despite massive changes in banking and the financial sector. Although space and time are transfigured within the information-based electronic world of contemporary commerce, classical architecture remains a viable style for communicating financial values.

Architecture provided a strategic style for banks to communicate key attributes of stability, strength, and security. Customers entrust banks with their savings, hopes, and goals—this distinguishes banking from most other business concerns. Each of these strategic banking values—stability, strength, and security—has a psychological dimension as well as a material solution. Stability, expressed in visual form by a sturdy structure, provides a metaphor for long-term endurance—colossal columns, heavy materials, and symmetrical form contribute to a building's appearance of strength. Of course, bank customers also desire financial strength and an ability to withstand economic cycles. Security, for so long largely dependent on architecture fortresses, walled cities, and massive structures, also relates to psychological anxiety about financial matters. The closed form of most banks was meant to signal protection—a secure institution to entrust one's future. Furthermore, the use of the temple form created a visual of a special building protecting its valuables, allowing only certain people access to the interior space, and promoting a ritual element of bank visit. Banks are not just depositories of money; they are repositories of hopes, dreams, and anxieties—a modern temple.

Information technology drove many changes in the banking industry—money and financial matters are no confined to pieces of paper that must be sorted and stored in ways that leave a ledger and an audit trail. Instead, they are electronic entries, generated via computers, and disconnected from particular spaces or buildings. The small town bank of the past, where customers knew the tellers, and met personally with the loan officer to discuss your mortgage, is gone, replaced by automated teller machines (ATM), online banking, secondary markets for mortgages, and credit default swaps. Perhaps this points to the continuing significance of classical architecture—it alone remains to symbolize banking's connection with the past by tapping into classicism as a powerful referent system. Although the premises of banking have changed, the promises of the banking industry have not.

Banks adopted classical architectural form to persuade the public. In the electronic age, architecture no longer confines banking, nor do most banking transactions take place within a bank's headquarters. Therefore, a change might be expected in communicative tools—classical style might seem outmoded or old-fashioned for the information society. However, banks have shifted the symbolic domain from the building to the strategic message, adopting architectural symbols for use in digitized images that carry on the communicative tradition of classical forms. In the aftermath of the credit crisis, many financial institutions are turning once again to classical style to reassure customers of their traditional values.

Banks today are in the business of building brands as much as physical structures. Classical style reinforces this notion, linking an ancient past to the present via rhetorical devices perfected during in classical era. Of course, these persuasive visual rhetorical tools are augmented via marketing information technology, selling the past to the future. Classicism remains a central cultural referent structure. Architecture provides spatial, historical, and psychological images easily appropriated by visual media. Furthermore, architecture is a basic metaphorical structure for perception and cognition— indeed, it "presents embodiments of thought when it invents and builds shapes" (Arnheim, 1977, p. 371). These shapes, translated into two dimensions, abstracted and isolated, are the building blocks of meaning making. By tracing visual genealogies such as classicism, we gain an appreciation of the complex composition of current branding strategies (Davison, 2009; DeCock et al., 2009; Schroeder, 2002, 2003, 2005, 2008a).

FETISH STYLE AS STRATEGY

The visual vocabulary of fetish has become a staple of the culture industries, television, fashion, film, music video, comic books, and advertising, which often draw on the cultural stereotype of the fetishist, a male whose sexual identity is linked with the fetish object. This projection—of lust, of desire, and of want—onto a fetish object seems the simplest way to present such imagery, which is usually recruited to lend an edgy sexuality to the advertised product. Fetishization in popular communication is often associated with *commodification*—associating objects and humans with markets and mass consumption. For example, strategic communication often fetishizes goods by eroticizing and *reifying* consumer goods, products, and brands. Products and brands are worshipped for their ability to complete the self, to help consumers gain satisfaction—or even ecstasy—and revered for their capacity to project desired images. In this way, consumer goods function similarly (in a psychoanalytic sense) to the fetish object, which promises gratification but ultimately is unable to deliver, forever displaced within a fetishized relationship. Once again, a brief historical genealogy of fetish style helps situate fetishization and clarifies its contemporary power.

Ads for many products, from cologne to telecommunications networks, feature fetish themes of high-heeled shoes, stockings, tight leather, sadism and masochism (S and M), and bondage (e.g., Schroeder and Borgerson,

2003; Schroeder and McDonagh, 2006). These images draw on motifs developed by such photographers as Helmut Newton, Horst, and Jean-Loup Sieff, who featured women in corsets, leather, and lingerie in their photographic work for mainstream fashion magazines. By the 1980s fetish imagery had established a firm place in the visual pantheon of fashion, music video, and film, as adopted by such celebrities as Grace Jones, Madonna, and Annie Lennox, and showcased in photography of Robert Mapplethorpe. Today, fashion companies such as Thierry Mugler, Versace, Jean-Paul Gauthier, and Sisley regularly include fetish-themed apparel in their clothing lines and ad campaigns; currently, tight leather leggings and latex stockings are *au curant,* and mainstream movies and television shows *the Matrix, Underworld, Watchmen,* and *Buffy the Vampire Slayer* feature fetishized outfits as standard hero (or villain) apparel.

Fetishized objects often symbolize control and release, power and helplessness, and sexuality and infantilism. In psychoanalytic terms, a fetish may be a dysfunctional response to sexuality, eventually replacing human contact for arousal. Further, a fetishized relationship, in some cases, interferes with the ability to have more 'human' relations. Typically linked to sexuality, fetishized items are often contextually isolated—the shoe that by itself arouses, the disembodied body part, or the black stocking unconnected to any recognizable body. Visual communication often further displaces these objects via fetishization, by which an image replaces the physical object. The study of fetishization can be particularized by focusing upon clothing items, but widespread communication processes are also implicated.

Fetish style emerged as an important tool of organizational communication, via direct representations of fetish objects, and the fetish-like worship and power of consumer goods inherent in contemporary advertising (Schroeder, 2002). Photographic techniques such as close cropping, lighting, and depth of field help fetishize objects by isolating and reifying them. Two factors underlie the visual power of fetish: associations made through repeated usage of stock items in fashion, photography, and pornography and what has been called the *liminal* element of fetishization (Schroeder and Borgerson, 2003). The word liminal reflects a gap, a space between, or an edge. Liminal zones are often spaces of uncertainly, creativity, danger, and passion. The space between—a space to be entered or crossed—can be exciting and unnerving simultaneously. Many fetishized objects—particularly items of clothing—represent a powerful liminal zone. Shoes, boots, corsets, stockings are typical fetishized items—usually colored black or bright red. In popular discourse fetish clothing is usually desired by men on women.

The long running and spectacularly successful Absolut vodka brand campaign provides a classic example of fetish style in strategic communication (Schroeder and Borgerson, 2003). One iconic Absolut ad, 'Absolut Au Kurant,' exemplifies how fetish style works. Introduced in 1997, the ad circulates widely and is reproduced on many Web sites, including Absolutad.com. The ad consists of a color photograph of a human torso dressed in a black leather corset with lavender lacing, tightly cropped to show only a small bare patch of white skin, perhaps an inch at the top and two inches at the bottom of the image. The words 'Absolut Au Kurant' run along the bottom of the ad, in lavender capital letters that match the corset's laces. A subtle lavender filter gives the corset a purplish cast. The corset's metallic hooks appear to form the shape of a bottle—the Absolut Vodka bottle—with a bow tied at the bottom of the corset. Thus, the laces represent the bottle in the ad.

In a fairly simple and straightforward image, Absolut links itself to leather corsets, fetishism, alternative sexuality, and sexual allure. In this way, fetish style assumes strategic force. The message of the ad centers on the resonance between opening an Absolut bottle and consuming the product and opening the black corset and consummating a relationship. The lace-bottle opens up the person within, undressing for potential intimate activity. The Absolut bottle serves as the key prop for sexual readiness. The magic, fetishized properties of the Absolut bottle are hinted at by these elements, a common theme in liquor advertisements. Style, for many fast-moving consumer goods, is everything, and visual styles such as fetishism often make powerful links to communicative strategy.

SNAPSHOT AESTHETICS AND PHOTOGRAPHY THEORY

Snapshot aesthetics represents a successful style for organizational communication. Brands in wide ranging industries—from finance to footwear—embrace this strategic style. Even iconic luxury brands such as Marc Jacobs and YSL turn to the humble snapshot for their corporate campaigns. The turn to style offers research an multidisciplinary gaze for understanding images and organization. Within this project I embrace a genre-based perspective influenced by art historical methods and assumptions. As part of my broader research project on style and strategy, this paper builds upon efforts in photography theory to systematically explore:

> the entire social, spatial, temporal and phenomenological context in which these technological forms are variously viewed and received; the psychic determination by which modes of spectatorial identification and projection are secured; and not least, the industrial (or alternatively, independent artistic) structures that underwrite, shape, manufacture and disseminate them. (Solomon-Godeau, 2007, pp. 268–269)

How photographs *address* viewers remains a key concern, as well as the strategic ambiguity of photographs in corporate communication (e.g., Eisenberg, 2007). Photography itself is often overlooked within organizational communication; I, along with a few other researchers, have insisted that visual rhetoric constitutes a key issue within strategic brand communication (e.g., Borgerson and Schroeder, 2005; Buchanan-Oliver et al., 2010; Davison, 2008; McQuarrie and Phillips, 2008; Pracejus et al., 2006; Schroeder, 1998; Scott and Batra, 2003).

Might we say snapshot aesthetics reveals the power of marketing communication to co-opt and appropriate popular forms, even colonize formerly private, family rituals?

Contemporary strategic snapshots embody a doubleness—spontaneous yet composed; authentic yet constructed; realistic yet sophisticated—that refers to the basic problem of photography. As Roland Barthes argues "The more technology develops the diffusion of information (and most notably of images) the more it provides the means of masking the constructed meaning under the appearance of the given meaning" (Barthes, 1977, p. 46). Strategic use of the snapshot masks the constructed nature of organizational communication. In what Nigel Thrift (2008) calls a *calculated sincerity*, these images often seem to offer a clear message—*this is an authentic act.*

The staged spontaneity of the snapshot offers powerful synergy with corporate strategy. Thus, snapshot aesthetics offer a useful window into how visual images perform identity work for organizations by capitalizing on historical notions of photography and realism, that is, by invoking the twin conceptions of photography as recording nature and photography as aesthetic creation. For much of its history, photography has assumed a pervasive presence in public discourse and commercial publishing. Photographs quickly became part of everyday life. As influential British photographer Nick Knight exclaims "[t]he most exciting way to see a photograph is passing a billboard in a car, flicking past it in a magazine . . . That's how its delivers it power, when it becomes part of the vernacular of everyday life" (in Muir, 2006, pp. 341, 400). Yet, often these ubiquitous images are overlooked in management research, as mere "pictures."

CONCLUSION

Stylistic analysis helps illuminate how organizational communication acts as a representational, performative, and aesthetic system that produces value beyond the realm of the product, service, or brand, connecting images to broader aesthetic and cultural codes that help create meaning and value. A style-based approach promotes interdisciplinary understanding of strategic brand communication, here focusing especially on photography as an engine of value creation. From this perspective, it is imperative to understand the visual genealogies—the history, legacy, or memory—of contemporary visual strategy and corporate expression. Style helps focus attention on how strategic communication taps into aesthetic, historic, photographic, psychological, and representational codes to create meaning and value.

Future research on style and strategy must acknowledge images' representational and rhetorical power both as perfomative artifacts and as engaging and deceptive bearers of meaning, reflecting broad societal, cultural, and ideological codes. Along with brand identity and brand image, the realm of brand culture serves as a necessary complement to understanding brand meaning and brand creation (Schroeder and Salzer-Mörling, 2006). Research focused on the rhetorical, social, and economic implications of images, fueled by an understanding of the historical conditions influencing their production and consumption may require an art historical imagination to uncover the intricate connections between strategy and style.

ACKNOWLEDGMENTS

This project has been benefited from seminar comments at University of Exeter, University of Bath, Lund University, Innsbruck University, University of Michigan-Flint, University of California-Davis, Bocconi University, London School of Economics, and the Photographers Gallery, London, as well as from the members of the International Network of Visual Studies in Organization. In particular, I want to thank Eric Guthey, Daved Barry, Sam Warren, Janet Borgerson, Janet Lorch, D. J. Trela, and Amelia Jones for comments and suggestions. Thank you to Cyril Cabellos at YSL Paris, Alex Small at Ray-Ban, Dan Barile at Mercedes Benz, and Vanessa Tebesceff and Beverly Don at Merkley + Partners, as well as Dr. Martens for kind permission to reproduce images in this chapter. Every attempt to trace all copyright holders was made. Thanks also to Emma Gregg for her picture research.

REFERENCES

Arnheim, R. (1977). *The Dynamics of Architectural Form*. Berkeley: University of California Press.
Barthes, R. (1977). Rhetoric of the image. In S. Heath (Ed. and Trans.), *Image, music, text* (pp. 32–51). New York: Hill and Wang.
Batchen, G. (2008). Snapshots: Art History and the Ethnographic Turn. *Photographies, 1*(2), 121–142.
Borgerson, J., and Schroeder, J. E. (2005). Identity in marketing communications: An ethics of visual representation. In A. J. Kimmel (Ed.), *Marketing communication: Emerging trends and developments* (pp. 256–277). Oxford: Oxford University Press.
Borgerson, J., Schroeder, J. E., Escudero Magnusson, M., and Magnusson, F. (2009). Corporate Communication, Ethics, and Operational Identity: A Case Study of Benetton. *Business Ethics—A European Review, 18*, 209–223.
Braddock, K. (2002). Vision Express. *The Face*, October, 157–161.

Buchanan-Oliver, M., Cruz, A., and Schroeder, J. E. (2010). Shaping the Body and Technology: Discursive Implications for the Strategic Communication of Technological Brands. *European Journal of Marketing, 44*(5), 635–652.

Campbell, D., McPhail, K., and Slack, R. (2009). Face Work in Annual Reports: A Study of the Management of Encounter Through Annual Reports, Informed by Levinas and Bauman. *Accounting, Auditing and Accountability Journal, 22*(6), 907—932.

Cohen, K. R. (2005). What Does the Photoblog Want? *Media, Culture and Society, 27*(6), 883–901.

Cotton, C. (2004). *The Photograph as Contemporary Art*. London: Thames and Hudson.

Currie, N., and Long, A. (2006). *fotolog.book: A Global Snapshot for the Digital Age*. London: Thames and Hudson.

Davison, J. (2008). Rhetoric, Repetition, Reporting and the "Dot.com" Era: Words, Pictures, Intangibles. *Accounting, Auditing and Accountability Journal, 21*(6), 791–826.

———. (2009). Icon, Iconography, Iconology: Visual Branding, Banking and the Case of the Bowler Hat. *Accounting, Auditing and Accountability Journal, 22*(6), 883–906.

De Cock, C., Fitchett, J., and Volkmann, C. (2009). Myths of a Near Past: Envisioning Finance Capitalism anno 2007. *Ephemera: Theory and Politics in Organization, 9*(1), 8–25

Deighton, J., and Kornfeld, L. (2009). Interactivity's Unanticipated Consequences for Marketers and Marketing. *Journal of Interactive Marketing, 23*, 4–10.

Dr. Martens and Daisy Lowe. (2008). (YouTube video) From http://www.youtube.com/watch?gl=GB&v=1Ib-jFUySqY (accessed June 6, 2012).

Dr. Martens Singapore Web site. (2009). From http://www.drmartens.sg/. (accessed November 29, 2009).

Eisenberg, E. M. (2007). *Strategic Ambiguities: Essays on Communication, Organization, and Identity*. Thousand Oaks, CA: Sage.

Fineman, M. (2004). Kodak and the Rise of Amateur Photography. In *Heilbrunn Timeline of Art History*. New York: The Metropolitan Museum of Art. From http://www.metmuseum.org/toah/hd/kodk/hd_kodk.htm. (accessed May 20, 2010).

Guthey, E., and Jackson, B. (2005). CEO Portraits and the Authenticity Paradox. *Journal of Management Studies, 42*, 1057–1082.

Holt, D. B. (2004). *How Brands Become Icons: The Principles of Cultural Branding*. Boston: Harvard Business School Press.

Horyn, C. (2008, April 20). When Is a Fashion Ad Not a Fashion Ad?. *New York Times*, online. http://www.nytimes.com/2008/04/10/fashion/10TELLER.html (accessed March 29, 2011).

Kismaric, S., and Respini, E. (2008). Fashioning fiction in photography since 1990. In E. Shinkle (Ed.), *Fashion as photograph: Viewing and reviewing images of fashion* (pp 29–45). London: I. B. Tauris.

Lagerfeld, K., and Newton, H. (2007). *Helmut Newton (Photofile)*. London: Thames and Hudson.

Lloyd, C. (2004). *Enchanting the Eye: Dutch Paintings of the Golden Age*. London: Royal Collections Publications.

McQuarrie, E., and Phillips, B. J. (2008). It's not your Father's Magazine Ad: Magnitude and Direction of Recent Changes in Advertising Style. *Journal of Advertising, 37*(3), 95–106.

Mills, E.. (2006, April 4). Perhaps the Best Sony 'Ad' Last Year Was Created by a Consumer. *CNET News*. From www.news.com (accessed September 20, 2006).

Mora, G.. (2007). *The Last Photographic Heroes: American Photographers of the Sixties and Seventies*. New York: Abrams.

Muir, R. (2006). The Image Makers. *Vogue* (UK Edition), September, pp. 337–341, 400.

Nickel, D. R. (1998). *Snapshots: The Photography of Everyday Life 1888 to the Present*. San Francisco: San Francisco Museum of Modern Art.

Nochlin, L. (1971). *Realism*. New York: Penguin.

Petrecca, L. (2006, March 3). Amateur Advertisers Get a Chance. *USA Today* online. From www.usatoday.com (accessed September 20, 2006).

Pracejus, J. W., Olsen, D. G., and O'Guinn, T. C. (2006). How Nothing Became Something: White Space, History, Meaning and Rhetoric. *Journal of Consumer Research, 23* (1), 82–90.

Schama, S. (1988). *The Embarrassment of Riches: An Interpretation of Dutch Culture in the Golden Age*. Berkeley: University of California Press.

Schroeder, J. E. (1998). Consuming Representation: A Visual Approach to Consumer Research. In B. B. Stern (Ed.), *Representing consumers: Voices, views, and visions* (pp. 193–230). New York: Routledge.

———. (2002). *Visual Consumption*. London: Routledge.

——— (2003). Building brands: Architectural expression in the electronic age. In L. M. Scott and R. Batra (Eds.), *Persuasive imagery: A consumer response perspective*, , (pp. 349–382). Mahwah, NJ: Erlbaum.

———. (2005). The Artist and the Brand. *European Journal of Marketing, 39*(11/12), 1291–1305.

——— (2006). Critical visual analysis. In R. W. Belk (Ed.), *Handbook of qualitative research methods in marketing* (pp. 303–321). Aldershot, UK: Edward Elgar.

———. (2008a). Visual analysis of images in brand culture. In B. J. Phillips and E. McQuarrie (Eds.), *Go figure: New directions in advertising rhetoric* (pp. 277–296). Armonk, NY: M. E. Sharpe.

———. (2008b). Brand culture: Trade marks, marketing and consumption. In L. Bently, J. Davis, and J. Ginsburg (Eds.), *Trade marks and brands: An interdisciplinary critique* (pp. 161–176). Cambridge: Cambridge University Press.

———. Value creation and the visual consumer. In K. Ekström and K. Glans, (Eds.), *Beyond the Consumption Bubble* (pp. 137–148). London: Routledge.

———., and Borgerson, J. (2003). Dark desires: Fetishism,representation, and ontology in contemporary advertising. In T. Reichert and J. Lambiase (Eds.), *Sex in advertising: Perspectives on the erotic appeal* (pp. 65–87). Mahwah, NJ: Lawrence Erlbaum Associates.

———. and McDonagh, P. (2006). The logic of pornography in digital camera promotion. In T. Reichert and J. Lambiase (Eds.), *Sex in consumer culture: The erotic content of media and marketing* (pp. 219–242). Mahwah, NJ: Erlbaum.

———., and Salzer-Mörling, M. (Eds). (2006). *Brand Culture*. London: Routledge.

———., and Zwick, D. (2004). Mirrors of Masculinity: Representation and Identity in Advertising Images. *Consumption, Markets, and Culture 7*(1), 21–51.

Scott, C. (2007). *Street Photography: From Brassai to Cartier-Bresson*, London: I. B. Tauris.

Scott, L. M., and R. Batra (Eds). (2003). *Persuasive Imagery: A Consumer Response Perspective*. Mahwah, NJ: Erlbaum.

Smith, J. (2001). Roll Over: The Snapshot's Museum Afterlife. *Afterimage* 29(2), 8–11.

Solomon-Godeau, A. (2007). Ontology, Essences and Photography's Aesthetics. In James Elkins (Ed.), *Photography theory* (pp. 256–269). London: Routledge.

Thrift, N. (2008). The Material Practices of Glamour. *Journal of Cultural Economy, 1*(1), 9–23.

West, S. (1996). *The Bulfinch Guide to Art History*. New York: Bulfinch.

Zwick, D., .Bonsu, S. K., and Darmody, A. (2008). Putting Consumers to Work: 'Co-Creation' and New Marketing Govern-Mentality, *Journal of Consumer Culture, 8*(2), 163–196.

7 Icon, Iconography, Iconology
Banking, Branding and the Bowler Hat*

Jane Davison[**]

These days, you can't think of *Bradford and Bingley* without thinking of bowler hats. But why?[1]

I am the unnoticed, the unnoticable man:
The man who sat on your right in the morning train:
[...] I am the man too busy with a living to live,
Too hurried and worried to see and smell and touch:
The man who is patient too long and obeys too much
And wishes too softly and seldom.
I am the man they call the nation's backbone
"The Man in the Bowler Hat" A. S. J. Tessimond

Visual branding represents an interesting point of crossover and interconnection. It is a pivotal point in the complex relationship between culture and economics and aesthetics and commodities (Bennett et al., 2008, Bourdieu, 1984; Power, 2004), where new intangible values may be created that are more than a 'dismal science of profit and loss (Thrift, 2008, p. 9). It is a point of intersection between the visual arts and marketing, and the blurred boundaries between 'high art' and the everyday, image and photograph, authenticity and copy. Brands are inherently visual (Schroeder, 2005). It is surprising, therefore, that there has been a 'blind spot' in organization studies regarding the import of the visual (Guthey and Jackson, 2005; Strangleman, 2004), and it is a relatively new field even within marketing, with a few notable exceptions, such as Schroeder's exploration of the interface between artist and brand in the work of Warhol, Kruger, and Sherman (Schroeder, 2005), analysis of art as commodity (Schroder, 2006), and examination of snapshot aesthetics in brand images (Schroeder, 2007).

Visual images perhaps elude scholarly activity in organization studies because they are enigmatic, from both theoretical and interpretive perspectives (Davison and Warren, 2009). Derided by some as eye candy, their capacity to captivate and enchant is intuitively acknowledged by the layman, and indeed research in psychology has shown the power of the visual

Figure 7.1 Wolfgang Suschitzky Man in Charing Cross Road c 1936. Courtesy W. Suschitzky.

image in memory and cognition (Anderson, 1980; Spoehr and Lehmkuhle, 1982; Tversky, 1974). Advertising has long appreciated the role that the work of art may play in product promotion, as in, for example, the famous use of Millais' 1885–1886 painting *Bubbles*, still in Unilever's ownership, to promote Pears' soap in the nineteenth century.

This study advances interdisciplinary links between visual branding and theory from arts disciplines. *Visual perspectives* examine the theoretical intermingling of the visual and the verbal (*icon* and *logos*) and construct a framework of *icon, iconography,* and *iconology*. A case study of the *Bradford and Bingley* Bank demonstrates marked innovation in their visual branding that accompanies innovation in their lending and funding practices in the period following privatization in 2000; it explores the rich cultural values and messages conveyed by the *Bradford and Bingley*'s bowler hat and its enduring charm and malleability.

VISUAL PERSPECTIVES

The relation between images and value is among the central issues of contemporary criticism, where it is a commonplace that present-day society is saturated with visual images (Mitchell, 2005). Whether investigation is in the fine arts, the organizational arena, or sociology and economics, 'we live in a culture of images, a society of the spectacle, a world of semblances and simulacra' (Mitchell, 1994, p. 5). Critical work has ranged from analysis of the role of the then new 'mechanical reproduction' in replacing the magic or authentic 'aura' of the artistic image with the 'exhibition value' of its mass reproduction (Benjamin, 1999, first published 1936), to exploration of the value-promoting image in the media (McLuhan and Fiore, 1967), and the role of the image in fostering a consumer society (Debord, 1967) where all is illusion and simulacra (Baudrillard, 1981). The image has always been immaterial in one way or another (Mitchell, 2005), but the unprecedented power of the new electronic means of reproduction and media of today, and their use in contemporary organizations and society make for marked turning points.

The evident prevalence of the image makes the need pressing for picture theories, or at least critiques of the visual image and conceptual frameworks of visual rhetoric, to be developed to underpin systematic analyses of the *modus operandi* of the visual. Yet, the pictorial image has been peculiarly resistant to efforts at explanation or theorization. Even a definition of image is problematic:

> We speak of pictures, statues, optical illusions, maps, diagrams, dreams, hallucinations, spectacles, projections, poems, patterns, memories and even ideas as images, and the sheer diversity of this list would seem to make any systematic, unified understanding impossible. (Mitchell, 1986, p. 9)

Some might refer to a lower, external, and physical concept of the image and others to a higher, internal and mental or spiritual concept; sometimes a material object is understood to be the original focus, but others would regard the eye and the seeing subject as the point of departure (Mitchell, 1986). Just as the interpretation of literature is now well recognized to be a question of readership as much as of authorship (Barthes, 1984; Eagleton, 2003), so should spectatorship similarly be recognized with regard to the meaning of images; subjective, multiple, and changing points of view are intrinsic to the production of meaning, together with the cultural baggage of each individual and of a given society.

Icon and Logos

If images are in themselves of problematic definition, the boundaries between *icon* and *logos*, or image and text, are also less clear than they might appear; indeed, it could be said that image and text are inextricably interlinked, and 'all media are mixed media' (Mitchell, 1994, p. 14) and produce meaning by association and inter-relationship. Derrida insists on the visibility and materiality of the 'traces' of written language (Derrida, 1967); in hieroglyphics language comes close to the pictorial, and the importance of calligraphy and printing fonts are well established. Texts may be manuscripts where key letters are ornately designed, or illustrations may coincide with text, exemplified in the illuminated works of the painter-poet Blake, or 'poem-drawings' such as Apollinaire's *Calligrammes: poèmes de la paix et de la guerre* (1925; Figure 7.2).

Cinema rapidly adopted the linguistic soundtrack; in printed form, text and image come together in the cartoon strip, where series provide a time dimension to the visual image, and linguistic meaning is given through ballooned speech and associated text. Painting frequently contain words and

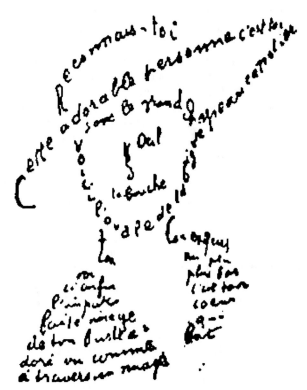

Figure 7.2 'Reconnais-toi', Apollinaire 1915.

signatures; Magritte's famous pipe (Magritte, 1928–1929) puts image and text in juxtaposition to examine both media and their interrelationship, through questioning the representative function of painting, and simultaneously forming a visual image from words. Pictures are generally titled or captioned; the absence of a title or use of 'Untitled' still implies acknowledgment of language through resistance (Mitchell, 1994).

Yet while the two domains may be intermingled in practice, they remain isolated from each other in theory. One of the problems in establishing critical models for the analysis of the icon has been the traditional rooting of the study of the visual image in art history, thus privileging historicism over structuralism or semiotics (Crary, 1990). With the rise of the 'linguistic turn' (Rorty, 1979) in critical analysis and move away from sources and history in the study of literature, attempts have been made to adapt semiotic models based in linguistics for the study of the visual. The visual image has, however, been in many ways resistant to these efforts, and for several profoundly structural reasons.

First, language and literature have an inherent temporal dimension that is absent from many forms of visual image; the latter generally presents its components simultaneously rather than sequentially as in the case of narrative. Second, the visual arts are perceived as domains where space and spatial relations normally have a more predominant role than in language and literature. It should be noted, however, that while these broad differences of time and space are intuitive for many, they are not universally accepted (see Mitchell, 1986). A third distance between the icon and the logos is conceptualized by Goodman (1968) as the difference between a dense system (visual images) where there is an infinite number of meaningful marks and a differentiated and discontinuous system (language) with a finite number of alphabetic characters. Finally, there is the problem of meaning and the difficulty of conceiving of a significance of the visual that may be expressed independently of language (Barthes, 1982b). These difficulties, among others, have led Foucault to conclude:

> The relation of language to painting is an infinite one. Not that words are imperfect, and in the face of the visible in a position of deficit that they cannot regain. Neither can be reduced to the other's terms: it is in vain that we say what we see; what we see never resides in what we say. And it is in vain that we attempt to show, by the use of images, metaphors, or comparisons, what we are saying; the space of their splendour is not that deployed by our eyes but that defined by the sequential elements of syntax. (Foucault, 1966, p. 25)[2]

Perhaps the central puzzle regarding images is precisely the question of their meaning (Roque, 2005). If, following Saussurian linguistics (1995), the signifying sign consists of two elements, a *signifiant* or *signifier*, and a *signifié* or *signified*, then how may the *signifié* be apprehended in the case of the visual image? As in the case of music, many question whether it is possible to speak of meaning with regard to images, leading to a self-referential 'art for art's sake' understanding of the visual image; others would argue that pictorial meaning cannot be conceptualized in linguistic terms and hence moot the notion of 'picturing theory' (Mitchell, 1994). Nonetheless, the ideology of advertising images has been fruitfully analyzed from a Marxist perspective (Berger, 1972) and through a combination of semiotics and psychoanalysis based in the French critical thought of Barthes, Lacan, and others (Williamson, 1978).

Icon, Iconography, Iconology

It has been suggested that this resistance of the visual arts to the 'linguistic turn' could mean that the visual image will itself come to occupy a position of centrality in a 'pictorial turn' (Mitchell, 1994). Indeed, given the growing interest in visual media that has spread from the humanities into other disciplines, this would appear to be in evidence. The icon behaves like a 'repressed memory' that keeps returning to the surface of our consciousness, and it might even be suggested that the ultimate reference in the mind is the image (Mitchell, 1994). Various models have been put forward for their analysis, which have points of similarity.

There has been a recent resurgence of interest in the work of the art historian and essayist Panofsky (1939), who discerns 'various levels of understanding within the visual image' (Hasenmueller, 1978). The first he calls *Pre-iconography*, or the primary or natural meaning that consists of the recognition of pure forms. The second level of meaning he names *Iconography*, or the secondary or conventional meanings that consists of the intellectual interpretation of a shared cultural context. The third level of meaning or *Iconology* is a symbolic, intuitive and deeper level of meaning accessible only to subjective understanding and often associated with the collective unconscious of a period or nation (Hasenmueller, 1978).

Comparisons may be drawn with the theory of signs developed by the philosopher and logician, Peirce (1960). Peirce divides visual symbols into three categories: the *icon*, which physically resembles what it represents; the *index,* which indicates through some associated meaning, such as a red traffic light signalling 'Stop'; and the *symbol,* which is removable from its context and has no direct link, such as the *fleur de lys* being a symbol of the French monarchy.

Barthes, the critical theorist, identifies two types of code within the photograph: the literal or *denoted* representation and the symbolic or *connoted* suggestion (Barthes, 1982a). Elsewhere, in analyzing painting (Barthes, 1982b), he opposes *signification* (symbolic meaning that can be put into words) to *signifiance* (meaning that cannot be conveyed in words). A further analysis (Barthes, 1980) focused specifically on the photographic image contrasts rational codes, or *Studium*, with a personal reaction or *Punctum*.

Table 7.1   Icon, Iconography, Iconology

Synthesis used here	Panofsky	Peirce	Barthes
Icon	Pre-iconography	Icon	Denotation
Iconography	Iconography	Index	Connotation *Signification* *Studium*
Iconology	Iconology	Symbol	*Significance* *Punctum*

There are overlaps between the three writers. All agree regarding a primary level of representation (*Pre-iconography, Icon,* or *Denotation*). All discern a secondary level of codes (*Iconography, Index, Connotation, Signification,* or *Studium*). All three have also identified some form of less logical domain (*Iconology, Symbol, Significance, or Punctum*), but there is less agreement as to how this manifests itself: whether it is a collective unconscious (Panofsky), a symbolic association (Peirce), or a personal interpretation (Barthes); the role of the intuitive, the irrational, and the unconscious are nonetheless indicated by all three writers.

For the purposes of the following study, the terms, *Icon, Iconography,* and *Iconology* are employed to designate these three levels (Table 7.1). *Icon* refers to the level of primary representation. *Iconography* designates the secondary level of coded interpretation and connotations. *Iconology* refers to the role of the intuitive, the irrational and the unconscious. An awareness of the inter-relationship between *Icon* and *Logos* informs the analysis.

VISUAL BRANDING, BOWLERS, AND THE BRADFORD AND BINGLEY

The *Bradford and Bingley* has long been noteworthy for its visual branding through associations with the bowler hat, one of the best-known United Kingdom (UK) banking symbols. There are measurable financial values attached to its expenditure on visual branding, but the financial statements are silent regarding the brand, in-line with the current, and arguably inadequate, accounting treatment (International Accounting Standards Board (IASB), 2004; Lev, 2001). Beyond this, and more importantly, this chapter makes two arguments: first, that there are intangible economic values attached to such visual branding arising from a value transfer of the rich cultural associations evoked by the image of the bowler hat; second, that the visual branding and its shifts in the period following flotation accompanies shifts in the company's business model.

The *Bradford and Bingley Building Society* was formed in the UK in 1964 as a result of the merger of the *Bradford Equitable Building Society* and the *Bingley Building Society*, both established in Yorkshire in 1851 (Bradford and Bingley, 2008a). In 2000 the Society converted to a public limited company and was floated on the London Stock Exchange as *Bradford and Bingley plc*. After a period of rapid growth and a doubling of its share price from that at flotation, it did not survive the financial turmoil of 2008, and its shares were taken into public ownership on September 29, 2008.

Their iconic bowler hat, the emblem most closely associated with the identity of the company, originated in the invention, at the time of the merger in the 1960s, of 'Mr Bradford' and 'Mr Bingley,' who sported bowler hats. To underline this association with the bowler hat, for a long time Stan Laurel's bowler hat, reportedly purchased for £2000 in 1995 (British Broadcasting Corporation, BBC, 2008), was in the possession of the organization and on display in its offices.

Business Perspectives

Alongside the metamorphosis that occurred in the visual branding, discussed later, there occurred mutation in the company's business models. The *Bradford and Bingley*'s experience exemplifies the financial services sector's need to innovate, driven by intensified competition due to globalization and deregulation (Lev, 2001; Rajan and Zingales, 2000). Following the easing of regulation of the City of London in 1986, new banking practices developed during the 1990s and more especially the 2000s.

The lending mix of the *Bradford and Bingley* altered substantially during the period following flotation in 2000 and moved away from the former traditional building society practice. First, there was movement from standard mortgage lending to residential customers, commercial customers, and housing associations and development of a greater proportion of 'Buy-to-Let' and 'Self-certification' mortgage business. Intuitively, it might seem that these latter are more open to risk. However, the *Bradford and Bingley* found the greater rewards of higher interest rates on such business to be attractive compared to the risks, and in 2003 experienced significantly lower rates of arrears and repossessions in those areas than for the residential mortgage market as a whole (Bradford and Bingley *Annual Report*, 2003, p. 16). Nonetheless, as business and economic conditions tightened, arrears progressively rose.

Second, the sources of funding moved proportionately away from the less volatile and more long-term retail deposits of savers, toward securitized debt and bonds, a relatively new phenomenon in banking, and which provided more rapid and substantial sources of funding. Securitized debt allowed the bank to bundle up pools of mortgages to acquire new lines of financing by transferring the right to receive cash flows to special purpose vehicles; the mortgage originator retained substantially all of the risks and rewards of the securitized loans, which were therefore, like the special purpose vehicles, included in the group's balance sheet (Bradford and Bingley *Annual Report*, 2007, p. 58).

However, once the housing market began to decline, and the quality of these mortgage assets became more doubtful, the bank was more exposed both to the impairment of its lending and to sources of financing, which had become less liquid and more expensive in a period of global increased risk.

In sum, this was a period of considerable growth for *Bradford and Bingley*, when mortgage assets increased from £17381 million in 2001 to £40444 million in 2007 (Bradford and Bingley *Annual Reports*, 2001, 2007), but the mix of assets was less traditional, and the funding of continued growth less certain. In 2008 the bank attempted to raise additional capital through a rights issue, punctuated by a profits warning; only 28% of the rights were taken up (Bradford and Bingley *Press Release*, August 18, 2008). An interim report (*Bradford and Bingley*, 2008b) revealed that the six-month level of bad debts had risen from £5 million in 2007 to £75 million in 2008. The report also revealed a further marked decline in the net interest margin. As the global financial position worsened in September 2008, the bank's position deteriorated to the extent that it ceased to trade.

Visual Branding

The following analysis shows how a shift in visual branding accompanied this shift in lending and funding towards more innovative business models. The analysis first explores the *icons* and *iconography* in the stages of the development of the *Bradford and Bingley's* bowler hat brand, under the headings *Class, Detectives?, Music Hall, Bowler-Object* Second, an interpretation of the *iconology* of the bowler hat is proposed.

Icons and Iconography

Class

Mr. Bradford and Mr. Bingley first appeared in the 1960s and 1970s as part of the *Bradford and Bingley's* logo, which featured on letterheads and leaflets (Figure 7.3). As *icons*, a duo of anonymous but apparently male figures, viewed from behind, are denoted, both wearing bowler hats, and carrying one umbrella between them. The image is incorporated within the organization's name and head office address, to make a whole unit, by means of lines at top and bottom, and there is therefore association between image and text.

Figure 7.3 'Mr Bradford' and 'Mr Bingley'—logo 1970s. Medium: silhouetted image/photograph taken from behind plus interplay with text.

The duo are presented as black silhouettes, a style that dates back to 18th-century cut-paper shadow portraits drawn by candlelight. The silhouette provides a degree of abstraction, formalization, elimination of detail, and removal from reality. Yet it also injects mystery, in providing a tantalizing level of information that invites the spectator to complete the image according to his or her imagination.

The resulting *iconography* is a paradoxical *mélange* of classlessness and class consciousness. On the one hand, the bowler hat is associated with Everyman and ordinariness (Wollen, 2000), an erasure of signs of caste and class, the anonymity and facelessness of 'the man they call the nation's backbone' of Tessimond's poem, the petit-bourgeois of medium and conservative aspirations who is likely to form the bedrock of *Bradford and Bingley*'s mortgage business. At the same time, however, the bowler hat indicates a very British class awareness; the bowler hat and umbrella were the touches of class built into John Steed of the *Avengers,* a 'classier' type of intelligence agent than the seedier characters of John Le Carré or Graham Greene.

The bowler epitomized British middle-class aspirations to superiority, the class consciousness epitomized by Captain Peacock (BBC, 1972–1985) and Captain Mainwaring (BBC, 1968–1977), and parodied in 'The Ministry of Silly Walks' (BBC, 1970) or 'The Class Sketch' from *The Frost Report* (BBC, 1967), where dress is an important signal in intimating each stratum of society.

The wearer of the bowler hat is the middle manager, and with umbrella, too, the London 'City gent,' or civil servant that peopled London over several decades. The connotations are of the staid but solidly reliable reputation with which *Bradford and Bingley* would undoubtedly have wished to be associated and would also inject a City metropolitanism and intimation of old-boy networks (Maclean et al., 2006) into the identity of a provincial building society. The accompanying Times New Roman standard font adds to a sense of old-fashioned straightforwardness and integrity. *Bradford and Bingley* were not alone in perceiving the bowler hat to have such connotations, as it was also chosen as an emblem of quality and reliability by Homepride bread makers in their creation of Fred the Flour Grader.

In the 1990s the logo shifted in nature to some degree (Figure 7.4). The *icons* of Mr. Bradford and Mr. Bingley, again apparently male, although still silhouetted, are now a faceless front view, where bowler hats are augmented by shirts and ties. The color red has been added to the silhouette, which is again spatially linked with the organization's name, now in a shadowed Times New Roman font face. The *iconography* is similar to that of the original logo. The disappearance of the umbrella, very much City of London pomp and prop, softens its metropolitan traditionalism, yet the removal of the Yorkshire address lessens the provincialism associated with the address of its head office. In proclaiming its name in shadowed lettering intended to give a three-dimensional effect, the organization appears more sure of itself and of its place in the national scene.

Figure 7.4 'Mr Bradford' and 'Mr Bingley'—logo 1990s. Medium: silhouetted image/photography front view plus interply with text. *Source*: leaflets, letterheads.

Detectives?

Post-mutualization, the *icon* alters substantially (Figure 7.5). A sense of costume or disguise replaces that of silhouettes and shadows. Greater human form may be distinguished, and the male duo has metamorphosed into a male and female, both sporting bowlers, sharp suits, and dark glasses. Hands are in evidence for the first time, either folded or raising identity cards displaying 'Bradford' and 'Bingley'. We are told they constitute 'The advice squad'.

Figure 7.5 'The advice squad' Bradford and Bingley 2002.

The *iconography* shifts markedly too, away from a bowler hat and umbrella image that is class-conscious, and that for the *Bradford and Bingley* became 'too old-fashioned, sexist and stuffy to survive into the Millennium' (*Sunday Telegraph*, 1998). Over time, 'hats can change meaning,' and can, moreover 'hint at the fragility of human identity' and as in the music-hall, be 'amusing or troubling' when worn too big or too small (Worth, 1999, p. 73). Here, humour is injected by these bowler hats, crammed onto their wearers' heads in too uniform a manner and at odds with the dark glasses and identity cards. We endeavor to make sense of the image through interplay with the *logos* of the 'Bradford' and 'Bingley' identity cards and through the caption 'The advice squad,' which leads the reader to 'Vice squad' and 'Fraud squad.' From this perspective, the bowler-hatted duo would be Criminal Investigation Department (CID) detectives or even Military Intelegence, Section 5 (MI5) agents. There is a long tradition of bowler-hatted detectives, from Feuillade's filmic Fantomâs and Judex, to Hergé's Dupont and Dupond in *The Adventures of Tintin* and to Christie's fictional Poirot. Without the bowler hats, 'Bradford' and 'Bingley' could be top-secret 'MIB' agents from the cult film *Men in Black*. We recognize this to be a comic scenario from its very disjunction with the more mundane reality of the *Bradford and Bingley*; the 'shocks and jokes of the unrelated' (Robinson, 1993, p. 135) add to the power of the image.

The softer values of old-boy networking are replaced with hard-edged professionalism. The revamped 'Bradford' and 'Bingley' appeared at a time when the commercial director is quoted as remarking that 'it's a seriously aggressive market out there' (Marshall, 2001).

Music Hall

The icon of the most recent incarnation of Bradford and Bingley's bowler hat branding now consists of a fully visible and smiling woman, dressed in a lime-green suit and bowler hat. There is inter-reaction with the text of the web page.

The *iconography* no longer plays with shadows, mystery, anonymity, and disguise, but presents a woman in full technicolor, attired, in total contrast to the erstwhile City gent, in a suit of feminine color and style, bowler hat worn jauntily at an angle. There is again incongruity between hat and wearer, this time through the donning of male apparel by a young woman. At a time when half of *Bradford and Bingley*'s workforce are women (*Telegraph and Argus*, 2002), selective borrowing of male clothing by women may be a sign of competence, status, or equality. Here, however, the disjunction affords not only the humor already mentioned in the depiction of 'The advice squad' but also an allure, even a demure but incipient eroticism along the lines of bowler-hat wearers such as Madonna or Liza Minelli's Sally Bowles in *Cabaret*.

In this move to connotations of the music hall, we have a full shift compared to the values of the original bowler hat branding: male has become female, anonymity has become identity, and the traditional and reserved City scene has become more proactive seduction. The sense of vaudeville was already presaged in *Bradford and Bingley*'s hiring of a juggler for a press launch in 2001, whose routine 'is a throwback to the good old days of music hall and vaudeville of the 1920s using three bowler hats and a suitcase' (Marchant, 2001). The bowler hat has an eminent past in the vaudeville tradition: Chaplin's dramatic knockabout routines exploit the class tensions of the bowler hat, in a coincidence of vagrancy and respectability, comedy and pathos, a poignancy that was further exploited by Laurel and Hardy (Robinson, 1993; Wollen, 2000).

The Chaplinesque bowler hat is now likely to be as much associated with Beckett as with silent film. Beckett's stage directions for *En Attendant Godot* require that all four major characters wear bowler hats. Yet if Beckett locates his bowler-hatted men in the music hall, it is to indicate that to be bourgeois is to be comic, and that 'aspirations are tripped up by realities' (Robinson, 1993, p. 159). Beckett's personages relate to inanimate objects as though they were extensions of themselves, so that for Lucky in *En Attendant Godot* thinking and his hat are interrelated; the boundaries between animate and inanimate are fuzzy.

Bowler-object

The blurring of boundaries between inanimate and animate observed in Beckett's work occurs too in the visual branding of *Bradford and Bingley*. A set of images parallel to those discussed above emerged in their visual branding from the late 1990s, and which transformed the bowler hat into an abstract form. Thus, 'as the bowler hat emerged from its specific social matrix, as it entered the world of art and entertainment and became a cultural icon as well as a social subject, it became more and more abstract in its semantics' (Robinson, 1993, p. 149).

Figure 7.6 displays '20 colored bowler hats,' used in the *Bradford and Bingley*'s logo from the late 1990s. Here the *icon* of the bowler has been separated from its wearer to acquire a life and importance of its own in these repetitive stylized motifs. The *icon* has shifted in nature, to become abstract shape rather than representative art or photography. Repetition provides emphasis and memorability as the foundation of rhetorical devices since ancient times, and emblematic of a society of mass production (Davison, 2008). The style of Warhol (for example, *Green Stamps*, 1965), avantgarde and anti-tradition in the 1960s, has now been absorbed into the establishment in the Bradford and Bingley's repetitive bowler hats.

The *Bradford and Bingley*'s bowler hat makes more autonomous appearances on the front covers of the 2005, 2006, and 2007 annual reports. In 2005 the *icon* of the bowler, which has reverted to a realistic representation,

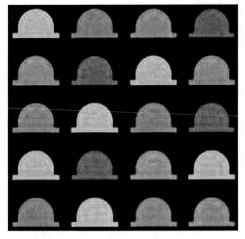

Figure 7.6 Bradford and Bingley logo from 1990s '20 coloured bowler hats'. Medium: Abstract visual images of the bowler.
Source: annual reports, letterheads.

sits in solitary but partial splendor (Figure 7.7). Harking back to the silhouettes and disguises of prior years, it is not wholly visible, combining a sense of snapshot authenticity (Schroeder, 2007) with intrigue and hide-and-seek. It has been jettisoned by its owner, at least temporarily, but in having been sartorially abandoned acquires even greater *iconographical* weight and importance. Now it is the bowler alone which represents the *Bradford and Bingley*.

Annual Report
& Accounts
2005

Bradford & Bingley®

Figure 7.7 Bradford and Bingley annual report and accounts 2005. Medium: Photograph.
Source: Front cover.

In 2006 the bowler is in triplicate, and 2007 further multiplied, in friezes of dancing movement where tumbling vaudeville hats, again partially viewed, acquire lives of their own, reminiscent of Walt Disney's *Fantasia*. These front covers are a testament to the way in which the object has now become 'value, fetish, totem' (Brown, 2001). Everyday objects have, since Ponge (1942) and Sartre (1938) had a capacity to inspire both philosophical delight and nausea, witnessed by a recent abundance of books on everyday things from the pencil and the banana to the potato and the bowler hat (Brown, 2001).

Moreover, the *Bradford and Bingley*'s latest logo, presented in simple lowercase font, is adorned by a bowler hat, which has almost fused itself with the lettering of the name. The words have become visual, and the hat has become an adjunct to the letters; this synthesis of *logos* and *icon* is now symbolic of the visual identity of the *Bradford and Bingley*.

Iconology

How may *iconology* be interpreted in the case of *Bradford and Bingley*'s bowler hat? For Panofsky, one way of understanding *iconology* is a historicist interpretation of a visual image in the context of a particular epoch or society (Panofsky, 1939). In this sense, *iconographies* of the bowler hat have already overlapped with *iconologies* relating to the culture of particular periods and popular images of *class, detectives, music hall,* and *bowler-objects*. Beyond this historical understanding of *iconology*, Panofsky suggests further interpretations may be shaped by resonances in the individual and collective unconscious. Writers such as Barthes (1984) stress the co-creative role of the reader or viewer of cultural artefacts such that works of art have a kind of 'unconscious,' which is not under the control of their creator but depends also on the reader, viewer, or listener.

In psychology, the hat has featured as an image of self, and more importantly 'as an emergence of the unconscious' (Jung, 1974, p. 122), analyzed in annual reports (Davison, 2004). The surrealists are known for their exploration of the unconscious. The surrealist painter Magritte (who had a background in advertising) frequently explored the image of the bowler hat. Magritte's work was a direct inspiration for the 1999 film version of the *Thomas Crown Affair*, which culminates in a crowd scene of multiple bowler-hatted figures. Magritte's work stimulates associational rather than logical and causal thinking and disrupts notions of everyday reality by creating oneiric environments (Robinson, 1993, pp. 125–126). Everyday respectability may be emphasized by a weight of massed staring and expressionless faces attired in suits and bowler hats, as in *Le Mois des Vendanges* (1959); elsewhere bowler-hatted figures are placed, childlike, in mid-air, simulating weightlessness and 'raining' from the sky, in *Golconda* (1953).

Repetition is itself a sign of the irrational and the unconscious, whether as Freudian repetition compulsion (Freud, 2003), or a Barthesian notion of a pleasure principle, and has been shown to be prevalent in the irrational exuberance of the 'dot.com' era (Davison, 2008).

Thus, Magritte's exploration of the bowler hat goes beyond social commentary to deeper levels of the psyche. He developed methods of thinking and painting 'employed to establishing a contact between the outside and inside worlds' (Magritte, 1985). Familiar everyday objects have lives that extend beyond their utilitarian function (Breton, 1969), and everyday objects can be suddenly imbued with mysterious significance. The surrealists 'transformed the bricolage of dreamwork into everyday life through working on things' (Brown, 2001).

Hats have long been associated with magic powers, whether in wizardry and witchcraft, Danish fairy tales (Stroebe, 1999), Harry Potter's 'sorting hat' (Rowling, 1997), the black top hat of the music hall, or Oddjob's use of a steel-rimmed bowler hat as a weapon in the James Bond film *Goldfinger*. The most recent incarnation of the *Bradford and Bingley's* bowler hat in a television advertisement is in precisely the role of a fairytale hat of magic powers that has the capacity to make dreams come true. The words of people's dreams become visual objects which blow around in a dreamlike fashion to arrive at the green-suited representative of the *Bradford and Bingley*; as she rubs the enchanted bowler, in the manner of Aladdin and the lamp, she is transported to the house of her dreams and finally pictured posed on that time-honoured emblem of freedom, the swing (Fragonard, 1766). In making illogical leaps and drawing on magic, and in making the everyday and the mysterious interact in this way, the *Bradford and Bingley's* technique is analogous to that of Magritte's 'authentic dream advertisements' (Gimferrer, 1987). The power of dreams and magic are explicitly evoked, by *logos* transformed into *icon*.

SUMMARY

Visual branding provides organizations with intangible values, even though it may not be possible to express these values in an objective and/or numerical form. The visual image is enigmatic and a full understanding of its *modus operandi* crosses the specialisms of many academic fields (Mitchell, 1986, 1994, 2005). Analysis of the visual image from a historicist perspective has always been a central preoccupation in the fine arts (Crary, 1990), but in recent decades there has been growing interest across disciplines in the development of theoretical models that go beyond historical placing to capture universal elements in the interpretation of visual images, especially their meaning.

This chapter has explored elements of the 'infinite inter-relationship between picture and word' (Foucault, 1966) and has drawn on the critical thought of Panofsky (1939), Peirce (1960) and Barthes (1980, 1982a, 1982b) to construct a framework of the visual sign in the three dimensions of *icon* or level of primary or literal representation, *iconography* or secondary level of coded meaning, and *iconology* or unconscious resonances. Just as the reader contributes to the meaning of a literary text, so does the spectator have a central role in contributing to the meaning of an image (Barthes, 1980, 1982a, 1984).

Bradford and Bingley provides an interesting case study. In line with regulation, the annual reports are almost silent regarding the company's visual branding, which is not included as an asset in the balance sheet, nor is information provided regarding expenditure on branding. Analyses of the financial statements demonstrate developments in the bank's practices, to incorporate more innovative models in a more competitive global and deregulated environment (Lev, 2001; Rajan and Zingales, 2000), as the lending mix moved from traditional residential mortgages to buy-to-let and self-certification, and the funding mix moved away from retail deposits to securitization and bonds. As business and economic conditions tightened, these innovative practices proved more susceptible to asset impairment and funding cost. Yet the visual branding still retains value.

The recasting of *Bradford and Bingley*'s visual branding over time to reflect and appeal to a changing society, and a more competitive business environment, is illuminated, in the use of logos, letterheads, leaflets, annual reports, web pages, and television video. The early use of the bowler hat may be viewed in the context of *class* and associations with the 'City gent' and his old-boy networks, reflecting the society and business world of the 1960s and 1970s. This is followed by a recasting of the male pair as a duo of mixed gender in the *detective* mould, with more aggressive yet humorous connotations, as the mortgage market-place became more competitive. The mixed duo metamorphose into a solo, bowler-hatted fun-promoting female in the *music-hall* tradition, reflecting gender shifts in society. The shadowy anonymity of the early 'Mr Bradford and Mr Bingley' that might be associated with a business environment shrouded in a certain mystery and mystique gives way to the more open and colorful identity of 'Ms Bradford & Bingley'. Alongside these developments, the bowler becomes an autonomous and powerful *object*, with the weight to represent *Bradford and Bingley* in its own right.

The bowler hat is recognized to have a quintessential Britishness, acknowledged in its nomination as a cultural icon of England (Icons, 2008), and resurfacing only recently in discussion of royal attire as Princes William and Harry sported bowlers at a cavalry parade in May 2007. The image of the bowler hat sparks *iconological* resonances of class and identity that exist in the collective unconscious, subverted and explored in its dreamlike and irrational manifestations by Magritte. The bowler hat may be interpreted as a 'special thing' which may range from a sacred, magical, uncanny object, to a modern commodity or souvenir (Mitchell, 2005).

There is increasing recognition of the need for an understanding of the points of crossover between culture and economics, aesthetics and commodities (Bennett et al., 2008; Bourdieu, 1984; Power, 2004; Thrift, 2008), which are epitomized in visual branding. The fetishism of the commodity and the domination of society by 'intangible as well as tangible things' attains its ultimate fulfilment in such spectacle (Debord, 1967).

ACKNOWLEDGMENTS

* A version of this chapter is published in *Accounting, Auditing and Accountability Journal* as 'Icon, Iconography, Iconology: Visual Branding, Banking and the Case of the Bowler-Hat,' 22(6), 883–906.

** I am grateful for helpful comments from the editors, and from Christopher Napier, Christopher Nobes, Len Skerratt, and participants at an European Institute for Advanced Studies in Management (EIASM) workshop *Imagining Business* at Saïd Business School, Oxford, and at a research seminar at Royal Holloway, University of London. I should like to express my thanks to Bradford and Bingley for kind permission to reproduce material from their annual reports and elsewhere.

NOTES

1. http://www.bradford-bingley.co.uk/tv/html/aboutus.htm. Accessed February 18, 2008.
2. Author's translation of 'Le rapport du langage à la peinture est un rapport infini. Non pas que la parole soit imparfaite, et en face du visible dans un déficit qu'elle s'efforcerait en vain de rattraper. Ils sont irréductibles l'un à l'autre : on a beau dire ce qu'on voit, ce qu'on voit ne loge jamais dans ce qu'on dit, et on a beau faire voir, par des images, des métaphores, des comparaisons, ce qu'on est en train de dire, le lieu où elles resplendissent n'est pas celui que déploient les yeux, mais celui que définissent les successions de la syntaxe', Michel Foucault, *Les Mots et les choses*, Paris: Gallimard, 1966, p. 25.

REFERENCES

Anderson, J. (1980). *Cognitive Psychology and Its implications*. San Francisco: Freeman.
Apollinaire, G. (1925). *Calligrammes: poèmes de la paix et de la guerre (1913–1916)*. Paris: Gallimard.
Barthes, R. (1980). *La chambre claire. Paris:* Le Seuil.
———. (1982a). Rhétorique de l'image. In *L'obvie et l'obtus* (pp. 25–42). Paris: Le Seuil.
———. (1982b). Droit dans les yeux, In *L'obvie et l'obtus* (pp. 279–283). Paris: Le Seuil.
———. (1984). La mort de l'auteur. In *Le bruissement de la langue* (pp. 61–67). Paris: Le Seuil.
Baudrillard, J. (1981). *Simulacres et simulations*. Paris: Galilée.
BBC (1967). The Class Sketch [Televison series episode]. In *The Frost Report*. Written and directed by M. Feldman and J. Law. UK: BBC.

————. (1968–1977). *Dad's Army* [Television series]. Written by J. Perry and D. Croft. Directed by Directors H. Snoad and B. Spiers. Norfolk, UK: BBC.

————. (1970). The Ministry of Silly Walks. [Televison series episode] In *Monty Python's Flying Circus.* Written and directed by G. Chapman, J. Cleese, T. Gilliam, e. Idle, T. Jones, M. Palin. UK: BBC.

————. (1972–1985). *Are You Being Served?* [Television series]. Written by J. Lloyd, D. Croft, M. Knowles, J. Chapman. Directed by R. Butt, H. Snoad, B. Spiers, J. Kelby, G. Elsbury, M. Shardlow. UK: BBC.

————. (2008), Who'll get custody of Bradford and Bingley's bowler hat? *News Magazine.*, From http://news.bbc.co.uk/1/hi/magazine/7641493.stm (accessed November 8, 2008).

Benjamin, W. (1999). The work of art in the age of mechanical reproduction, (Das Kunstwerk im Zeitalter seiner Reproduzierbarkeit). In Arendt, H. (Ed.), *Illuminations,* Trans. from the German by H. Zorn. (pp. 211–244). London: Pimlico.(Original work published 1936)

Bennett, T., McFall, L., and Pryke, M. (2008). Culture/Economy/Social. *Journal of Cultural Economy, (1),* 1–7.

Berger, J. (1972). *Ways of Seeing.* London: Penguin.

Bourdieu, P. (1984/1979). *Distinction: A Social Critique of the Judgement of Taste,* (R. Nice, Trans.). London: Routledge.

Bradford and Bingley plc (2001–2007). *Annual Reports.* Bingley, Yorkshire, UK: Bradford and Bingley.

————. (2008a). Group profile. From www.bbg.co.uk/bbg/ob/grpprofile (accessed December 2, 2008).

————. (2008b), *Interim Report.* Bingley, Yorkshire, UK: Bradford and Bingley.

Breton, A. (1969). Magritte's Breadth of Vision, (S. Watson Taylor, Trans.), *Studio International, 177*(908), 72–73.

Brown, B. (2001). Thing Theory. *Critical Inquiry, 28* (1), 1–22.

Crary, J. (1990). *Techniques of the Observer: On Vision and Modernity in the Nineteenth Century.* Cambridge, MA: MIT Press.

Davison, J. (2004). Sacred vVestiges in Financial Reporting: Mythical Readings Guided by Mircea Eliade. *Accounting, Auditing and Accountability Journal, 17*(3), 476–497.

————. (2008). Rhetoric, Repetition, Reporting and the 'dot.com' Era: Words, Pictures, Intangibles. *Accounting, Auditing and Accountability Journal, 21*(6), 791–826.

————., and Warren, S. (2009). Imag[in]ing accounting and accountability. *Accounting, Auditing and Accountability Journal, 22*(6), 845–857.

Debord, G.-E. (1967). *La société du spectacle.* Paris: Editions Buchet-Chastel.

Derrida, J. (1967). *De la grammatologie.* Paris: Editions de Minuit.

Foucault, M. (1966). *Les Mots et les choses.* Paris: Gallimard.

Fragonard, J. H. (1766). *The Swing.* London: Wallace Collection.

Freud, S. (2003). *Beyond the Pleasure Principle and Other Writings.* London: Penguin.

Gimferrer, P. (1987). *Magritte.* London: Academy Editions.

Goodman, N. (1968). *Languages of Art: An Approach to a Theory of Symbols.* Indianapolis: Bobbs-Merrill.

Guthey, E., and Jackson, B. (2005). CEO Portraits and the Authenticity Paradox. *Journal of Management Studies, 42*(5), 1057–1082.

Hasenmueller, C. (1978). Panofsky, Iconography and Semiotics. *The Journal of Aesthetics and Art Criticism, 36*(3), 289–301.

International Accounting Standards Board (IASB). (2004). *Intangible Assets: International Accounting Standard 38 (Revised).* London: Author.

Icons (2008). From www.icons.org.uk (accessed February 2, 2008).

Jung, C. J. (1974). *Dreams,* (R. F. C. Hull, Trans.). In G. Adler (Ed.) London: Routledge and Kegan Paul.

Lev, B. (2001). *Intangibles: Management, Measurement and Reporting.* Washington D. C.: Brooking Institution Press.

Maclean, M., Harvey, C., and Press, J. (2006). *Business Elites and Corporate Governance in France and the UK.* New York: Palgrave Macmillan.

Magritte, R. (1928–1929). *La trahison des images.* Los Angeles, CA: Los Angeles County Museum of Art.

———. (1959). *Le Mois des Vendanges.* Paris: Private Collection.

———. (1985). La ligne de vie. In S. Gablik, (Ed.), *Magritte.* London and New York: Thames and Hudson.

Marchant, I. (2001). *Bradford & Bingley Press Launch.* From http://www.contrabandevents.com/performer.php?name=Ian+Marchant+-+Juggler+-+London&group=Circus&category=Jugglers+%26+Contact+Jugglers (accessed October 18, 2007).

Marshall, A. (2001, April 18). Corporate Profile: How Mr Bradford and Mr Bingley Lost Their Hats. *The Independent.*

McLuhan, M., and Fiore, Q. (1967). *The Medium Is the Massage: An Inventory of Effects.* London: Penguin.

Mitchell, W. J. T. (1986). *Iconology. Image, Text, Ideology.* Chicago and London: The University of Chicago Press.

———. (1994). *Picture Theory.* Chicago and London: The University of Chicago Press.

———. (2005). *What Do Pictures Want?* Chicago and London: The University of Chicago Press.

Panofsky, E. (1939). *Studies in Iconology: Humanistic Themes in the Art of the Renaissance.* New York: Oxford University Press.

Peirce, C. S. (1960). *Collected Papers of Charles Sanders Peirce.* Cambridge, MA: Harvard University Press.

Ponge, F. (1942). *Le parti pris des choses.* Paris: Gallimard.

Power, M. (2004). Counting, Control and Calculation: Reflections on Measuring and Management. *Human Relations, 57*(6), 765–783.

Rajan, R., and Zingales, L. (2000). The Governance of the New Enterprise, working paper 7958. Cambridge, MA: National Bureau of Economic Research, .

Robinson, F. M. (1993). *The Man in the Bowler Hat. His History and Iconography,* Chapel Hill and London : The University of North Carolina Press.

Roque, G. (2005). Boundaries of Visual Images: Presentation. *Word and Image, 21,* 111–119.

Rorty, R. (1979). *Philosophy and the Mirror of Nature.* Princeton: Princeton University Press.

Rowling, J. K. (1997). *Harry Potter and the Philosopher's Stone.* London and New York: Bloomsbury.

Sartre, J.-P. (1938). *La Nausée.* Paris: Gallimard.

Saussure, F. de (1995). *Cours de linguistique générale.* Paris: Payot (Originally Published in 1916).

Schroeder, J. (2005). The Artist and the Brand. *European Journal of Marketing, 39*(11–12), 1291–1305.

———. (2006). Aesthetics Awry: The Painter of Light™ and the Commodification of Artistic Values. *Consumption, Markets and Culture, 9*(2), 87–99.

———. (2007). Images in brand culture. In B. J. Phillips, and E. McQuarrie, (Eds.), *Go figure: New directions in advertising rhetoric* (pp. 277–296). Armonk, NY: M. E. Sharpe.

Seethamraju, C. (2003). The value relevance of trademarks. In Hand, J. R. M., and B. Lev (Eds.), *Intangible assets: values, measures and risks* (pp. 228–247). New York: Oxford University Press.

Spoehr, K. T., and Lehmkuhle, S. W. (1982). *Visual Information Processing,* Freeman, San Francisco.

Strangleman, T. (2004). Ways of (Not) Seeing Work: The Visual as a Blind Spot in WES? *Work, Employment and Society*, 18(1), 179–192.

Stroebe, C. (1999). *The Magic Hat and Other Danish Fairy Tales*. Mineola, NY: Dover Publications.

Sunday Telegraph (1998, May 3).

Telegraph & Argus (2002, October). Now it's Mr Bradford and Ms Bingley!

Tessimond, A. S. J. "The Main in the Bowler Hat." *Not Love Perhaps*. London Faber and Faber.

Thrift, N. (2008). The material practices of glamour. *Journal of Cultural Economy*, (1), 9–15.

Tversky, B. (1974). Eye Fixations in Prediction of Recognition and Recall. *Memory and Cognition*, 2, 275–278

Warhol, A. (1965). *Green Stamps*. New York: Museum of Modern Art.

Williamson, J. (1978). *Decoding Advertisements. Ideology and Meaning in Advertising*. London and New York: Marion Boyars.

Wollen, P. (2000). Magritte and the Bowler Hat. *New Left Review*, 1, 104–121.

Worth, K. (1999). *Samuel Beckett's Theatre: Life Journeys*. Oxford: Oxford University Press.

8 Modernizing the Grocery Trade with Cartoons in Wartimes

Humor as a Marketing Weapon (Progressive Grocer, 1939–1945)

Franck Cochoy

The very mission of business organizations is to adapt ceaselessly to, but also shape, a moving world. In this respect, their essence is much more the process of "organizing" than the institution "organization" (Czarniawska, 2008). There even exist some organizations aimed at organizing all the others, like governments, consulting agencies, professional associations, and trade press. Among these organizations, the latter deserves particular attention. At the turn of the 20th century, the rise of modern companies was accompanied by a parallel proliferation of some journals and magazines, which proposed to help businessmen share their experiences and build the common language they needed to promote, exchange, standardize, and forward some new kinds of business practices. These journals were oriented toward general business and managerial issues, of course, like *System, The Magazine of Business*, a publication launched in 1903 by the businessman and Harvard Professor Arch Shaw (*System* later became the well-known *Business Week*). But trade press journals also flourished as a series of publications specialized in different business sectors (automobile, architecture, retailing, etc.; Laib, 1955).

In this chapter,[1] I propose to focus on one of these journals: *Progressive Grocer*. This journal was launched in 1922 to help independent grocers to modernize their businesses. I would like to show that *Progressive Grocer*, like many other trade-press journals, promoted a performative rhetoric, i.e., a narrative aimed at accounting for business evolutions while shaping them at the same time (Callon, 1998; Cochoy, 2010). More particularly, I will focus on one aspect of this rhetoric: the use of figures, pictures, and cartoons as a way to both describe and transform business practices. Because the "business model" of trade press generally rests on advertising rather than subscriptions (Laib, 1955), *Progressive Grocer* is full of ads and pictures aimed at showing many types of professional equipment to grocers as a way to improve their efficiency and profitability. Because its readership is made up of practical-minded hard-working men rather than intellectuals, *Progressive Grocer* has to find the means to have its readers agree to stop working and start reading as a detour toward improved business practices. Along this route, pictures and cartoons play an essential role, since visual arguments reflect practice in a faster, concrete, and more "telling" way than abstract narratives. Indeed, visual elements help people both see and imagine what their future could be; they also work as a moment of both leisure and apprenticeship.

As we will see, the pictorial rhetoric of *Progressive Grocer* is aimed at loosening and overcoming the tensions of a world facing two successive types of wars. The first war is the battle of independent grocers against the threats of chain stores in the 1920s and against the Great Depression in the 1930s. The second war is the real worldwide conflict of the Second World War and its possible impact on business activities. *Progressive Grocer* systematically took these dramatic contexts as arguments pointing toward the modernization of the grocery business. It seized and staged historical developments as calling for the introduction of new business devices and practices. It presented the latter as the necessary means for the survival and development of the grocery business. Insisting on wartimes is focusing on contexts of crisis and disorganization. In such circumstances, images play a prominent role: as Martin Giraudeau shows in his chapter, bi-dimensional representations help temporarily represent and stabilize a mutable world; hence, reassuring the actors and hopefully helping them to hold on and take action. In order to explore the pictorial rhetoric of *Progressive Grocer*, I will first present the journal and its role, or more exactly, I will account for how the journal presents itself, through an astute use of figures and pictures. Then, I will focus on the particular role of humor and cartoons: on the one hand, at times when business is a serious affair in a dangerous and frightening environment, humor appears as a way to have a break, take a breath, and reassure oneself; on the other hand, far from being purely recreational, the cartoons of *Progressive Grocer* play a decisive role in the definition of new business attitudes and practices.

PROGRESSIVE GROCER: *IMAGINING THE NEW GROCERY TRADE IN CRISIS TIMES*

Progressive Grocer was founded in 1922 by journalists who thought that there was a market for a publication oriented toward the modernization of small retailing, along the modernizing rhetoric of the "Progressive Era" (see the journal's title). One of its key contributors was Carl Dipman, a man trained in journalism with previous experience in retailing who soon became its editor-in-chief because he knew the grocery field and the people involved.

Carl Dipman reasoned that the food trade could be best served not by preaching, not by sermons, not by theorizing—but by seeking out successful men and ideas, by investigating and analyzing, and by factual reporting to the readers of PROGRESSIVE GROCER. Grocers, Carl often smilingly recalled, were not always as eager for new and better ideas, nor were they the avid, responsive readers and doers that they are today. Many had to be lured into and through the magazine with a generous sprinkling of jokes and extensive cartoon spreads (1954, 09, p. 36).

As we will see, these ideas were carefully put to work in the journal which made great use of facts reporting (often with figures and graphics), photographic demonstrations and, more interestingly, with many lovely cartoons.

Carl Dipman had an aesthetic and visual approach to retailing: his main concerns were for shop arrangements, better display, adapted furniture, and adequate lights rather than price setting, cost management, and other managerial strategies and economic issues; one of his distinct accomplishments was the building of a scale model of an ideal shop that he used extensively as a demonstrator; he thought that such a device was more convincing than long discourses and theoretical justifications (1930, 06, pp. 24–25). But at the same time, he never forgot the economic purpose of this qualitative, decorative, and visual approach: each innovation was systematically presented as an occasion for higher profit. This profit concern may be found in the many ads the journal published in the early 1930s to celebrate its own financial success as an argument to entice its partners to invest in *Progressive Grocer* and benefit from its growth. For instance, a 1930 double-page advertisement entitled "MORE MONEY EVERY YEAR" proudly

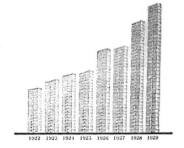

Figure 8.1   More money every year (1930, 01, pp. 2–3).

displayed a chart showing the exponential rise of its advertising turnover from 1922 to 1929.

Of course, this self-advertisement largely relies on text, along the "copy writing" feature of most advertisements of that time (Strasser, 1989). But the role of images is nevertheless prominent. A quick reading easily and surely associates the growing piles of dollar bills, the name of the journal "PROGRESSIVE GROCER" and its distinctive logo: that of a booklet which, far from being a boring set of abstract and obscure concepts, is rather a tool that any grocer may have in his pocket, ready to use when necessary, just like a gun. This first illustration reflects Dipman's approach of trade press: being aimed at "practice oriented" professionals, *Progressive Grocer* prefers a particular form of writing, where words are supplemented with pictorial elements. Arguments are complemented with shows, demonstrations, and visual representations, which are presented as open windows to the world.

Our first example of such windows is the graphic evidence of statistical figures. But even numbers and words could also be used in a graphic and somewhat "imaginary" manner, with short messages aimed at making a strong impression. On the first page of its November 1930 issue, the magazine wrote in large bold characters: "In spite of the well-advertised business depression, manufacturers have again invested more money in the Progressive Grocer in the first 11 months of 1930 than in any previous 11-month period" (1930, 11, p. 1). This "counter ad" mimicked press headlines to smartly confront the "advertising-like" information of the press with its own "information-like" advertisement and thus suggest *Progressive Grocer*'s amazing success in times of economic crisis. The idea was of course to put these few words in the minds of the advertisers and readers in order to have them work as an implicit device: "one could win at a time when everybody is losing" (or rather fears to do so) . . . provided, of course, one read and applied *Progressive Grocer*'s solutions (and more importantly advertise in its pages)[2].

The entire effort of the magazine is to fit into business history as well as to fill and to fix it. Its mission is to articulate the performativity of its words to the performance of business practice, either by using this performance as a proof of its own power, or by using the power of its narratives to promote business performance (or more exactly by playing in a circular manner on these two figures). The success of this endeavor is far from certain. There is a structural discrepancy between this press outlet (which as a "shop window of shop windows" well deserves its name of "Progressive Grocer"), and the true shops, that were far less "advanced" than the ones the journal put forward. Indeed, a close look at some dry statistics shows that the classical form of counter service was rather slow to abandon its place to the modern arrangements of semi-self-service and self-service. In 1939, counter service was still the solution used by almost half of the shops, with only a small 13% using full self-service (and the remaining 42% the hybrid solution of semi-self-service); it was only in 1947 that pure self-service became the most common form. Now, as early as 1939 and despite these figures, counter service had long since disappeared from the pages of *Progressive Grocer* (except in a very few cases devoted to recollections of the good old "past", see Figure 8.2 below; 1949, 04, p. 59).

This distortion between what the journal shows and what statistics tell could be attributed to the supply side logic of a free publication. Indeed, giving the journal for free does not oblige it to reflect exactly on its demand. However, the magazine was proud to reach 68,000 retailers as early as in 1930 (1930, 08, pp. 2–3), that is: almost a third of the 250,000 independent grocers of that time (1930, 02, 14–15). This is a very remarkable potential readership, that probably no other form of circulation would have been able to approach. Even if it is plausible that a large percentage of this readership ignored the journal or looked at it absentmindedly, like for any other advertising publication (Canu, 2009), it is likely that the journal had a strong real impact in the grocery world, as its growth, the enduring and rising confidence of its advertisers (see Figure 8.1 above), and more certainly the progressive migration of the advertised innovations in the photographed scenes (see Figure 8.2 below) bear witness.

The reason for the discrepancy between what the journal shows and the reality of trade should thus be sought elsewhere, in its very style and mission. In order to modernize the American groceries, *Progressive Grocer* uses a particular visual rhetoric: the idea is to rely on photographs to *make an impression* (on the pages and on the public who reads them); it is to encourage the advances of grocery techniques in showing the present as the image of far-off times (see the counter service sale in the 1930s), in exhibiting some rare initiatives prefiguring the wanted future as the present state of affairs (see the "open display" concept during the same decade), or in bridging these two strategies into the staging of some spectacular developments by means of the dramatic figure of the "before/after" framework, as in picture 8.2.

However and paradoxically, the spectacle of such a discrepancy does not disqualify the ability of the journal to represent the world it is talking about. On the contrary, it outlines its aptitude to "re-present" this world efficiently, in the latourian sense of the verb (1993): the journal presents the world a second time, and differently, so that the actors may recognize the world shown to them as their own, and thus adjust their practices to it accordingly.

The journal's re-presentation of the grocery business is all the more efficient in that it is addressed to a grocer whose view is as limited as the one of Lippmann's public (Lippmann, 1993). Indeed, this grocer is isolated and sedentary in his shop, going out rarely and working a lot, thus seeing his competitors from far away, or from his window, while this brochure he regularly receives each month offers him, by contrast, an omniscient and miraculous view of the grocery business of America at large—a view that

Figure 8.2   Sales jumped 50% (1936, 01, p. 19).

he can only receive as an adequate image of the external world. *Progressive Grocer* presents to him thousands of images and reports on experiences and equipment, which are as many possible (if not necessary) practices and identifications. *Progressive Grocer* thus leads our grocer to take the vanguard of distribution as the present state of commerce and consequently his own state as the rearguard. Since the poor man worries about the competition and the innovations reported in the journal, he has no other choice, if he wants to remain in the business race and still be worthy of his profession, but to engage his person, his shop, and his clients in this irresistible modernization movement that has apparently already taken hold of most of his fellow grocers. Our grocer is thus pushed to buy and set up the furniture, products, and techniques, which are presented to him, in a still-life manner, as the means to overcome his worries and accomplish his projects[3].

This tension between what the journal shows, and what the state of commerce is, may be traced from some interesting discrepancies between the papers and the many ads and pictures the journal reproduces. The advertisements published in *Progressive Grocer* are often ahead of the articles that will later focus on the equipment they present. New practices and equipment often appear in the form of "pictorial externalities": For instance, while the journalists of *Progressive Grocer* completely disregarded such a decisive innovation as shopping carts, the same carts nevertheless spread as soon as they were introduced into photographs of grocery stores figuring in articles on other subjects (Cochoy, 2008). The same is true for the use of carts to transport children (1940, 02, p. 86; 1945, 10, p. 102). But such discrepancies are rather exceptional. Because external realities may generally be seized only through their translation (Callon, 1986), especially in the advertising sector (Canu and Mallard, 2006), the classical distinctions between rhetoric and reality, pictures and life, theory, and practice are in fact untenable. When reading *Progressive Grocer*, we are most of the time no more informed and certain about the state of affairs than the actors themselves. Now, this uncertainty should not be regarded as a limitation of our knowledge, but rather as the comprehensive reduplication of the state of affairs, as the intimist sharing of the grocer's point of view.

CARTOONS: *SMILING TOGETHER AS A WAY TO LIVE (BETTER) IN A WORLD AT WAR*

The journal displays a pictorial rhetoric, and the real effects of it. A distinctive feature of this rhetoric is the use of humorous cartoons. I mentioned above that far from being a peripheral activity left to cartoonists, these cartoons were part of a deliberate strategy of the journal's editor-in-chief Carl Dipman. To my knowledge, the role of humor in social life has not attracted enough attention from the (too?) serious social sciences, at the risk of missing some important figures of the very objects they pretend to study. As we will see, cartoons are aimed both at diverting and educating people, at lighting up their faces, and changing their minds, the former of these aims being the condition of the latter. And they succeed in doing so when they happen to widen the gap between their inherent fictitious character and the hard realities they refer to, especially in these times of economic crisis, market competition, and business transformations. The humorous treatment of the threat that self-service represented is particularly spectacular in this respect.

Figure 8.3 shows a drawing which addresses the very problem *Progressive Grocer* had to overcome: this journal endlessly presented self-service arrangements, techniques, and equipment as means to modernize the grocery trade and help grocers solve their difficulties, resist competition, and improve their results, but the same grocers often saw self-service not as a solution but as a real threat, especially because of the risk of theft: if customers serve themselves, will they not be tempted to leave the shop with the

**"How did they know
we were coming along?"**

Figure 8.3   How did they know we were coming
along? (1939, 10, p. 195).

goods without paying for them? This cartoon is a particular way to deal with this fear[4]. It features two thieves who don't know what "help yourself market" means. But the cartoon is funny only if it suggests by antiphrasis that in the real life of the late 1930s, "everybody should know that everybody knows" (real thieves included) what self-service meant! There was no alternative: on the one hand, without the sharing of such knowledge, there is no reason to smile; but on the other hand, the picture at hand is a cartoon, and to see it as such, to extract the fun of it, one has no other choice than to adopt the proper reading which makes smiling possible. In other words: in order to be the proper reader with a sense of humor, one has to admit that the featured situation is nonsense. The cartoon thus indirectly promotes a view of self-service as a reality that is already there and thus should be neither avoided nor feared but rather controlled and domesticated.

To put it differently, humor is about the sharing and understanding of a situation between two persons: the one who tells the story and the one who has to grasp its meaning and return his smile. As such, humorous stories are always some little self-service devices: their proper meaning is to mean nothing themselves. They need the reader's cooperation and creativity to fully express what they are all about. See the next cartoon (Figure 8.4) that

"I think this store is carrying self-service a little too far."

Figure 8.4   Self-service too far (1942, 03, p. 186).

features another fear about self-service, that is: the idea that the disappearance of service may lead to the appearance of dissatisfied customers.

Putting a living cow in a grocery store and asking customers to draw their own milk makes no sense in itself[5]. Or rather, it does not make sense until the reader reframes what he sees, completes the narrative, and constructs his proper meaning: it is the cartoon, rather than the economy, that carries self-service a little too far. Humor, more than any other form of language, consequently stages a kind of "joint performativity": what is meant is produced both by the story teller and by the reader. All the pleasure of humor comes from this complement, from this game of "guessing" the secondary/complementary meaning, of producing oneself the true message of the story. If the message is explained by someone other than the reader, humor just vanishes: as everybody knows, one does not explain a good joke. This distinctive character of joint performativity of humorous speeches has some strong and serious social implications, since it is used as a means to enroll the public into the very production (and acceptance) of the meaning not only of a story, but more importantly of the hard world the story refers to. Showing self-service stores where customers have to draw their milk themselves from the cow is to give readers the full experience of the uncertainty surrounding the development of the grocery business and the extension of the self-service movement. In so doing, the cartoons format and channel true worries in a cathartic manner, and more importantly they stage a collective test of what self-service is and could be. The figuration of some extravagant forms of self-service is both a means to remind indirectly what its contemporary forms really are, and to explore the limits of their acceptable future. The cartoon particularly plays on the second feature, since it invites readers to frighten themselves about the development of self-service. But doing so in a humorous manner is also a means to reassure them. Implicitly, the cartoon suggests that the development is already there and should be accepted rather than resisted. In exaggerating the future, the cartoon de-dramatizes the present, and helps grocers to accept it. What is not "performable" works as a support for what can really be performed, in accordance with the logic that things could be worse anyway and that one had better take them positively.

But it is essential to insist on the importance of the first feature: if cartoons are fictions, these fictions are paradoxically strongly connected to the world, as a parallel between a variant of the preceding cartoon and a true 1944 billboard makes it both clear and spectacular (Figure 8.5).

There are two ways to read this parallel. On the one hand, the cartoon refers to the same real problem as the billboard . . . which itself is just a true picture of a real shop window in a country that was certainly at war. What is said in both representations does nothing but confirm a fact that may be traced to a whole series of information and papers published in *Progressive*

Will it come to this?

SELF-SERVICE IN PRODUCE dept. is encouraged by above sign. All items possible are pre-priced.

Figure 8.5   Will it come to this? (1943, 10, p. 215; 1944, 12, p. 54).

Grocer during the war period. This fact is as simple as it is significant: the war played a great role in the conversion of American grocery stores to self-service. Because of the war, many men had left the labor market, thus raising the problem of their replacement.

If this problem was only alluded to in the cartoon ("due to labor shortage"), it is clearly put forward in the billboard ("we have lost some of our clerks to the service"). Both pictures just present in their own way what they see as the necessary solution of the lack of workforce: the amount of service that grocers cannot provide anymore has to be rendered by the customers themselves (sweep out the floor, turn out the light in the cartoon, picking and weighing the fruits and vegetables oneself in the billboard). The effort to acknowledge/trace a relationship between labor shortage and self-service, far from being restricted to the cartoon and billboard, is a pervasive motto in many papers that *Progressive Grocer* published all through the war period (1942, 04, p. 136; 1942, 08, pp. 46–47; 1943, 01, p. 28; 1943, 05, p. 58 sq.).

Two sub-periods may be distinguished in this respect. At the beginning of the war, the problems were anticipated rather than dealt with, and self-service was presented as a possible "theoretical-like" solution: a 1942 paper entitled "How War Affects the Food Trade" forecasted that "With gas rationing and tyre shortage service stores will adopt more supermarket technique, more self-service features, perhaps greater inducements to cash-and-carry buyers" (1942, 04, p. 136). In August of the same year, another paper entitled "Employing more women? Here are the suggestions" noted that "One of the most important changes war is bringing to food merchants is the change in personnel." This statement led the author to conclude that time had come for the "necessity of employing women." At first glance, employing women was an alternative to self-service in the effort to counterbalance the departure of male clerks. But in fact, *Progressive Grocer* closely linked the idea of female employment to that of self-service. Indeed, the journal asserted that women could not exactly replace men, or rather that they could do so by means of some technical adjustments . . . like the help of self-service devices:

> A woman can, of course, be taught and adapted to food store work to an extent, but her physical limitations require that the merchant employing her must also learn and must change some of his methods of operation to get the most of his new employee [. . .] Much unnecessary carrying can be avoided, however, by permitting the women to use gliders or supplying them with some sort of flat rolling truck for moving case goods. (1942, 08, pp. 46–47)

In 1943, things became a little bit different: what was one year earlier envisioned as a possible abstract solution was reported as an actual and tangible practice. In January, a paper entitled "Women can replace men in most jobs, grocers find" (1943, 01, p. 28) used a questionnaire to account for the feminization of the labor force ("the number of women employees in the large-volume food stores has about doubled in the past year, jumping from an estimated 75,000 to 150,000"). In May, *Progressive Grocer* issued a paper gathering testimonies with the following title: "12 food merchants say 'Self-service solves many of our wartime problems'" (1943, 05, pp. 58–61). All the "picked up" testimonies supported this idea with some particular personal experiences like this one:

> when the present labor shortage came along, we soon learned that it was impossible to handle our business in a counter-service store with the limited help available. The self-service arrangement enables us to do half again as much business with actually less help than we had in the counter-service store. (1943, 05, p. 58)

On the one hand, the cartoon, the billboard and the many other articles seize the war as a "necessary" force driving the move toward self-service: labor shortage, in particular, is meant to "push" groceries to employ more women and self-service devices, the one being related to the other, thanks to the use of gliders (see above) and cashiers as a way to counterbalance the supposed physical differences between men and women. But on the other hand, self-service did not start with the war, and it did not end its development after. Similarly, *Progressive Grocer* did not wait for the war to promote self-service, and, of course, it did not stop promoting it when it was over. During the war, labor shortage is just taken as an additional argument among many others to develop self-service[6]. This is best expressed in the very cynical caption which goes with the billboard. This caption implicitly suggests reproducing the rhetoric of the billboard, i.e., playing on wartime patriotic feelings to do more business and make more money ("SELF-SERVICE in produce dept. is encouraged by above sign" . . . that you have thus to take as an inspiration for your own store).

CONCLUSION

As we saw, talking to business people is presenting them with some arguments, but (and more importantly?) it is also showing them figures, pictures, and cartoons. The process at stake is very close to that of writing history. When you account for history, you have no other choice than to transform a discrete and incomplete series of elements into a coherent, articulated, and continuous discourse. You thus have to fill the holes; you have to both seize and construct the reality at stake. Images work along the same logic. Like any account, they "re-present" reality: they transport some elements of the entities they refer to and give them another form and meaning. In so doing, they "reduce" the latter (some aspects of real life are left out), but at the same time they also "amplify" them: the represented reality, because it is simplified, receives some new properties like (in our case) exemplarity, understandability, usability, etc. (Latour, 1993). *Progressive Grocer*'s figures, pictures, and cartoons transport the world, frame and fix images. As such, they work as "references" in the latourian sense: they "re-present" the world they refer to in a different and often simplified way. But *Progressive Grocer*'s representations of the grocery business also work as "reference points": they provide grocers with a selection of "views" aimed both at making them look at their world differently and helping them "fill the holes" and complete the narrative they suggest through proper action. Cartoons play a prominent role in this latter process. Indeed, they not only "reduce" and "amplify" the world at stake or play on double sided references, but they also assume and stage a voluntary distortion. In classic references, the distortion of facts may be seen as a negative and unplanned externality: to account for something, we have to accept to "stylize" what we account for, and thus transform the referred reality into something different and

"I understand their clean-up man has been drafted."

Figure 8.6 Their clean-up man has been drafted (1944, 03, p. 211).

"twisted" through simplification. In the very same way that accounting figures and statistics, in "extracting" information, cannot but leave out the substratum it is extracted from (Quattrone, 2009), taking a picture cannot but exclude what is out of its frame, or what is not in its field and focus. Cartoons work along the same logic, but they do so voluntarily. More importantly, they immediately point to this voluntary distortion, or rather they invite us to do so with them. In other words, they implement the well-known feature of *"larvatus prodeo"* that was so dear to Roland Barthes (1972): "I move forward with a mask, but I show this mask with my finger at the same time." More exactly, the cartoons slightly change the formula in *"We*, the cartoon *and its reader* move forward *together* in *sharing* the same mask of humor, and we join our fingers to show this mask at the same time." Cartoons are all the more humorous in that they appear in a codified frame (mask) reserved to make fun of the world, and that people agree to join their own understanding to the framed situation. In other words, cartoons and their humor exist only if they present themselves as humorous on the one hand, and if they are read as such on the other hand. Given this very special mode of existence, they are continuously reenacted, along the fragile but powerful process of Butlerian's performativity (1988). They call for "imagin-action," as Paolo Quattrone (2009) nicely puts it, thus helping the readers to transform in an oblique way the world they see into the world that is coming.

NOTES

1. This study is the result of a research mission to the University of California at Berkeley, which took place from July 14 to August 8, 2006. I thank Catherine Grandclément for the idea and the Education Abroad Program for funding the research. I am also very grateful to Jutta Wiemhoff, Martha Lucero (Northern Regional Library Facility [NRLF]), Steve Mendoza (main library), and three other anonymous librarians of the Business/Economics Library and Environmental Design Library at Berkeley. Finally, I am indebted to David Vogel for his support and the Haas School of Business for its material help. I warmly thank *Progressive Grocer* for granting me the permission to reproduce the images this publication rests upon. When writing this text, I benefited from the material and intellectual support of the School of Business, Economics and Law, University of Gothenburg, Gothenburg, Sweden.
2. Of course, the journal did not say that at this time the effects of the economic crisis were moderate: the sales of grocery and combination stores dropped from $9 billion to 8 billion only between 1929 and 1931 (estimates from a graphic chart [1951, 03, p. 43]). During the same period, independent grocers abandoned only 2% of this business to chain stores (68 to 66%). It is only in 1933 that the depression effect became severe for them: sales went below $6 billion, with a stronger impact on independent grocers whose share dropped to 63%.
3. In order to give a more complete picture it should be noted that *Progressive Grocer* controls not only the grocers but also the advertisers who follow and

finance the journal, while the effectiveness of the messages they put in it is no way guaranteed to them.

4. It is of course not the only one. *Progressive Grocer* published at the same time several articles on the topic, and attempted to present some solutions to handle this risk (1939, 07, p. 43; 1941, 10, p. 81 sq.; 1943, 11, pp. 48–49).

5. Although contemporary situations may prove the contrary (see Cochoy, 2007, for the presence of live cows in supermarkets, and Dujarier, 2008, for the pervasiveness of consumers' hard work!).

6. For some excellent studies on the introduction of self-service, see Du Gay, 2004, Kjellberg, 2006, and Grandclément, 2008.

REFERENCES

Barthes, R. (1972). *Le Degré zéro de l'écriture*, Paris, Seuil [first published in 1953].

Butler, J. (1988). Performative Acts and Gender Constitution: An Essay in Phenomenology and Feminist Theory. *Theatre Journal*, 40(4) 519–531.

Callon, M. (1998). Introduction: The embeddedness of economic markets in economics. In M. Callon (Ed.), *The laws of the markets* (pp. 2–57). Oxford, Blackwell.

———. (1986). Some elements of a sociology of translation: Domestication of the scallops and the fishermen of St Brieuc Bay. In J. Law (Ed.), *Power, action and belief: A new sociology of knowledge* (pp. 196–233). London: Routledge and Kegan Paul.

Canu, R. (2009). La manipulation des documents publicitaires. Contribution à une sociologie du travail marchand. *Revue Française de Socio-Economie, 3*, 147–167.

Canu, R. et Mallard, A. (2006). Que fait-on dans la boutique d'un opérateur de télécommunications. Enquête ethnoraphique sur la mise en référence des biens marchands. *Réseaux, 24*(135–136), 161–193.

Cochoy, F. (2007). A sociology of market things: On tending the garden of choices in mass retailing. In M. Callon, Y. Millo and F. Muniesa (Eds.), *Market devices* (pp. 109–129). Oxford, Blackwell.

———. (2008). Driving a shopping cart from STS to business, and the other way round. On the Introduction of Shopping Carts in American Grocery Stores (1936–1959). *Organization, 16*(1), 31–55.

———. (2010). How to build displays that sell: The politics of performativity in American grocery stores (*Progressive Grocer*, 1929–1946). *Journal of Cultural Economy, 3*(2), 299–315.

Czarniawska, B. (2008). *A Theory of Organizing*. Cheltenham, England: Edward Elgar Publishing.

Du Gay, P. (2004). Self-Service: Retail, Shopping and Personhood. *Consumption. Markets and Culture, 7*(2), 149–163.

Dujarier, M.-A. (2008). *Le travail du consommateur, De McDo à eBay: comment nous coproduisons ce que nous achetons*. Paris: La Découverte.

Grandclément, C. (2008). *Vendre sans vendeurs: sociologie des dispositifs d'achalandage en supermarché*, thèse pour le doctorat en socio-économie de l'innovation. Paris: École Nationale Supérieure des Mines de Paris.

Kjellberg, H. (2006, September). *The Mode of Exchange and the Shaping of Markets: Introducing Self-Service in Swedish Post-War Food Distribution*. Paper presented at the 22nd IMP Conference, Milan, Italy.

Laib, J. (1955). The Trade Press. *The Public Opinion Quarterly, 19*, (1), 31–44.
Latour, B. (1993). The 'Pedofil' of Boa Vista—A Photo-Philosophical Montage. *Common Knowledge*, 4(1), 145–187.
Lippmann, W. (1993). *The Phantom Public*. Library of Conservative Thought, Transaction Publishers [first published in 1925].
Quattrone, P. (2009). Books to Be Practiced: Memory, the Power of the Visual, and the Success of Accounting. *Accounting, Organizations and Society*, 34(1), 85–118.
Strasser, S. (1989). *Satisfaction Guaranteed: The Making of the American Mass Market*. New York: Pantheon Books.

Part IV

Inscriptions, Emotions and Passions

9 Imagining Passion in Action
An Analysis of Translation and Treason

Consuelo Vásquez and François Cooren

Over the past decades, Science and Technology Studies—especially through Latour's (1987, 1994, 1996, 2005) work—have largely contributed in highlighting the need to revisit the notion of agency. By taking into account the role of nonhumans—artifacts, architectural elements, machines, texts—in the construction of socio-technical phenomena, this theoretical framework has shifted from an *internal* view of action, as being reserved to human condition, to an *external* one (Robichaud, 2006), which includes the participation of entities with variables ontologies (human, nonhuman, discursive, material). In organizational studies, this hybrid perspective on action has had a major influence in defining organization as a complex and heterogeneous phenomenon, what Law (1994) defines as an "heterogeneous ontology" and Cooren (2006) calls, in reference to Garfinkel (1988), "a plenum of agencies." As Cooren argues,

> [A]n organization's identity can . . . be understood through all these entities that can act and speak in its name. The organization, in this specific sense, is a kind of monster, a Leviathan, to the extent that its mode of being can be extended to whomever or whatever ends up representing it. (p. 83)

From this ontological standpoint, a key notion that takes account of the hybrid character of organization is representation or, as Cooren et al. (2008) label it, *presentification*, that is, the "process by which something or someone is made present to someone else" (p. 6). In coining this neologism, the authors focus on the experience of materiality as being intimately associated to the process of *presentification*. In this sense, they argue "it is always *through* a specific material form that something—God, our dog, an idea, the Microsoft Company—will be made present to us" (p. 6, italics in the original). If we acknowledge this mode of 'being' and 'doing' of organizations, we must then recognize the diversity of material forms in which it is embodied. In fact, it is through various humans, artifacts, technologies, spatial elements and texts that an organization can be said to exist and act (Cooren, 2006; Cooren et al., 2007).

Taking this perspective as a starting point, we would like to draw our attention to a specific material form though which organizations are widely *presentified*: images. Be they logos, corporate colors, signatures, mascots, posters, trademarks, and many more, there are multiple visual figures that populate the organizational world. In this chapter, we reflect upon images not only as privileged spokespersons (or should we better say *spokesobjects*?) representing organizations (Quattrone, 2004, 2009) but also—and by doing so—as generating passions, which participate in the unfolding of organizational actions and processes. Following Greimas and Fontanille (1993), we recognize that passions appear in discourse as carrying specific meaning effects. Furthermore, we agree that they are not "the exclusive property of subjects (or of the subject), but properties of all of discourse" (p. 1). And in this sense, passions can be projected either onto subjects or objects or onto their junction.

In keeping with this focus on junction, we propose to problematize passion as *attachment*, that is, what *ties* people to specific "things" because they *hold to* them, whether these things are values, principles, collectives, projects, or artifacts (Cooren, 2010). As we will see, these attachments, these passions, seem to play an important role in people's conduct, especially when *presentification*/incarnation is at stake. For instance, the way a project is made present or incarnated is not a neutral matter to the extent that people who are partaking in its achievement are, most of the time, attached to it. Because of this passion/attachment, the various incarnations of a project can become the object of fierce disagreements and debates, with important organizational consequences.

It is particularly this relational dynamic that we approach in this essay to seize "passional fragrances" (Greimas and Fontanille, 1993, p. 2) on the *terra firma* of interactions. Instead of reducing passions to a nuisance or an obstacle to organizational processes, we thus show that passion/passivity is actually constitutive of any action/activity to the extent that it is what provides a form of intelligibility/accountability/reasonability to what people collectively do. To do so we analyse two consecutive episodes related to a science and technology diffusion project—the National Science and Technology Week—in *Explora*[1], a Chilean governmental organization committed to children's valorization of science and technology. More specifically, these two episodes focus on the poster designed by *Explora's* central committee for this event. In both episodes we can see how passions move from objects to subjects to the junction between them as they interweave with a series of states and doings: accusations, frustrations, anger, manipulations, seductions, tortures, construction of scenarios, and so on. Through this analysis we

review the "passional fragrances" of images as they represent and/or
betray specific groups—*Traduttore, traditore*!

PASSION IN ACTION: THE INTERWEAVING
OF STATES AND DOINGS

Traditionally passion has been associated with the internal state of
an individual, the affective aspect of consciousness (Solomon, 1998).
Clearly embedded in the discussion of vice and virtue in ancient philosophy, the analysis of passion moved in the 17th century to questions
of self-knowledge and self-control (Gherardi et al., 2007). The 17th century also marked a removal of passion and emotions from the public and
organizational sphere—removal sustained by the individual control and
the public regulation of emotions (Elias, 1994). Passions have then often
been neglected or attacked as primitive, dangerous, or irrational.

In organizational studies, passion has particularly been circumscribed
to the display (and control) of emotions or feelings in organizational settings. Starting with Simon's (1989) notion of bounded rationality, passions
have been reduced to an affective response to organizational settings, often
associated to an irrational dimension, which causes poor decision making.
As Mumby and Putnam (1992) note, "bounded rationality is utilized by
researchers to frame emotions as producing 'bad long-run consequences for
the organization'" (p. 471; Simon, 1989, p. 35). The bounded rationality
concept treats emotional experience as either a weak mode of reasoning or a
means to serve organizational ends (Kisfalvi, 1995). In the former case, passions are devalued and consequently are treated as something to be removed
or silenced. In the later case, passions are instrumentalized and treated as
ways to achieve efficiency, profit, and productivity. This instrumental view
of passion is known as emotional labor, a form of organizational control
of the heart in which passions become a commodity exchanged for organizational ends (Van Maanen and Kunda, 1989). In both cases, however,
emotions (and passions) still remain confined to a human (unavoidable)
response to organizational settings.

Another trend in organizational studies that has firmly criticized this
functionalist vision of emotion and passion is the feminist approach
(poststructuralist, critical, or constructivist). But if this approach proposes to deconstruct mainstream discourse by revealing its gendered construction and the power issues related to its production, it still focuses
on individuals (or structures that constraint individuals). Let's take for
example (and following the previous discussion), the neologism coined
by Mumby and Putnam (1992) as an alternative to Simon's bounded
rationality: "bounded emotionality." This concept, as the authors argue,
refers to "an alternative mode of organizing in which nurturance, caring,

community, supportiveness and interrelatedness are fused with individual responsibility to shape organizational experience" (p. 474). Here, the concept of 'bounded' is associated to that of intersubjective limitation, that is, "the constraints that individuals must exercise in a community" (p. 474). In this perspective, emotions are considered to be outgrowths of these intersubjective relationships and the interpretative schemes of the community. The focus shifts here from the individual (through the self-control and management of emotions) to the individual and its community and how emotions emerge trough this interaction. However, emotions (and passion) are still confined to human expressions and affective responses.

In taking a discursive approach to passion we argue, following Greimas and Fontanille (1993), that passions are "properties of all of discourse, and that they emanate from discursive structures, from a certain 'semiotic style' that can be projected either onto subjects or onto objects or onto their junction" (p. 1). Defining passion as a discursive property allows us to open up the realm of passion to include other actants—objects, texts, principles, rights and hopes, and so forth—as generating passions.

If passions are the properties of all discourse, we contend that we first need to conceive of a more inclusive conceptualization of the term. Using etymology, one could note, for instance, that passion has the same root as passivity and suffering (pathos), which conveys the idea that someone is acted upon (Greimas, 1983, Spinoza, 2004/1677) or subjected to something. According to this approach, passion therefore becomes a sort of mirror of any action to the extent that whenever someone acts, it is for a specific reason, even if this reason is not something that she knows about or appears to control.

For instance, if X asks Y to bring him a file, and, following this request, Y brings it to X, one can retrospectively say that *X made Y bring her the file* (which is what linguists would call "factitiveness"). In such sentences, Y is positioned as *moved or led* by X's request, which positions Y as *relatively* passive. Of course, this is only one way to describe what happens, and we could depict the same situation in more actional terms for Y by simply saying "Y is bringing X the file." According to this description, it is now Y who is active (he is positioned as the agent) while X is now more passive (she is positioned as the recipient). A priori, the factitive construction tends to bypass something important, which is the *reason(s)* why Y brought the file to X, but, interestingly enough, reasons can also be positioned as agents. For instance, if Y is retrospectively asked, "Why did you do that?" which is another way to ask "What led you do that?" Y could answer, "Because X asked me to do so," which positions X's request as what retrospectively explains his behavior, i.e., led him to bring Y the file (of course, other reasons could be invoked, like "because she is my boss" etc.).

What this example illustrates is that action, passion, and reason are intimately tied to each other, so to speak. Whenever there is action, there is passion (and the opposite is also true, of course), and whenever there is passion (and action), there are reasons, given that reasons are supposed to be what leads people to do what they do. According to this approach, reasons are types of "little passions" or, more prosaically, animations, which can account for our behavior (Cooren, forthcoming). However, one could also note that we tend to speak of "real" passions (in the common and somewhat loaded sense of the term) when one reason keeps superseding all the others. For instance, if someone is a collector and is ready to sell everything she owns to buy very rare stamps, one can say that she is, in general, moved or led by her passion for stamps. In this case, what makes us speak of (real) passion is that she keeps being positioned as moved by the same reason, the same logic, i.e., her passion for stamps.

As we also see, passion presupposes a form of *attachment* to things, values, ideas, and principles that seem to (relatively or absolutely) possess or tie us. We thus speak of (real) passions when someone appears to be absolutely attached to something to the detriment of many other potential objects of attachment. However, when someone's attachment appears relative, that is, when many different sources of attachment potentially exist for her, passions then appear to be multiple and her behavior more "reasonable" or even "rational," because more "calculated" (as we know, *ratio* means calculation in Latin). While passion implies *heat*, calculation implies a certain and relative *coldness* or *coolness*, to the extent that people are then weighing different sources of attachment.

But note that the passionate person is also creating coldness around her, given that her absolute attachment to a specific object *detach* her, by definition, from other objects (in other words, as it is the case for a fridge, coldness is produced by heat, and the opposite is true). Both calculation and passion can therefore lead to heat and coldness. Someone who appears to be a "cold calculator" is someone who will not hesitate to detach herself from possible sources of attachment in the name of what she perceived to be her interest, her passion (revenge is a good example). But calculation can also lead to warmth, so to speak, when one manages to maintain various sources of attachment compatible in our decisions, a sort of *diffuse heat* that maintains a balance between absolute coldness and absolute heat.

Interestingly, when we pay attention to the way people interact with each other, we realize that interactants are presented or present themselves as being moved or animated by specific passions or sources of animation (Cooren, 2008b) that function as many reasons explaining their behavior. A discursive approach to passion also allows us to consider junction—the association of those heterogeneous actors—as a key to understanding its dynamic on the *terra firma* of interaction. In this sense, passion can result from the beings and doings of these associations and can also lead to an act. In fact, passion itself, as we just saw, can be considered an actor (Greimas and Fontanille, 1993). Consequently, a passional discourse can be considered as a series of acts (a chain of state and doings), where manipulation, seduction, torture, sanction, revenge, and so on are at stake.

Drawing upon this latter definition of passion, Cooren (2008, 2010) explores the action/passion tension in the interactional realm. He proposes to open up the scene of interaction as many different types of actants, such as passions, can be identified by interactants as doing something, as making a difference in a given situation. In this context, he argues

> If we therefore acknowledge that people are literally 'moved' by feelings, emotions and even passions, nothing should prevent us from identifying [these latter] as actants, that is, as at least partly responsible for what is said and done and how something is said or done. (p. 5)

A way to capture the hybridity of action (and passion) thus consists of mobilizing the concept of ventriloquism (Cooren 2008b, 2010), defined as the process by which someone or something *makes somebody or something speak.* Consider a married couple arguing about the dishes that he or she was supposed to wash. We can probably imagine that after this discussion one of them would argue, in looking for forgiveness, that anger or frustration led him or her to say what he or she said. A form of ventriloquism is here at work, to the extent that anger—a passion—is positioned as having expressed itself through him or her at a specific moment. This argument does not elude the strategic mobilization of passions, feelings, and emotions by interactants. It opens up the analysis in both ways, in considering that "interactants make feelings say things as much as feelings might make interactants say things" (p. 6). So the question might then be: Why did she or he say that? And the answer leads us to look upstream (or downstream) in the chain of agencies.

In a similar logic, Greimas (1983) proposes in his study of anger to separate the discursive sequence constituted by the intertwining of states and doings in order to identify the elements of passion and then recompose it into a passional configuration, which will be taken as its definition. In this context, something like anger, for example, appears to be a sequence of frustration (passional state), discontent (passional pivot) and agressivity (passional realization). Prior to frustration Greimas identifies an original state of non-frustration, "a state of passion *ab quo*" (p. 149) from which the story of anger seems to unfold. Now, what makes the difference between this original state and frustration is the meeting (or not) of expectations, expectations that, we would contend, are always related to objects of attachment.

Going upstream, expectation appears as the starting point to understanding the discursive sequence of anger. For Greimas (1983), an expectation is not a simple wish; it presupposes a pseudocontract of confidence between at least two subjects, one who has expectations (X) and one who is supposed to act according to these expectations (Y). Ultimately, this fiduciary expectation implies that X believes that s/he can count on Y for the realization of his rights and hopes vis-à-vis a specific object of desire or passion (to which he or she is attached). So, when these expectations are not met and, therefore, the confidence contract is broken, dissatisfaction and disappointment appear, both triggered by a state of frustration and leading to the realization of anger. Going downstream in the discursive sequence of anger, Greimas places *aggressiveness* as the sanction of this sequence. In this sanction phase, the regulation of passion takes place to reinstitute the language of trust.

Greimas's analysis is interesting in its understanding of passion as the articulation of a sequence of states and doings, which allow us to go upstream and downstream in the chain of agency. However, his analysis tends to remain at the abstract and conceptual level. How the doings and beings related to passion are actualized and enacted in interaction is still yet to be explored. We therefore propose in the following analysis to explore *in interaction* this relational dynamic as it moves from objects to subjects to the junction between them in the interweaving of states and doings.

PASSIONAL FRAGRANCES *OF THE NATIONAL SCIENCE AND TECHNOLOGY WEEK*

To seize on the *terra firma* of interactions the dynamic of "passional fragrances" (Greimas and Fontanille, 1993, p. 2) we analyze two consecutive episodes related to the diffusion of a science and technology project—the National Science and Technology Week (NSTW)—in *Explora*, a Chilean governmental organization committed to children's valorization of science and technology. These two episodes are related to the poster designed by *Explora's* central committee for this activity, a poster which is being distributed to *Explora's* 14 regional branches. The first episode coincides with the arrival of this poster to one of these branches—namely *Explora Sur*—a couple of weeks before the beginning of the NSTW. Through this episode, we see how the members of the *Explora Biobio* branch vividly react *vis-à-vis* this poster which, they contend, misrepresent their local project. This section starts with Claudia, *Explora Biobio's* secretary, announcing to Alejandra, the regional director of the program and project manager of the NSTW at *Explora Sur*, the poster's arrival. Then, Gerardo, a Journalism Professor who is very implicated with *Explora* , Lorena, *Explora Sur's* designer, and Claudia share their comments with respect to the poster. (The transcript is an English translation, since all interaction took place in Spanish. The passages in bold are the passages considered to be key to the analysis).

1	Claudia:	Madame Alejandra, **more posters are coming.**
2	Alejandra:	What?
3	Claudia:	**More posters are coming?**
4	Alejandra:	**They're here?** [XXXX
5	Claudia:	[Now
6		((Claudia takes out some cookies from the drawer. She and I talk while we
7		walk through the alley towards the main entrance. There, the deliveryman
8		is bringing the last box filled with the NSTW posters, which were sent
9		to Alejandra by *Explora's* central committee, located in Santiago (Chile's
10		capital city). The deliveryman gives Claudia a form she has to sign to
11		confirm the reception of the boxes. They check that the codes in the form
12		correspond to the ones in the boxes. Claudia signs the form. The
13		deliveryman leaves the premises. Claudia goes to the kitchen and gets a
14		pair of scissors. Gerardo is approaching through the alley)).
15	Gerardo:	There are thousands!—but these are the posters **from here? The one you**
16		**did?** ((He is asking Lorena, *Explora-Biobio's* designer who has just
17		walked in to see the posters)).
18	Claudia:	**No, from Santiago.**
19	Lorena:	Are these the thematic ones?
20	Claudia:	Hum ((She takes a poster out of one box and hands it to Lorena)) Take it,
21		Lorena. ((Lorena unfolds it and looks at it, so does Gerardo))
22	Claudia:	And the other one must be the same one we've just seen now. ((She is
23		referring to a vertical and bigger poster that arrived previously that day))
24		(0.7)
25		((The poster there are looking at is horizontal, smaller than the vertical
26		one. It shows in big and colorful letters the NSTW slogan for this year:
27		"New Materials. The atom's game". The main colors of the poster are
28		black and orange. In the right size there is a space, a ¼ of the poster area,
29		where the information about the activities is presented, as well as the
30		contact information. This specific zone will be presented as an important
31		identity issue with regard to *Explora's* regional branches versus the central
32		committee, located in Santiago.))
33	Consuelo:	Comments?
34	Claudia:	What does Lorena say?
35	Gerardo:	**That this is a shame that they make a poster for Santiago.** ((Lorena
36		smiles. She puts the poster on the desk that is near the window where
37		there is a better light)).
38	Claudia:	**They continue to get better in spending money in horrible things.**
39	Gerardo:	((Who approaches the table to better see the poster)). By the way, **look.**
40		**((He points out the right area of the poster** where the contact
41		information and activities are presented))
42	Lorena:	What **utility** is this for us?
43	Claudia:	It looks like a window valance.
44		(0.3)
45		((Lorena moves her hand as to say "I don't know"))
46	Lorena:	If we put here another little paper hiding this ((She points to the area)). Is
47		that the idea? ((She looks at Gerardo, trying to make sense of the utility of
48		this area))
49	Gerardo:	But look at the extension they put ((**He points again to the area,** but more
50		specifically to the URL address that refers to *Explora's* regional branches
51		information)). **Aren't they stupid! ((He walks away))**

52		((Claudia points out the URL in the poster to show to the camera. It reads:
53		www.explora.cl/exec/explora/memoria.e3. Lorena is still looking at the
54		poster. She does not talk. She smiles ironically, takes the poster in her
55		hands and shows it to the camera.))
56	Claudia:	We should put here a paper so it would have **our activities, our contact**
57		**information.**
58	Lorena:	((Looking at the poster she is holding)). Information with Claudia.
59		((She laughs. She puts the poster on the table again. Looks at it and
60		scratches her head)).
61	Claudia:	There's no way, ah?
62	Lorena:	It's an innovation. Do you think that ((She takes the poster again))—I
63		think that they did a lot of work to get this result. It's like, because=
64	Claudia:	= Yes, it's true. It doesn't matter anymore.
65	Consuelo:	I think it's nice. I like the title.
66	Claudia:	Yes, but **how is this useful for us,** Consuelo, if they only send us the
67		**information of Santiago's activities.**
68	Lorena:	Well, I ((She looks at the poster again)). I don't know.
69	Claudia:	**We are going to have to do what they did in Journalism and cut.** They
70		did cut (inaudible). ((Laughs)).
71		((Claudia is referring to a previous situation when, at the Journalism
72		Department, they cut another poster just to keep the information they
73		thought was useful to their department. The part that was taken off
74		corresponded to the different organizations and institutions that sponsored
75		the event: *Explora*, the Government of Chile, and so forth. This
76		explains why they are laughing about the situation.))
77		((Lorena moves her hand simulating that she is cutting the right area of the
78		poster.))
79	Lorena:	It already looks cut. It misses some air. ((She shows the bottom area)). Ok,
80		let's see. I thought that they would make it with an empty space ((She
81		shows the right area, again)).
82	Claudia:	So that we would at least, [we would
83	Lorena:	[we would write. Even more, in this thing you
84		can't write because it's thermo-laminated and bright. So you can't write
85		here because it's going to spill out.
86	Claudia :	((She approaches the table where Lorena has put again the poster)).
87		((inaudible))
88	Lorena:	It should have been in opaque *couché* paper.
89	Gerardo:	((He is coming through the alley)) What happened?
90	Lorena:	That this paper does not work for writing on it. ((She takes the poster
91		and walks to the panel in the main entrance where the vertical poster is
92		clipped)). In the case of this poster they left a blank space. ((She touches
93		the vertical poster, takes the horizontal one and puts it over. She walks
94		away)).

The first five lines of this excerpt are very explicit in giving us a sense of the atmosphere of this sequence. By saying "more posters are coming" (lines 1 and 2), Claudia is implicitly orienting to the posters as an actor; something they were expecting, and that is now arriving. Alejandra's reply confirms this orientation: "They're here?" (line 4). Both Claudia and Alejandra's expressions could have been used to refer to human actors, like the students or the teachers they work with. But in this case, they refer to the poster they have been waiting for and for which they have, of course, expectations.

Was is interesting to note is that the expectations related to the poster concerns not only the material arrival of this actor—the poster being physically there—but also its characteristics—the *Explora* members are all supposed to have more or less in mind an image of what this poster should look like. The word *attente* (expectation, in French) better captures this double meaning related to the action of waiting (*attendre*) and what one is expecting about what we are waiting for, i.e., some specific characteristics that this object should be endowed with, characteristics that one is supposed to be attached to. Hence, once the posters are finally there (line 5), the *attente* is not over. It is, in fact, just beginning, since now expectations are at work. As we can see from lines 15 to 99, the posters are being evaluated in conformity to these expectations as each member of *Explora Sur* reacts *vis-à-vis* this expected (but suspicious) actor. As in Greimas' study of anger, the poster can be said to generate passion because of the expectations that are associated with it. Let us see now, in further detail, how this generation of passion is at work in this excerpt.

The first one to react is Gerardo, as he asks about the author of the poster (lines 15–16). With this question, we could contend that he is not only looking for a specific information that would help him evaluate the poster (i.e. expectations), but also framing the following comments in terms of representation. From now on, whom or what the poster does (or does not) (re) present will become a critical issue regarding the meeting of expectations. So once the authorship is established (line 18: ". . . from Santiago"), the opinions about the poster will often aim directly at whom it represents, in this case *Explora's* central committee (for example, lines 40, 43, 54–56, 67–68, and 71–72). Therefore, the meeting (or not) of people's expectations with respect to the poster will be in fact measured by taking into consideration the relationship between *Explora Sur* and the central committee (in this case, from *Explora Sur's* point of view). Setting the authorship of the poster is of crucial importance to understand the basis of the fiduciary expectation of *Explora Sur's* member (Greimas, 1983) as the evaluation of the poster will depend on the *pseudocontract* of confidence between this regional branch and the central committee.

This is exactly what we see in line 35. When the researcher (Consuelo) asks for comments, Gerardo answers that it is a shame that they [the people from Santiago] made "a poster for Santiago." With this statement, he is implicitly questioning the poster's representativeness. The poster that was supposed to represent every regional branch of *Explora*, only (re)presents *Explora's* central committee. In doing so, the poster is implicitly positioned as a traitor as it does not meet what should be expected from a "national" spokesperson (or *spokesobject*) of *Explora* (i.e., that it should represent them all). Also, by referring to *Explora's* central committee as *they* (which presupposes an *us*), he is also positioning *Explora Sur* and the central committee in a relationship of antagonism.

Now that Gerardo has voiced his opinion about the poster, we see him explaining or justifying his viewpoint. On line 44, he points to the specific area in the poster that is problematic and implicitly blames the authors (referred to as "they", meaning the Santiago team): ". . . they put . . . . aren't they stupid" (lines 54–56). Responsibility is associated to the authors of the poster and the specific area in the poster pointed by Gerardo is presented as the material proof of the treason. We can feel here Gerardo's frustration and anger, as the expected relationship of confidence (Greimas' fiduciary expectation) appears again to be broken. Note also how Gerardo walks away as if nothing more could be said and nothing more could be expected. Walking away could also be interpreted as "not being able to stand this anymore" as if Gerardo wanted to protect himself from additional anger and emotions. One way to interpret his behavior would consist of saying that he appears to be carried away by his emotions. In taking a ventriloquism analysis, we could say that what is here acting upstream is his anger an anger that carries him away and is triggered by the poster's treason.

Interestingly, Claudia and Lorena, who, as we will see, both appear to agree with Gerardo with respect to the non-representativeness of the poster, do not "walk away" as if nothing else could be done. They frame the representation issue in terms of functionality (lines 47 and 51–52) and by doing so react by discussing different strategies to make the poster more functional and, therefore, more representative (lines 61–62 and 74). We see how the poster's uselessness is here implicitly presented as the cause of its non-representativeness. According to Claudia and Lorena's expectations, this poster is supposed to be functional, an agent that is going to faithfully do what it is supposed to do, i.e., representing *Explora Sur* during the NSTW. It is therefore expected to be an organizational agent that can be *imbricated* in *Explora Sur's* program of action (Taylor and Van Every, 2000). If it only presents (i.e. re-presents) Santiago's activities, then it is useless (since it cannot be imbricated), as Claudia states in lines 71–72: "Yes, but how is this useful for us, Consuelo, if they only send us the information of Santiago's activities."

Now, the positioning in terms of *they* versus *us* is still present in Claudia's statements ("*our* activities, *our* contact information"; "*they* continue to get better in spending money in horrible things"; *they* only send *us* the *information of Santiago's activities*). This relationship of antagonism presupposes some sort of expectation about what she thinks Santiago *should have done* with respect to poster's design. As Gerardo, she is holding the central committee responsible for the poster's treason. In a different way, Lorena's statements do not explicitly and directly aim at *Explora's* central committee. Instead, she repeatedly focuses on the poster ("*It's* an innovation"; "*It* already looks cut. *It* misses some air"; "*It* should have been in opaque *couché* paper") and especially presents design/functional issues ("I thought that they would of *make it with an empty space*"; "Even more, in this thing you *can't write* because it's *thermo-laminated and bright*. So you can't write here because it's going to spill out"). Lorena's expectations, while still aligned with Gerardo and Claudia's, appear different. They refer to her area of expertise and to her expectation of what an organizational (functional) image should do in terms of design.

The strategies discussed by Claudia and Lorena—to stick a blank paper on the problematical area (line 51), to put their information (line 61), to cut the area (line 74)—can be said, using Greimas' (1983) nomenclature, to be a sanction vis-à-vis this act of treason, i.e. the realization of passion: here, frustration related to the non meeting of expectations concerning the poster. The sanction is also present in the following excerpt. Here, Alejandra and Claudia are discussing different scenarios to transform the betraying poster, to make more functional, i.e., more representative.

```
113 Alejandra:  You know Claudia, directly, Journalism's style ((She laughs)).
114 Claudia:    Journalism! That was the same thing I told Lorena. We are going to have
115             to cut it on the side as they did in Journalism, we cut it on the side.
116 Alejandra:  And we put Explora's logo.
117 Claudia:    And there is another one this size? Because you say that the other-
118 Alejandra:  It's because the other is different ((Alejandra walks towards the verti-
119             cal poster, the one clipped near the main entrance)).
120 Claudia:    ((She follows her)). This one, this one
121 Alejandra:  This one. Here, it has a space to paste a—it's done for that.
122 Gerardo:    Forget it!
123 Alejandra:  Yes, they designed it for that purpose ((She responds to Gerardo'
124             comments)). But, you know, I don't think it's that bad to cut it ((She
125             laughs)). Of course, Conicyt (( acronym for the National Science and
126             Technology Research Committee)) is going to be eliminated. But, but,
127             you know I would cut it ((She makes the gesture of cutting the right area
128             of the poster)). And I would paste a logo of Explora here ((She shows it
129             on the poster)). A sticker.
130 Claudia:    But don't they want to get rid of the logo?
131 Alejandra:  ((She looks at the camera smiling humorously)) This year=
132 Claudia:    =We put the logo.
133 Alejandra:  Journalism's style. ((They laugh)). But, I tell—Claudia, let's use Jour-
134             nalism's methodology. The knife methodology ((She laughs))
135 Claudia:    What isn't useful, what isn't useful, we cut it ((She takes a poster and
136             starts folding it to hide the right area)).
137 Alejandra:  Because, look at it, it's not bad, it's not ugly, like this. Because, all
138             this thing ((She points to the right area of the poster)) it's only about
139             Santiago.
140 Claudia:    This is what I say, why don't they leave us=
141 Alejandra:  =and we have many!((referring to the many activities organized))
142 Claudia:    But why don't they leave us the space so that we can put our new, our
143             regional contact information.
144 Alejandra:  We cut it here and we put a logo of Explora, so we don't put something—
145             Well no! It has the Explora-Conicyt here ((She shows another area of the
146             poster, where it reads Explora-Conicyt)).
147 Gerardo:    That's what I was telling you.
148 Claudia:    Yes, it says it here. Yes, it says it.
149 Alejandra:  Yes, it says it. We don't' paste anything, then.
150 Claudia:    No, if it says it here.
151 Alejandra:  You know what? I think that they- this is cute for the 1,000 scien-
152             tists ((an important activity of the NSTW consisting of encounters
153             between scientists and young students))
154 Claudia:    What are we going to do with the 1,000 scientists, you say?
```

155	Alejandra:	That we always send them a poster, do you remember? No? Better the
156		calendar that we are going to make.
157	Claudia:	No, better something **that comes from us**. Because, also they are going to
158		see it and they are going to realize that we cut it. Because they are going
159		to see it, because in *Explora's* Website-
160		(2.0)
161	Claudia	Do you think they are not going to see it?
162	Alejandra:	No, no, it's like=
163	Claudia:	Can you swear it?
164	Alejandra:	Oh no, no. I can't swear it.
165	Claudia:	See, you can't swear it, see.
166	Alejandra:	((inaudible)). ((She sits down)).
167		((**Claudia has finished folding the poster. The "non-representative"**
168		**area is now hidden. She takes the poster and puts in on a wall to see**
169		**the effect.))**
170	Claudia:	It does look weird. It's like squeezed. Well. ((She leaves the poster on the
171		table with the others and goes back to her desk.))

From the beginning of this excerpt, Alejandra (who is looking at the posters for the first time) appears to align with Claudia. She even refers, several times (lines 113 and 132–133), to the same "cutting" strategy, alluding to the Journalism episode Claudia talked about before. It is interesting to note that, in contrast to Gerardo's anger reaction, Alejandra appears quite amused by the situation (she laughs at lines 113, 124–125, and 132–133 and smiles humorously at the camera at line 130). She even finds that the poster is cute (line 150), not bad and not ugly (line 136). Her expectations with respect to the poster (and *Explora's* central committee) appear clearly different than Gerardo's. We can speculate that she promptly assumes that the poster is not representative (and this does not surprise her, since it has happened many times before. Note that Alejandra has been working at *Explora* from the beginnings of the program). Consequently, she believes that they (*Explora Sur*) have to do something to make it functional, i.e., to imbricate it in their program of action. However, in the second episode, as we will see next, her reaction will be much more similar to Gerardo's when she presents this case during *Explora's* national meeting. Even her arguments will be aligned with his as she will focus on the uniform resource locator (URL) extension presented in the poster to position it as the proof of the treason and even more, as an example of *Explora's* regional branches' exclusion from the organization's identity.

For Alejandra, the poster's functionality and, therefore, its representativity imply that they cut the information about Santiago's activity and put a sticker with *Explora's* logo. To understand these moves, we should acknowledge that at the time when this interaction took place *Explora's* central committee was working on a new corporate image and one of the steps toward this new image was to change the logo. This explains why the actual logo is not present in the poster. It just says in big letters: *Explora-Conicyt*. The reference to the logo (to put it back) is a very contested one. This is why Alejandra smiles humorously when suggesting it (line 130). She knows that *Explora's* central committee staff (especially the communication department) will not approve this *bricolage*, which she characterizes as not being "bad" (line 124). What is interesting to note, is that for the poster to re-present *Explora Sur,* it must now betray *Explora's* central committee. It is as if the poster could not be reliable to both this regional branch and the central committee. This says much about the organization's national identity and the 'natural' differentiation by region (which is a common issue in Chilean national organizations).

Again, Claudia insists on the poster's functionality and while she intensely affirms, "what isn't useful, we cut it" (lines 134 and 135), she actually takes action and folds the poster to hide the "betrayal" area. A physical and material sanction is now at work: the poster is being amputated. It is the consequence of its treason and the arrangement that has to be made in order to imbricate it in *Explora Sur*'s program of action. However, even with this *bricolage*, the poster is still not a 100% reliable *spokesobject* for *Explora Sur.* This is why Claudia rejects Alejandra's proposition to send the 'amputated' poster to the scientists that will collaborate with them in the 1,000 scientists' activity. She argues, "No, better something that comes from us. Because, also they are going to see it and they are going to realize that we cut it . . ." (lines 156–157).

For Claudia, cutting off the area with Santiago's activities will not hide the poster's authorship. Furthermore, if they do send the poster without this area, they (*Explora Sur*) can be "caught" in a disloyal act. They could then be positioned as traitors. It is as if to operate, the sanction must remain coherent. To present the poster as the traitor there must not be any public evidence of *Explora Biobio's bricolage.* (In fact, the 'amputated' poster will finally be used as tablecloth during the Scientific Scholar Conference diner.) This is the story that *Explora Sur* wants to tell. As we will see in the next episode, Alejandra will publicly accuse the poster to have excluded *Explora's* regional branches. The second episode corresponds to a meeting held in Santiago the day after the posters arrived at *Explora Sur.* This meeting has been organized by the central committee to gather the regional branches' directors in order to discuss various organizational issues, one of them being *Explora's* new corporate image, a process that by the time of this meeting was being negotiated between *Explora's* central committee and the advertising company hired for this purpose. The extract begins after the presentation of Javier, the president of the advertising company, concerning the importance of the new corporate image. Alejandra opens up the discussion about inclusiveness and identity by mobilizing the NSTW poster, which happens to be the first visual work of the advertising company with *Explora.*

As we see, Alejandra frames the question she addresses to Javier, as well as her following arguments, in terms of brand development (this follows,

1	Alejandra:	Let's go to the other side ((She now points towards Gonzalo)). Now, with
2		respect to the brand's construction, **I am worried that in this brand**
3		**construction, in a way or another, the criteria used will exclude us.** And
4		when I say exclude us, **I mean the rest of us that is not Santiago**
5		((She shows everyone around the table corresponding to this description,
6		in this case *Explora*'s regional directors who are all sitting together)).
7		We have had a permanent discussion about the fact that the Program in
8		its graphic proposal- Just look at the Website. A **national program** where
9		the regions arrive only after three Web pages, **otherwise they do not exist. If**
10		**they don't exist in the contents, they don't exist practically anywhere.** Just
11		look at ((she turns her head looking for something)). **Where is the poster?**
12		This one, please, the long one ((She makes a gesture with her hand
13		horizontally)). No, the long one. ((There is some noise because people
14		are moving papers, whispering. Someone from the audience hands the
15		poster to Gonzalo)). This one. I think that, in fact, and I am very sorry
16		((She looks around the table)) **it's a joke.**
17	Javier:	Why?
18	Alejandra:	**A joke. Look what it says about the regions.** Please, look. In the last
19		line. ((She points out from where she is sitting towards the poster that
20		Gonzalo has in his hands)). There, the last line on the right hand
21		((whispers and comments from the audience)).
22	Javier:	Ah!
23	Alejandra:	**This is a joke, sincerely.**
24	Loreto:	**It's not useful.**
25	Alejandra:	This- Not even someone with a pen and a paper has the capacity—He will
26		not even want to write it down as a Web page ((She moves her hand as
27		if she was writing down something. She moves a lot her hand while she
28		talks. She seems very upset)). Like a reference, **better for it to not exist.**
29		**It does not make a difference if it's there or if it's not.** Sincerely. I
30		think that you agree with me?
31	Javier:	**Absolutely**
32	Alejandra:	**OK.**
33		((Laughs))
34	Isabel:	If not ((She touches Alejandra's shoulder as suggesting that it is not a
35		good idea to disagree with her))
36	Alejandra:	That's what I mean when I say that there is a very central vision
37		((Santiago, as the countries capital, is considered the centre of Chile
38		even if geographically it is not)). And **we feel excluded.** When I get 1,000
39		posters like these=
40	Loreto:	=**you cut them**
41	Alejandra:	This: **what** (.) **use** (.) **does** (.) **it** (.) **have** (.) **for** (.) **me** ((She pauses
42		between each word)). The only alternative I have is invest more money
43		and make a **sticker and paste it over it.** Or a cheaper alternative.
44	Loreto:	**Cut it.**
45	Alejandra:	Go to the printer and **decapitate this part** ((She makes the gesture with
46		her hand)). It's much more economic and I can use the piece, because if
47		not, in reality, **it makes too much noise** ((whispers and comments)). It
48		makes a tremendous noise because **it does not give me anything.** So,
49		when I say this, this is a concrete and clear example. A piece recently
50		done, **for which you have responsibility,** I am asking when you are
51		designing the brand and you are thinking about this brand, **what level of**
52		**incorporation of the regional imaginary is in it?**

consequently Javier's presentation on *Explora's* corporate image). By taking the brand construction as a starting point (lines 1–3), she is able to expose an important regional issue with respect to *Explora's* inclusiveness/exclusiveness in its graphical proposal, and, more specifically, she presents the poster's matter in a coherent and overall frame (and not as an isolated situation).

From the beginning she positions herself as the spokesperson of *Explora*'s regional branches. She even specifies on line 4 what she means by *us*: "The rest of us that is not Santiago". This formulation is quite interesting because it not only reveals an antagonistic relationship between *them* (Santiago, the central committee) and *us* (*Explora*'s regional branches), but it connotes a much deeper and traditional conflict between Chile's capital city and the rest of the country. (There is a common Chilean expression that says that Santiago is Chile.) By re-actualizing this sentence, she is in fact criticizing much more than *Explora*'s graphical proposal; it is Santiago's central vision (line 35) that is being questioned.

Note that Alejandra's positioning as a spokesperson is not the product of chance. Before the meeting started the regional directors were discussing about the poster (the discussion was triggered by Alejandra). They all agreed that the poster was useless, and Alejandra proposed she would put this topic on the table. Therefore, she knew she had her colleagues' informal support, which is explicitly manifested in Loreto (lines 23, 39, and 43) and Isabel's (line 13) alignment. In associating herself with the other regional directors she knows she is a priori authorized to speak on behalf of "the rest of us that is not Santiago" (line 4), which in this case corresponds to 90% of the people reunited in this meeting. Strategically, her argument is much more powerful than if she had only voiced her regional branch (Latour, 1986).

However, even if she acts as *Explora* regional branches' spokesperson, we see how she also allows herself to speak on her own behalf. Interestingly, she does so when expressing her feelings: I am worried (line 2). What appears to move her—or we could even say what authorizes her to speak in the name of the other regional branches about this specific topic—is positioned as her worryness. A form of ventriloquism is here at stake, since she implicitly positions herself as voicing this problematic issue *in the name of* a certain passion, but even more, in a subtle way, as voicing a principle of equity (Cooren, 2008b). In other words, it is as if both a principle of equity and her worries *were expressing themselves through her*. Passion is here implicitly expressed in terms of a personal attachment and a commitment to *Explora*'s national character, which presupposes a regional incorporation in its graphical proposal. Since, repeatedly this imaginary contract (Greimas, 1970) has been broken, she, that is what she says, worries. The relation between passion, expectation, and attachment is at work. Alejandra thus presents herself as moved by her worries and by this principle of equity, which can be both explained in terms of her attachments and her (broken) expectations.

With respect to the regional inclusiveness/exclusiveness in *Explora*'s graphical propositions, it is worth noting that Alejandra defines this in terms of *presence* (lines 8–9). If the regions are not present in those organizational images—they arrive after three web pages—they simply do not exist. Even more, if they are not in these images' content, they do not exist. As in the first episode, we can see how, for Alejandra (and whom she represents) the *presentification* (Cooren et al., 2008) in organizational images—the Web site and the poster—is crucial for the regional branches' existence. It is indeed an organizational mode of being through which *Explora's* regional branches guarantee their existence and continuity (Vásquez, forthcoming). This is why the non-representation of *Explora's* regional branches in the poster is of such importance. Note that in lines 15, 17, and 22, Alejandra qualifies the URL address (the only regional presence, i.e., representation, in the poster) as "a joke." In this argument, which she addresses specifically to Javier, we can find Gerardo's comments in the first episode. This is clearly a translation of Gerardo's "they are stupid" comment in the context of this meeting. Now, she expresses overtly her disapproval and her frustration. She presents herself as feeling deceived (once again) and looks for Javier's approval. With Javier's alignment in line 30 and the general laughs of the regional directors (line 32), the poster (and through it, the Santiago team) has been publicly established as the traitor.

As in the first episode, we see how treason is associated to functionality. First, it is Loreto (line 23) who aligns herself with Alejandra's definition of the poster as "a joke" by stating that it is useless. Alejandra insists on this specific point (lines 24–28, 40, and 46–47) and defines functionality in terms of action: "to make a difference." In referring to the URL address presented in the poster, she points out that it does not make a difference if it is there or not. If it cannot make a difference, it cannot act, and it cannot be an agent for *Explora's* regional branches. In this case, it should not even exist (line 27). She also refers to this as "making too much noise" and as "not giving me anything". She is here referring to Shannon's traditional model of communication where noise is something that has to be avoided to maintain the high fidelity in the transmission of the message (Alejandra is knowledgeable of Shannon's model). The URL address is the noise in the poster and because of it, it is useless, and therefore betrays the regional branches' expectations of functionality.

At the end of this excerpt, we see how Alejandra positions Javier as having his part of responsibility for the poster's treason. He, as a representative of the advertising company who designed the poster, is being held responsible of it. He is also being questioned about the incorporation of the regions in *Explora's* new corporate image (lines 49–51). In the following excerpt, Javier's answer to Alejandra's questions does not directly address the regional branches' concerns. Actually, he first argues about what he presents as an important issue in Explora's corporate branding, that is the differences between rural and urban children's imaginaries. He then addresses the question of his (supposed) responsibility in this poster's *affaire*.

63	Javier:	(. . .) Now, I, look, I have, Let's see. There are **two things that I should**
64		**address here.** One, with respect to this ((he points to the posters)), we are
65		in a **phase of the brand identity construction process** that goes in
66		parallel with this. In this case I cannot respond for the visions that are
67		more **administrative** or that are the consequences of a **part of the Web**
68		**system that existed before.** But for me, **this meeting** here is a clear
69		demonstration of the contrary. Precisely the point of me coming here
70		today and not simply resolving this in the office in Santiago was to make
71		you participate in a debate that will probably occur when I am probably
72		not here. And then, that's why I think it is important what you say. And
73		second that, I think, that we don't have to overestimate the differences
74		between urban and rural children, not even between Chilean and Russians
75		children, because=
76	Anita:	=Excuse-me, but I forgot the last part of my intervention. I know that a
77		good brand should be able to be [inclusive an to cover
78	Javier:	[It's more than that. Another thing,
79		every time and more and more, [I have been 20 years in
80	Anita:	[**What worries me**
81	Javier:	And I realize more and more that we consume the same images in spaces
82		that are completely different. See that a, it's very probable=
83	Anita:	= globalization is here, I understand it clearly
84	Javier: Ah?	
85	Anita:	globalization is here, I understand it clearly, I
86	Javier: Exactly, exactly	
87	Anita:	But independently
88	Javier:	=Then what we have to do is to balance the local identities with also
89		universal languages. And I think we are in this topic, in this debate with
90		respect to the web page.
91	Alejandra:	I completely agree with you. The point is that **we don't feel**, because you
92		are presenting it with respect to what our **perception is**, that **we do not**
93		**want to feel excluded.** When you send me a poster like this
94	Javier:	I think you have to be included
95	Alejandra:	When you send me a poster like this =
96	Javier:	=You feel excluded
97	Alejandra:	I feel excluded.
98	Javier:	Ok. **Now let's not confuse the inclusion in the debate and the collective**
99		**design.**
100	Alejandra:	That's why I wanted, I presented it as two directions.
101	Javier:	Because that is complicated.
102	Alejandra:	There were two directions in the discussion, let's say.

As mentioned previously, Javier only addresses two aspects in responding to Alejandra's question: the responsibility for the poster design and the differentiation between local and global, or rural and urban, or regional and central. With respect to the first accusation of responsibility—the poster's alleged treason—it is interesting to note that Javier frames it in terms of brand construction process in which there are, according to him, many independent actors involved: the administration, the Web site, and so forth (lines 63–68). He can only be held responsible for his area of expertise: the design and in this case, he says he has nothing to be reproached for. This common argument when talking about responsibility shows a strategic and rational detachment (without passion), which Javier uses to confront Alejandra's *attachment* (in terms of what she feels, what she is worried of and the principles and passion that move her). The binary opposition between passion and rationality is at work: as passion implies attachment and reason, detachment (Cooren, 2007). At least this is what Javier intends to do by framing his answer in what is supposed to appear as a more detached and rational way to express oneself *vis-à-vis* Alejandra's passionate arguments that tie her to her feelings and worries. However, at the end of the excerpt Javier will align with Alejandra, as he explicitly voices what she feels: being excluded (line 96). By doing so he implicitly validates this passional argument as a rational (and accepted) one.

Once he has responded to his accusation of responsibility, he will address *Explora*'s central committee's part of responsibility. It is interesting to see that from the beginning of this discussion between Alejandra and Javier, the central committee's responsibility has never been overtly addressed. (Let us remember that in the first episode this was not the case, as Gerardo and Claudia referred specifically to the central committee as the author of the poster and, therefore, the one to be held responsible for this treason.) In line 68, Javier orients toward the central committee's responsibility and acts as its defense. In a certain way, we can say he is speaking on behalf of the central committee since the question was directly addressed to him. He presents the meeting as a concrete example of the willingness of the central committee to include regions in the debate about the organization's image and national identity. The meeting-as-proof for his argument therefore confronts the poster-as-proof used in Alejandra's argument.

We can also find this strategy of attending to indirectly a much deeper and contested issue when Javier addresses the second part of his answer. Instead of framing it in terms of an antagonistic relationship between the regions and Santiago, and consequently the regions' feeling of exclusion, he structures his answer in terms of globalization and localization, rural and urban, yet another set of rational dichotomies to explain a similar phenomenon. Again, a rational argument is used (lines 88–89) to confront Alejandra's passionate intervention. However, from lines 91 to 97, passion appears to take over reason as Javier accepts that, in the case of the betrayer poster, the feeling of exclusion is rational and accepted. Still, he points out (lines 98–99) that the inclusion in the debate does not imply an inclusion in the design. By doing so, he reaffirms the task division in the brand construction process; therefore, he clearly differentiates his area of responsibility and the central committee's one. In recognizing passion (Alejandra's feeling of worry), Javier is enrolled in the regional branches' agenda. Sanction is completed; the traitor has been publicly declared guilty!

DISCUSSION

In this paper we have approached the realm of passion, images, and organizations from a discursive and pragmatic point of view to seize *passional fragrances* as they move from objects to subjects to the junction between them in the *terra firma* of interaction. Opening the definition of passion to its etymological roots—as to be acted upon–, we have focused on the interweaving of states and doings as they unfold in a series of interactions between multiple (inter)actants. This semiotic reading of interaction has led us to look at both human and non-human contributions to the passional flow.

We have seen, in analyzing two controversial episodes related to a project of science and technology diffusion, that not only humans can trigger passion. Images, as the poster in the previous analysis, can also inspire anger, frustration, discontent, dissatisfaction, and so on. This is possible because images do not act by themselves; they act on behalf of other actors, those who authorize them as *spokesobjects*. This is especially true with respect to organizations, since objects, as images, are supposed to be organizational agents for the organization (their principal) and therefore respond to functional orders. *Presentification* (Cooren, et al., 2008) is then the key to understanding how images can or cannot act as functional and reliable agents in the name of the organization they are supposed to (re)present. We especially saw that when objects do not fulfill their representational function as *expected—traduttore, traditore*—they can provoke strong reactions in those who relied on them.

We saw that expectations—as the upstream state in the passional discourse—are crucial in understanding how objects can trigger passion. In the previous analysis, expectations with regard to the poster (and whom it represented) framed the interactants' evaluation of the poster ("it's a joke"; "it's useless") as well as their passional reaction (walking away, cutting it, folding it). We also saw how expectations can be pervasive, as they permeate the passional flow from the beginning to the end. Following a ventriloquist logic, one could say that their expectations led the interactants to speak negatively about the poster, and act upon it. Consequently, expectations can also be considered as actant participating in this passional dynamic.

Another actor that strongly appears as a crucial contributor to this dynamic is passion itself. In the analyzed episodes (especially the second one), people were presented or presented themselves as being moved by specific passions. (Let us recall that Alejandra's first utterance, introducing the question she asks Gonzalo, explicitly refers to her worries). Furthermore, these passions were mobilized as justifying their acts or their sayings, in a certain mode of accountability (Quattrone, 2004). In this strategic use of passion as a rational and accepted argument, we can see how the passion/reason duality starts to disappear as we are moved by passions that can account for our actions (Cooren, 2007). Passion can be presented as what ties us to a principle, an idea, a value—an *attachment*—but it can also be presented as the justified reason for our actions—a *detachment*. Hence, this interactional analysis of passion has demonstrated that the passional realm is more populated than what we thought it was. Images, expectations, and passions themselves have also a word to say. So, the question is 'Why did they say that?' And the answer is upstream or downstream in the infinite chain of agencies.

NOTES

1. The data used for this analysis was collected during the first author's thesis field research. The thesis entitled "Spacing organization: trajectories of a science and technology diffusion project in Chile" was funded by the Social Sciences and Humanities Research Council of Canada.

REFERENCES

Cooren, F. (2006). The organizational world as a plenum of agencies. In F. Cooren, J. R. Taylor, and E. J. V. Every (Eds.), *Communication as organizing: Practical approaches to research into the dynamic of text and conversation* (pp. 81–100). Mahwah, NY: Lawrence Erlbaum Associates.

———. (2008a). Between Semiotics and Pragmatics: Opening Language Studies to Textual Agency. *Journal of Pragmatics, 40*(1), 1–16.

———. (2008b). The Selection of Agency as a Rhetorical Device: Opening Up the Scene of Dialogue through Ventriloquism. In E. Weigand (Ed.), *Dialogue and Rhetoric.* Amsterdam: John Benjamins.

———. (2010). *Action and agency in dialogue: Passion, incarnation and ventriloquism.* Amsterdam: John Benjamins.

———., Brumans, B., and Charrieras, D. (2007). *To Be or Not To Be: The Question of Organizational Presence.* Paper presented at the International Communication Association.

———, Brummans, B. and Charrieras, D. (2008). The coproduction of organizational presence: A study of Médecins Sans Frontières in action. *Human Relations, 61*(10), 1339–1370.

Elias, N. (1994/1936). *The Civilizing Process.* Oxford: Basil Balckwell.

Garfinkel, H. (1988). Evidence for Locally Produced, Naturally Accountable Phenomena of Order, Logic, Reason, Meaning, Method, etc. in and as of the Essential Quiddity of Immortal Society (I of IV): An Announcement of Studies. *Sociological Theory, 6,* 103–109.

Gherardi, S., Niccolini, D., & Strati, A. (2007). The Passion for Knowing. *Organization, 14*(3), 315–329.

Greimas, A. J. (1970). De la colère. Étude sémantique lexicale. In A. J. Greimas (Ed.), *Du Sens II. Essais Sémiotiques* (pp. 225–246). Paris: Éditions Du Seuil.

———. (1983). *Du sens II: essais sémiotiques.* Paris: Éditions du Seuil.

Greimas, A. J., and Fontanille, J. (1993). *The Semiotics of Passions. From States of Affairs to States of Feeling.* (P. Perron and F. Collins, Trans.). Minneapolis and London: University of Minnesota Press.

Kisfalvi, V. (1995). Laisser nos émotions à la porte? *Gestion revue internationale de gestion,* 20(3), 110–113.

Latour, B. (1986). The powers of associations. In J. Law (Ed.), *Power, action and belief: a new sociology of knowledge?* (pp. 264–280). London: Routledge.

———. (1987). *Science in Action: How to Follow Scientists and Engineers Through Society.* Cambridge: Harvard University Press.

————. (1994). Une sociologie sans objet: Remarques sur l'interobjectivité. *Sociologie du travail, 4,* 587–607.

————. (1996). *Aramis: Or the Love of Technology.* Cambridge: Harvard University Press.

————. (2005). *Reassembling the Social—An Introduction to Actor-Network-Theory.* Oxford, England: Oxford University Press.

Law, J. (1994). *Organizing Modernity.* Cambridge, MA and Oxford, England: Blackwell.

Mumby, D., & Putnam, L. (1992). The Politics of Emotions: A feminist reading of bounded rationality. *Academy of Management Review, 17*(3), 465–486.

Quattrone, P. (2004). Accounting for God: Accounting and Accountability Practices in the Society of Jesus (Italy, 16th–17th Centuries). *Accounting, Organizations and Society, 29*(7), 647–683.

Quattrone, P. (2009). Books to be practiced: Memory, the power of the visual, and the success of accounting. *Accounting, Organizations and Society, 34*(1), 85–118.

Robichaud, D. (2006). Steps toward a relational view of agency. In F. Cooren, J. R. Taylor, and E. J. V. Every (Eds.), *Communication as organizing: Practical approaches to research into the dynamic of text and conversation* (pp. 101–114). Mahwah, NY: Lawrence Erlbaum Associates.

Simon, H. (1989). Making management decisions: The role of intuition and emotion. In W. H. Agor (Ed.), *Intuition in organizations* (pp. 23–39). Newbury Park, CA: Sage.

Solomon, R. C. (1998). The politics of emotion. In P. A. French & H. K. Wettstein (Eds.), *The Philosophy of Emotion 22,* 1–20. Notre Dame, Indiana: Universty of Notre Dame Press.

Spinoza, B. (2004/1677). *Éthique* (R. Misrahi, Trans. 2nd ed.). Paris: éditions VIGDOR.

Taylor, J. R., and Van Every, E. J. (2000). *The Emergent Organization: Communication as its Site and Surface.* Mahwah: Lawrence Erlbaum.

Van Maanen, J., & Kunda, G. (1989). Real feelings': emotional expression and organizational culture. In B. M. Staw & L. L. Cummings (Eds.), *Research in Organizational Behavior* (Vol. 11). Greenwich, CT: JAI.

Vásquez, C. (Forthcoming). Spacing organization (or how to be here and there at the same time). In D. Robichaud and F. Cooren (Eds.), *What is an organization? Materiality, agency and discourse.* Oxford, England: Oxford University Press.

10 Imagining (the Future) Business
How to Make Firms with Plans?

Martin Giraudeau

Entrepreneurial finance is a market for virtualities. Investors, be they venture capitalists, business angels, or any other kind of financial institutions investing in new or rapidly developing ventures, spend their money on companies whose existence and profitability have yet to become empirically observable. The valuation of new ventures raises some classical problems. Moral hazard is of course the first one of these.[1] For strategic reasons, or just out of forgetfulness, the entrepreneur may keep from disclosing part of the information she has to the people from whom she expects to raise capital. Another classical evaluation problem is that new companies are complex "nexuses of contracts," (Williamson, 1986) mixing heterogeneous elements that can very hardly be evaluated according to a simple grid of criteria. Financial statements can of course provide useful information about the initial assets, liabilities, and expenses of the business, but they do not say much about the singular articulation of these elements in the business, about their actual use inside the new organization, about the evolutions presently happening in the markets the company aims to conquer, etc. In short, the assessment of a singular business "combination," as Schumpeter would have put it (Schumpeter, 1911), happens to be a hard task because of the difficulty to evaluate the quality of some elements of the business as well as of their mixture. But entrepreneurial finance is not just any market—with its moral hazard issues—nor is it just a market for qualities or singularities (Karpik, 1989, 1996, 2010; Musselin and Paradeise, 2002). The uncertainties market actors are confronted with on this market may be uncertainties about full disclosure of information or about the qualities of the new venture, but they are also and most importantly uncertainties about the future. Investors and entrepreneurs meet around strange products that are in a sort of existential twilight zone: they do exist, as projects, but they do not exist yet as operating enterprises. As businesses, they are still virtual. How can such an uncertainty-laden market actually function?

This paper shows that there is no straightforward answer to this question, but that market actors, over the years, have devised various ways to circumvent the problems of dealing with virtualities, by proposing various tools and methods for imagining the future business. To do so, they have notably relied on a specific tool: the business plan. The business plan is a paper or electronic mediation instrument designed to circulate between the individual actors of the supply and demand sides of the market, in order to make them meet and eventually reach an agreement. If one wishes to compare the funding of new ventures with a market for goods, then the business plan is best compared with the packaging of a product: it is a two dimensional *pack*, covered with inscriptions about the product's ingredients, qualities and price. But it is specific in that it is an *empty* box, which will only end up being filled with what is promised on the cover if and once funding is actually secured.[2] The question therefore is how does the business plan account satisfyingly enough for the future? How does it reduce the uncertainties inherent to the virtuality of the companies it intends to describe? Put bluntly: what is a good business plan? As all entrepreneurs and venture capitalists know, answers to this question may be found in the normative literature on business plans, and especially in business plan guidebooks. We propose, in this paper, to follow the actors in their quest for the good business plan, by having a look at the evolution of this literature. We will thus focus on the 40-year history of business plan guidebooks, from their emergence in the late sixties until the post-dot.com times of the last 10 years. This will unable us to emphasize the youth and fragility of present business planning norms, as well as to reveal some tensions inherent to the operational imagining of the future.

"THE BUSINESS PLAN PACKAGE"

Business plans have a long history. Merchants in Renaissance Venice prepared anticipated balanced sheets to assess their chances of success and discuss them with fellow merchants and bankers (Braudel, 1993). With the emergence of new types of companies, and the separation of ownership and control, other forms of documents were prepared. An often quoted example is that of Columbus' request of funds to the Spanish sovereigns for his transatlantic venture. A more recent and adequate example is that of Pierre-Samuel Du Pont de Nemours' written projects of 1797 and 1798, designed to secure funding from European merchants and bankers before settling in the newly born United States, where his son would end up founding the DuPont Company (Giraudeau, 2010). It was not until the late nineteen sixties, however, that business plans became identified objects deserving a specific name. Following the Second World War and thanks to growing state concern about both small business and technological innovation, a whole world of entrepreneurship started to emerge. The Small Business Administration was created in 1953, and new types of financial institutions appeared: venture capital firms on the one hand and the federally supported Small Business Investment Companies on the other hand.[3] Research and training in small business management and entrepreneurship simultaneously started to develop, both in academia and out of it (Vesper, 1993; Katz, 2003), and a new literature thus emerged to help entrepreneurs govern their businesses.[4] Providing advice on how to secure funding for new or rapidly growing businesses soon became an important matter of concern for some of the actors of this world of entrepreneurship.

By the seventies, hundreds of venture capital firms and Small Business Investment Companies already existed, and already asked for "business plans" from those who asked them for funding.

Investors, who received dozens of applications every day, were generally small and risky companies that couldn't afford to hire enough personnel to assess all the business projects they received and therefore felt the need to rationalize their screening of projects. Asking for a written proposal that could then be dealt with administratively and discussed internally was a helpful and obvious option. There was however quite some variability in what different investors meant when talking of "a business plan." Some barely expected entrepreneurs to send them a brief operational description of the future company, along with basic financial projections, while others required longer and more narrative documents, which would describe the proposed product or service, its market, the entrepreneur's curriculum, etc. Knowing what type of document investors wanted often proved tricky for entrepreneurs, who had to ask every new investor they contacted what his or her requirements were in this respect. But it was not long before consultants and academics, who were sometimes the same persons, spotted the information problem and sought to solve it. In 1973, for instance, a New York business information company called Technimetrics Inc. issued a *Business Plan Package* (1973), which started with brief information about the expectations of venture capitalists in terms of return on investment, and basic examples of ratio analysis.[5] The package then contained a 10-page long standard outline for a plan, which emphasized the necessity to put synthetic information about the financial prospects of the business at the forefront of the plan, before going into a detailed presentation of the business (products or services, operations, patents, etc.) and a market study (sales, markets, competition), first in a narrative way and finally to pro forma accounting statements. It finally provided entrepreneurs with more than 30 pages of "handy fill in the blanks tables," half of which were accounting tables, while the other ones were to be lists of personnel, recruitment schedules, and such. Today's standard format of business plans was starting to appear.

Such formats, initially made for companies with high return on investment prospects, soon came to be developed for more common business ventures, who sought investments from small business investment companies (SBICs) or even just loans from banks and state agencies. These formats were explained more thoroughly by their authors, in order to make them accessible to inexperienced and low qualification entrepreneurs. In 1976, the Federal Reserve Bank of Boston for example published what seems to be the first *Business Planning Guide. A Handbook to Help You Design, Write, and Use a Business Plan Tailored to Your Specific Business Needs* (Bangs and Osgood, 1976), which was co-authored by the bank's Urban Affairs manager, William R. Osgood, and David H. Bangs, coordinator of the Business Information Center of the Southeastern New Hampshire Regional Planning Commission. This 90 page long booklet was structured around the sample plan of a fictional New Hampshire company called "Finestkind Seafood Inc." The outline of the plan was similar to that of the *Business Plan Package*, but the first synthetic pages had disappeared and the plan was clearly divided in two parts, the first one being narrative and the second one made of pro forma accounting statements and ratio analysis. The business plan was here conceived of as a means to attract investors but also to allow entrepreneurs to assess their businesses themselves, less from a financial standpoint than in terms of day-to-day operations, general structure of the business, and fit with its markets. The planning process was thus meant to become a formative period for the entrepreneurs, who had to take a leading part in it:

> YOU must do the planning / This means that you must make the time available. (. . .) Others can assist you in the process, but you must do the actual planning./ If you are not in business, but are trying to determine whether of not your business idea makes sense—or are getting ready to get started—following the planning process outlined is the most important thing you can do./ PLAN what's going to happen— Then do it. (Bangs and Osgood, 1976)

"HOW A BUSINESS PLAN IS READ"

With the growing number of support services for entrepreneurs, some authors even developed what they called "a systems approach to venture initiation," (Osgood and Wetzel, 1977) or considerations about "guided entrepreneurship" (Timmons, 1975).[6] The idea was to have "professional business development teams" frame entrepreneurs in the business planning process or at least to provide entrepreneurs with external feedback on their plans in specifically tailored workshops. First critiques of the use of excessive framing in the preparation and formats of business plans however started to emerge as early as the mid-seventies. Another paper from the *Business Horizons* review, which was created in 1958 with a target audience of small and medium business owners but started like many others to publish more articles about new venture formation from the beginning of the seventies,[7] stated these critiques clearly. Its author, Joseph R. Mancuso, was himself an entrepreneur, who had founded in 1959 one of the first business "incubators" and is actually said to have coined that word.[8] Less interested than others in how complete and detailed a business plan had to be, Mancuso made interviews with venture capitalists and focused on "How a business plan is read." (1974). His conclusion was straightforward:

> Most articles concerned with the writing of business plans focus on checklists, blank forms, and sample plans. As guides, they help catch items that might be overlooked because they force a full and balanced consideration of the many intertwined issues. To be helpful, they must be broad in scope; but this also decreases their effectiveness for a particular reader. (Mancuso, 1974, p. 34)

Such a reader would indeed spend on average five minutes reading a plan written in more than five weeks, and sometimes months, and these five minutes would be devoted to the following steps:

> Step 1—Determine the characteristics of company and industry./Step 2—Determine the terms of the deal./Step 3—Read the balance sheet./ Step 4—Determine the caliber of the people in the deal./Step 5—Determine what is different about this deal./Step 6—Give the plan a once-over-lightly. (Mancuso, 1974, p. 36)

According to Mancuso, the wise business planner therefore had better to produce a synthetic plan that made such a quick reading possible, rather than lose time in preparing a more systematic document.[9]

Such a critique was however followed by one of another type. If the planning process wasn't to be too formal and excessively framed, it also had to lead to more than a quick and synthetic document. For some authors, Joseph Mancuso was "more of a cheerleader," who neglected the importance of thorough business planning more than was preferable from the actual point of view of investors. This was the point of view that was developed in 1985 by Stanley R. Rich and David E. Gumpert in their catchily entitled book: *Business Plans that Win $$$. Lessons from the MIT Enterprise Forum* (1987). Stanley Rich, a technology-oriented business entrepreneur and Massachusetts Institute of Technology (MIT) graduate, was the chairman of the MIT Enterprise Forum, which he had participated in launching in 1978 with the MIT alumni and alumnae associations, and was designed as a meeting place for entrepreneurs, venture capitalists, and other people interested in venture formation. Rich's rather dissatisfied experience with the Forum made him want to write a book to educate entrepreneurs, and he asked for Gumpert's help in order to do that. David Gumpert, a former *Wall Street Journal* journalist whose parents owned a retail store and who had always had a specific interest in small business issues, had been hired by the *Harvard Business Review* in 1979 as its "small business and entrepreneurship" editor, a newly created post. The book contained almost no fill-in-the blank tables and showed no sample business plan. It did articulate, classically, around the various successive parts of a business plan: "What do you want to be when you grow up?" "What's the user benefit and other marketing issues," "Selling and supporting your product," "Product development and manufacturing," "What's the management team like?" and "Those %&*#@! Financial projections," which reflected the general dislike of accounting among the population of entrepreneurs. But the book's focus was much less on the methods and technicalities of market and competition studies or of financial accounting than on the general impression of credibility the business plan was meant to attain. The authors thus developed what they called "The Rich-Gumpert evaluation system," which aimed at summarizing the expectations of venture capitalists and other potential investors when they appraised a business plan. The "system" emphasized two dimensions in the evaluation of plans:

the "product/service status" and the "management status," which could be confronted in a four-by-four table.

> First comes a qualitative assessment, based on the status of the product and the management team. (. . .) Thus, most desirable is what we might refer to as a '4/4'—a business with a Level 4 product and a Level 4 management team. This venture has an accepted product in a proven market, run by a first class and fully staffed management team and is clearly the likeliest combination to win investment funds at the lowest cost for the money. / At the other extreme is a single entrepreneur with an unproven idea—a 1/1. This venture has barely a chance to obtain investment funds unless the founder has a magnificent track record. All the other combinations will range between these extremes. (Rich and Gumpert, 1987, p. 165)

The authors insisted here on the importance of "proof" in an interesting way: the product, the market and the team all had to be convincing and they could only be so if they actually existed. The product had to have already met its market and the management team had to be constituted. The business plan thus had to, first of all, describe an attested present in order to make credible claims about the future.

"A BUSINESS PLAN FOR AMERICA"

This position, held in the mid-eighties, however went against the general tendency of recommendations that were made to entrepreneurs in this decade as well as in the following one. By this time, business plans had indeed stopped to be a local tool used in the very specific market for risky-venture finance. The tool had indeed become a symbol for the "new economy," and so much so that business planning was even turned into an actual economic and social policy "programme" (Miller and Rose, 1992) to fight against the recession. A book entitled *Business Plan for America: An Entrepreneur's Manifesto* was published in 1984, which was a plea for the promotion of individual initiative through new venture formation, in order to let the "ingenuity," "ideas," and "desires" of the American people express themselves against the forces of the "establishment" (Gevirtz, 1984). This "manifesto," which called on the ideals of the founding fathers of the United States (US) and especially on those of Benjamin Franklin, thus conceived of the business plan as the modern technology that could make Adam Smith's invisible hand real, with Smith's butcher, baker, and brewer just replaced, first, by the engineers of Silicon Valley and, then, by all the "efficient hedonists" the American people was made of. The business plan, which allowed for emergent relationships between finance and entrepreneurs, was to be both the symbol and the tool for "twentieth century capitalism," as the hammer and sickle had been those of another ideal world. The "new spirit of capitalism" had thus found an instrument in which to embody itself (Boltanski and Chiapello, 1999).

This celebration of business plans went along with an intense proliferation of business plan guidebooks, that where now aimed at all types of entrepreneurs. More than 20 of them were published in the US in the 1980s, and twice as many in the 1990s. One of the first authors to propose such a guidebook was William Osgood, who recycled part of his material from the 1976 *Business Plan Guide* he had co-authored with David Bangs, and it wasn't long before Bangs himself published his own guidebook, that was to be re-edited numerous times until today (Osgood, 1980; Bangs, 1985). These authors mainly focused on providing entrepreneurs with a precise format, which was first a checklist of all the information they had to provide in the plan. The checklist also respected the already standardized order in which this information was expected by potential investors and thus served as an instrument of comparability of plans the ones against the others. The role of formats was particularly important for the accounting parts of the business plans and new ways to enforce these formats were soon developed. As soon as the first spreadsheet software came out, Osgood indeed issued new guidebooks that explained how to design prospective accounting tables with such software and thus automate part of the required computations (Osgood and Curtin, 1984; 1985; Osgood and Maupin, 1985). Other authors relied on older tools, but all moved in the same direction of proposing detailed and explained business plan formats. It was even the case of Joseph Mancuso who, in spite of his previous critiques against business plan formats, published *How to Prepare and Present a Business Plan* in 1983, and *How to Write a Winning Business Plan* just two years later, both of which provided entrepreneurs with predefined plan structures. David Gumpert, who had then started working for *Inc.* magazine, was asked by the magazine's editor to write a new business plan guidebook aimed at a broader public than the one he had co-authored with Rich, and he thus also started to focus less on the provision of proofs of existence of the business than on the business plan format itself (1990). The writing of business plans was thus mainly a matter of filling in the blanks of a pre-established and stable document structure.

The titles of business plan guidebooks that were published over the years are quite telling about this delegation of part of the business planning process to the paper and computer technologies embedded in the guidebooks. Most of them, of course, claimed to propose methods for the production of a "successful business plan," a "winning business plan," a "powerful business plan," "your best ever business plan," or even "a great business plan," when it wasn't simply "the perfect business plan." This efficiency of the plan took, in some other titles, a more explicit form: the good business plan was sometimes the one "that others [would] want to read and invest in," that would enable entrepreneurs "to win [their] investor's confidence," made for "attracting equity investors" or "raising venture capital." Elsewhere, the good business plan was the one who made it possible primarily to attain internal goals for the business: it was a business plan "for profitability," or more generally "the start of something big": "start with a vision, build a company" said another title. But business plans were also recognized as having some dark sides: business planning required rather thorough writing and computation from entrepreneurs, which made it seem like a complicated or at least fastidious task. Business plan guidebooks therefore insisted on how they could make things easier for the writers of business plans. They would explain *Business Plans for Dummies* or *The ABC's of Writing Winning Business Plans* and claim that thanks to them the writing of business plans had "never been easier." The length of the business planning process was itself a major issue and guidebooks insisted on their ability to reduce it thanks to methods "in 30 days," "in 15 days," "in 60 minutes or less . . ." or even "in no time" with the "instant business plan"! These miraculous methods were said to be "easy-to-follow," structured around a limited number of "steps"—often seven!—and relied heavily on the use of workbooks, as well as on a growing number of spreadsheets and software when, from the mid-nineties, the use of computers had been democratized. A real market for business planning tools and methods had developed, that gave birth to a whole generation of newly equipped entrepreneurs.

"THE DEFINITIVE BUSINESS PLAN"

The growth of this market led to evolutions in the contents of business plan guidebooks. Even though most of the titles of their books sounded alike, authors indeed progressively tried to differentiate from one another. Differentiation went in various and sometimes opposite directions, depending mainly on the type of entrepreneurs guidebook authors were aiming to sell their tools and methods to. Some thus tried to simplify as much as possible the business planning process. *The One Page Business Plan. The Fastest, Easiest Way to Write a Business Plan* was first developed by its author, previously a senior financial executive in various large firm, as a consultancy tool that he ended up publishing in 1997 (Horan, 2006). The aim of the book was to facilitate the writing process, i.e., to help entrepreneurs design their plans on paper, in order to enable then to assess and improve their projects, especially in a marketing perspective—so that they could become understandable to someone else.

> Things get clearer when you write. Of course at first the process can feel very awkward, and the results seem poor and anything but clear. But given time and patience, the process results in a connection of the mind with the reality of the paper. Thoughts begin to develop into images. Images turn into keywords and short phrases. An outline begins to emerge, and the clarity builds. (Horan, 2006, p. 21)

In order to make this possible, *The One Page Business Plan* proposed around a hundred preformatted pages, where precise writing exercises where given to entrepreneurs, quite in the same way as in writing exercise-books for school children. A good example of these exercises was the one that aimed at facilitating the production of an initial "vision statement" for the new business. The entrepreneur was asked to state his general vision of the future of his company in three different ways: first, in a pre-ascribed fill-in-the-blanks format, second "in [his] own words," and third in a "wildly optimistic, no limits, outrageous" way. With the additional help of a dozen of examples of vision statements given in the book,[10] the entrepreneur could thus phrase and rephrase his or her statement without being afraid of confronting a white page. Besides writing, (ac)counting was also to be simplified and, like many other guidebooks since the mid-1990s, *The One Page Business Plan* was accompanied by a tool-kit CD containing Microsoft Excel spreadsheets with, on the one hand, an empty monthly profit and loss statement for one year—joint with predefined charts to show the evolution of sales, overhead and profit before tax, as well as "key financial percentages" (cost of goods sold, gross profit, etc.)—and, on the other hand, a more synthetic version of the profit and loss (P and L) made to automatically generate a breakeven chart. The simplified representation of the future business had been advocated since the early days of business planning guidebooks, who already referred, although rapidly, to such tools as ratios, charts, and synthetic statements but didn't go as far in equipping entrepreneurs with automated or quasi-automated methods to produce these.

Providing simplified tools for the written and charted visualization of venture projects was the intention of many a guidebook, and this proved to be a source of commercial success for them, the *One Page Business Plan* for instance ending up as an Amazon.com bestseller, even though it wasn't published by a well established editor. Other guidebooks however opted for more sophistication. First published in 1986 and re-edited a number of times, *Anatomy of a Business Plan* (Pinson, 2005) was thus a 300 page long A4 volume with extremely detailed advice and worksheets on all the sections of a business plan. This guidebook emphasized precision and depth of analysis much more than clear synthesis. It was not until the late 1990s, however, that a first up-market business plan guidebook emerged, aimed at entrepreneurs with a high level of business education and experience. By that time, entrepreneurship research and education had developed all over the world, and business school students could use a more academic business plan handbook. *The Definitive Business Plan. The Fast Track to Intelligent Business Planning for Executives and Entrepreneurs* (2007) with its telling title that places it at the top of intellectual hierarchy, was first published in 1999 by Richard Stutely, an author whose background was for once not in entrepreneurship, journalism, or management, but in finance.[11] The book, with a classy black cover and a foreword by Sir Paul Judge, is full of quotes on strategy by great men and refers more than any other one to the academic tradition, be it in a humoristic way when, in the final sample plan it exhibits, it describes a management team made of Machiavelli—the CEO, who "brings strategic insight which will help the company to gain market share . . ."—Karl Marx, Adam Smith, and Descartes (p. 308). But the academic ingredients of the guidebook are more than a matter of style. The advice given to entrepreneurs is indeed much more sophisticated than in other guidebooks. Breakeven analysis, for instance, is not only explained on the basis of the simple straight-line method, and no software is provided to which entrepreneurs could delegate

part of their work. Moreover, some elements of economic theory are introduced in the advice given to entrepreneurs, with a notable suggestion on how
to introduce marginal analysis in the plan, based on the abstract example of a
coconut seller—i.e., some sort of a Robinson Crusoe on the market.

> You certainly want to think about marginal analysis when you plan and
> run your business. The calculations are usually more complex than the ex-
> ample here, but the conclusions will hit you like a coconut falling from the
> palm tree. Remember that average costs are not static. Watch for them to
> jump about when the stall owner suddenly increases the rent. It is a rare—
> and advanced—business plan that includes much marginal analysis. Nev-
> ertheless, you may find it useful to say a word or two about marginal
> costs, not least to demonstrate that you understand costs and prices—and
> that you have them well under control. (Stutely, 2007, p. 238)

The microeconomics of production attempt, in a late effort, to have a performative effect on business planning practices.[12] But the caution of the author
in proposing this "complex" method is telling as to the actual distance
between empirical business planning methods, based on discreet accounting data, and the computational requirements of micro-economics.

However sophisticated economic and accounting methods may be, they
are not the only components of Stutely's "scientific method" for business planning. Another major element of this method is the empirical grounding of the
assumptions made in the plan. This is obvious when one looks at the

> Ten reasons why business plans fail at first glance: / 1. The presentation
> is too scruffy or to slick—it feels *false*. / 2. The text is too long, with *too
> many generalizations*, too much waffle. / 3. The text is too short, too weak
> and *vague*. / 4. Whatever the length, there are not enough *hard facts and
> details*. / 5. There are *errors of fact* (a major sin). / 6. Specific omissions
> suggest that vital skills, resources or knowledge are lacking. / 7. There is
> not enough *"what-if?" analysis?* (What if sales drop 10% ? Increase 10%
> if interest rates rise one-percentage-point?) / 8. The financial projections
> are *unreasonably* optimistic, especially if sales or cash flow improve un-
> realistically smoothly—without *seasonal variation or downward blips*. /
> 9. The plans are obviously produced to raise finance, *not for running the
> business*. / 10. The plan was produced by professional consultants, raising
> doubt about the *management's own skills*. (p. 259—my italics)

The errors to avoid are all related to unsatisfying references to the reality
underlying the plan. Put shortly, the main recommendation is "You have to
prove that your plan will work" (p. 279). And, just as Rich and Gumpert
had in the mid-1980s, many other guidebooks insist on this same necessary
empirical grounding of business plans.

> In writing a business plan, your 'thesis' isn't a complex theoretical state-
> ment. Instead, it is a simple thought: 'My idea for a (insert your concept

here) business is a profitable one.' Your research goal is to prove this statement accurate. If you cannot, then you need to rethink your idea and revise it. (Fullen and Podmorott, 2006: p. 175)

But how can one prove the future success of a new business? And how does this grounding articulate, in the plan, with accounting and—eventually—economic methods of formalization?

"THE BUSINESS PLAN IS DEAD"

The main requirement, as is obvious here, is for the entrepreneur to undertake "research." As Stutely puts it, it is to "know [one]self" and "know the world": "If you got this right, it is a downhill ride to business success. Now you can have fun in converting the effort to date into strategy" (p. 84). In this perspective, the market study is the part of the plan that ends up being "the real 'meat-and-potatoes' of [the] business plan," (Fullen and Podmoroff, 2006: p. 71) i.e. the main source for data, and especially numerical data, that is then to be worked upon in order to produce pro forma financial statements. But how may this data be used to plan ahead? *The ABC's of Writing Winning Business Plans* provides an answer to this question:

> If you are writing your plan for a new business venture, you really have no choice but to extrapolate. Yet that extrapolation will still be based on real data. Any number you put into your business plan needs to be backed up by research and/or expertise. . . . / Guessing can kill a plan. . . . The minute any of your numbers are called into question, your whole plan is called into question. Remember that financial readers are trying to decide whether or not they can trust your business to return their money. If they can't trust your figures, they can't trust you. (Sutton, 2005, p. 117)

There is no such thing, here, as mere "trust in numbers" (Porter, 2005): all numerical data must be "backed-up," and the practice of "top-down forecasting" itself is meant to respect that rule, by relying on factual assumptions.

> Top-down forecasting is planning for the future with the end in mind. It starts with your goals for three years out and backtracks the steps it will take to go there. You start with the big picture—the industry—and your goals within it. With your market share goal, you can predict your revenue. From there, you work your way down the table, filling in exact numbers where you can and making your best predictions where you can't. Still, there are no guesses. Even the advertising section (one of the most variable sections of your projection) can be worked out logically. You know where you stand with the competition and the industry norms. So you know if you will need to spend more or less than the norm in order to increase your piece of the pie. How much more is a little murkier, but

your marketing section analysis should be able to guide you. / Top down forecasting allows you to work your goals into your company's expectations of the future. It also allows for some spin, but keep it real. (Porter, 1995, pp. 38–39)

"Keeping it real" is a methodological requirement that should be respected during the planning process, but it is also a requirement in terms of presentation of the plan, where references should be made to all data that may help justify the argument, and where this data should actually be presented, in order to allow for verification by the readers of the plan. Such factual information is indeed expected in the

> Supporting Documents: . . . These are the records that back up the statements and decisions made in the three main parts of your business plan [i.e. the executive summary, the narrative part, and the financials]. As you are compiling the first three sections, it is a good idea to keep a separate list of the supporting documents you mention or that come to mind. Many of these documents will actually be needed as you write your plan so that you will have solid financial information to use in your projections. For instance, discussion of your business location might indicate a need for demographic studies, location maps, area studies, leases, etc. The information in the lease agreement will state the financial terms. Once you have the location, you will also know the square footage of your facility and be able to project other associated costs, such as utilities and improvements. . . . You can sort them in a logical sequence, add them to your writing copy, and be ready to add any new ones that become pertinent during the lifetime of your business (Pinson, 2005, p. 114).

In the end, as it is summarized in another guidebook, "a good business plan contains dreams and ideas backed by facts and figures presented in a standardized format" (Fullen and Podmoroff, 2006: p. 37). The exact nature of the "back-up" that is to be provided in the business plan is however a problem. Depending on the tolerance of the readers of the document to "extrapolation" from facts, the issue is to know whether the business plan should just be realistic, or actually real. If all assumptions made in the plan have to be attested by supporting data, then the plan is no more a plan, but the description of an existing business. There is indeed a tension towards the immediate actualization of the plan in the "back-up" norm of business planning, which tends to imply that filling in the planning forms means fulfilling the planned firm. If, for instance, to be able to justify the planned amount of a lease, the entrepreneur is asked to include in the plan a copy of the said lease, then this agreement must exist, and an actual place to let must have been found. And this performative effect of contemporary business planning norms also works the other way: the transformation of "dreams" about the future into paper acts as a first actualization which calls for further actualization. Focused as he is on the role and difficulties of writing, *The One Page Business Plan*'s author says it well:

The written word also produces a contract with yourself that results in immediate action. Haven't you found that if you make up a grocery list and leave it at home you almost always remember everything on the list? Many users of the *One Page Business Plan* report that as soon as they begin to write their action items—some of which they have been thinking about for years—they start to take action on them. I think it's magic! (Horan, 2006, p. 21)

This "magic" may however have doomed the business plan. Norms about the backing-up of the plan indeed became more present in business plan guidebooks after the "dot-com bubble" burst, in early 2000. Fast and risky investment in new ventures, sometimes based on the sole reading of their business plans, created a general suspicion against these, as well as a collective move towards more prudence in entrepreneurial finance. In this context, some authors went even further than reinforcing the back-up norm for business plans. David Gumpert, who had long been an advocate of "proof" in business plans, as we have shown, issued a new book in 2002 entitled *Burn Your Business Plan!,* in which he proposes

a new approach in which the written business plan has much less prominence, having been replaced by other means of inspiring confidence in tentative investors. / In the traditional approach, entrepreneurs seeking to raise money invariably began the process by contacting prospective investors and then following up with copies of their business plans. Today, entrepreneurs increasingly begin the process by launching their ventures in some form, and then conducting formal presentations to explain their vision. . . . As you can see, the business plan hasn't disappeared from the landscape, but rather has assumed a much different role in the process of financing and building a business. Instead of being tackled at the start of the business development process, it is left to later stages, after more critical tasks have been dealt with and the business is up and running in some form. This new role for the business plan reflects the fact that professional investors will no longer assume technology and other significant risk; they demand sales or similar customer confirmation before committing. (p. 5)

The rising paradox of the business plan would therefore be the following: the good plan would be the one that has already been—at least partially—realised. Because of this, and according to another new venture planning guidebook written around the same idea by a Silicon Valley entrepreneur, one could therefore conclude that *The Business Plan Is Dead* (Wofford, 2008).

CONCLUSION

The business plan, as "scientific" as its construction may be, raises more questions than the scientific methods used to describe the present or past worlds.

Like the construction of facts by scientists, the construction of plans by entrepreneurs stands in a tension between reduction and amplification (Latour,
1995). The formalization of a business plan, which implies the production of
synthetic charts, tables, summaries, and brief stories, is an extreme reduction
of the future venture which also allows it to circulate better, be compared to
others, and thus possibly enrol new members. But this double movement is
perturbed, in the case of business plans, because the facts they constitute are
what we called virtualities, or what Gabriel Tarde called, in a beautiful oxy-
moron, "future facts" (1901). The possibility for their empirical grounding are
therefore scarce, and this is why the business plan, now long stuck in a tension
between excessive unreality and immediate actualization, may be said dead.
No empirical evidence however comes to support this claim of a decline in
the production of business plans in the United States or anywhere else around
the world. New venture planning, in its different guises, wasn't born during
the dot-com era, as we have shown, and it seems to be still going strong after
that. In spite of all the issues it may raise, the business plan has indeed prolifer-
ated on the market for entrepreneurial finance, as a tool sufficiently efficient
in making supply and demand meet and eventually reach an agreement over
the future. And its success may be attributed precisely to its ability to "colonise
the future," (Giddens, 1991) not only by providing a means to represent this
future, but also by fostering the continuous actualization of the future during
the planning process itself.

NOTES

1. Information problems in venture capital investment have long been noticed
   by economists, be it when applying decision theory to venture capital decision making (Meade, N., 1978; Cooper and Carleton, 1979); in the study
   of the dynamics of borrower-lender relationships, and in the appraisal of
   the contribution of financial intermediation to the resolution of these problems (Chan, 1983). Efforts to provide models to describe these relationships have lead, more recently, to their description through the prisoner's
   dilemma (Cable and Shane, 1997) and agency theory (Kaplan and Stromberg, 2001; 2003).
2. For a sociology of the mediation operated by packaging on markets for tangible goods, see Cochoy 2002.
3. For a brief introduction to the history of venture capital, see Gompers 1994;
   Gompers and Lerner, 2001. On public programs for the funding of new ventures, see Noone and Rubel, 1970; Leicht and Jenkins, 1998.
4. *How to Organize and Operate a Small Business* by Kelley, and Lawyer
   (1955) is arguably the first guidebook on new venture formation, after those
   of the *Starting and Establishing* series that were edited in the 1940s by the
   Department of Commerce (e.g., US Bureau of Foreign and Domestic Commerce (1945). *Establishing and operating your own business*, Washington:
   US Government Printing Office). But a new surge in entrepreneurship guidebooks started in the 1970s (see, for instance, Dible, 1971; Mancuso and
   Baumback, 1975; Timmons, et al., 1977).
5. Ratio analysis based on the financial statements of existing firms was born in
   the early 20th century and, in spite of some debates, had long been accepted
   by business professionals by the seventies (Miller and Power, 1995).

6. A member of faculty in management at Northeastern University, in Boston, Jeffry Timmons described in this article the activities that were taking place in the *Institute for New Enterprise Development* he had participated in creating at the university in 1972. He would, a few years later, publish an entrepreneurship guidebook that we have already come across (Timmons and Smollen, 1977), before co-authoring another guidebook with David Gumpert, whom the reader will soon get to know better (Gumpert, D. E., and Timmons, J. A. 1982).

7. Moreover, new magazines, specifically focused on entrepreneurship issues, started to be published in the second half of the seventies (e. g., *Entrepreneur Magazine* in 1976, *Inc. Magazine* in 1979 . . .).

8. National Business Incubators Association (2008), "NBIA Remembers Joe Mancuso," http://www.nbia.org/resource_library/review_archive/0608_02.php (accessed on April 1, 2011).

9. Similar critiques against pre-formatted business plans also arose in more confidential spaces inside the venture capital industry. Georges F. Doriot, for instance, who is often considered as the inventor of modern venture capital and who thus contributed actively to the proliferation of business plans, wrote the following memo to his staff just before he retired: "Looking back over the last two or three years, there is a new expression which has arisen in the so-called "venture capital world." When a project comes in, when a man with an idea calls on us, it seems that we cannot wait to ask the question: Do you have a business plan? If not, why not? Where is your business plan? . . . It is fashionable. One must have a business plan. . . . The Business Plans I see, the ones we seem to like, look so perfect that they are superficial, misleading and ridiculous. I do know that we are all searching for slogans, for life belts, for anything which does not require hard, difficult thinking and hard work. We are drifting into laziness and complete inability to be imaginative and constructive. We analyze worthless documents and waste our time doing so. A computer could do the job!! I do not want to hear about the modern conception of a business plan" (Baker Library Historical Collections Department, Harvard Business School Archives, Arch. GA 19.1: Georges F. Doriot American Research and Development Papers (1946–1991), Box 2, Folder 17, "GFD advice and memos").

10. E.g., "*Create a network of Creativity Cafes around the world that are live and cyberspace networking salons featuring educational entertainment and electronic cyber theatre. A fun place where people gather for play and work; where creative people, using the marriage of art and state-of-the-art technology learn from each other and have a forum for showcasing their work*" (p. 34) or "*Build a successful local business furniture company that specializes in providing competitively priced furniture with superior service to companies with 10 to 50 employees*" (p. 35).

11. Richard Stutely, a British economist, held management or director positions at NatWest and at Her Majesty's (HM) Treasury, before becoming senior economist in two American investment banks, and later chief economist in a commercial bank. He is the author of various guidebooks on financial decision making.

12. The desired convergence of business planning practices with the micro-economics of production was also promoted at the same time, but in the reverse way, as a means to give empirical grounds to the teaching of economics (cf. DeBoer, 1998).

REFERENCES

Bangs, D. H. (1985). *Business Planning Guide: A Handbook to Help You Design, Write, and Use a Business Plan and a Financing Proposal Tailored to Your Specific Business Needs.* Dover: NH: Upstart Pub. Co.

Bangs, D. H., and Osgood, W. R. (1976). *Business Planning Guide: A Handbook to Help You Design, Write, and Use a Business Plan Tailored to Your Specific Business Needs*, Boston: Federal Reserve Bank of Boston.

Braudel, F. (1993). *Civilisation matérielle, économie et capitalisme (XVe-XVIIIe siècle). 2. Les jeux de l'échange*. Paris: Librairie générale française.

Boltanski, L., and Chiapello, E. (1999). *Le nouvel esprit du capitalisme*. Paris: Gallimard.

Cable D. M. & Shane S. (1997), "A Prisonner's Dilemma Approach to Entrepreneur-Venture Capitalist Relationships," *The Academy of Management Review*, 22(1), 142–176.

Chan Y.-S. (1983), "On the Positive Role of Financial Intermediation in Allocation of Venture Capital in a Market with Imperfect Information," *The Journal of Finance*, 38(5), 1543–1568.

Cochoy F. (2002). *Une sociologie du packaging ou l'âne de Buridan face au marché*. Paris: Presses Universitaires de France.

Cooper I. A. & Carleton W. T. (1979), "Dynamics of Borrower-Lender Interaction: Partitioning Financial Payoff in Venture Capital Finance," *The Journal of Finance*, 34(2), 517–529.

DeBoer D. R. (1998), "The Business-Plan Approach to Introductory Microeconomics," *The Journal of Economic Education*, 29(1), 54–64.

Dible, D. M. (1971). *Up Your Own Organization!* Santa Clara, CA: The Entrepreneur Press.

Fullen S. L., and Podmoroff, D. (2006). *How to Write a Great Business Plan for Your Small Business in 60 Minutes or Less*. Ocala, FL: Atlantic Publishing Group Inc.

Gevirtz, D. (1984). *Business Plan for America: An Entrepreneur's Manifesto*. New York: Putnam's.

Giddens, A. (1991). *Modernity and Self-Identity: Self and Society in the Late Modern Age*. Stanford, CA: Stanford University Press.

Giraudeau, M. (2010). Performing Physiocracy. Pierre Samuel Du Pont de Nemours, From Politics to Business. *Journal of Cultural Economy* 3(2), 225–242.

Gompers P. A. (1994), "The Rise and Fall of Venture Capital," Business and Economic History, 23(2), 1–26.

Gompers P. A. & Lerner J. (2001). "The Venture Capital Revolution." *The Journal of Economic Perspectives*, 15(2), 145–168.

Gumpert, D. E. (1990). *How to Really Create a Successful Business Plan: Featuring the Business Plans of Pizza Hut, People Express, Ben and Jerry's Ice Cream, Celestial Seasonings, Software Publishing*. Boston, MA: Inc. Pub.

Gumpert, D. E., and Timmons, J. A. (1982). *The Insider's Guide to Small Business Resources*. Garden City, NY: Doubleday.

Horan, J. (2006). *The One Page Business Plan: Start with a Vision, Build a Company*. Berkeley, CA: The One Page Business Plan Company.

Kaplan S. N. & Stromberg P. (2001). "Venture Capitalists as Principals: Contracting, Screening and Monitoring," *The American Economic Review*, 91(2), 426–430.

———. (2003). "Financial Contracting Theory Meets the Real World: An Empirical Analysis of Venture Capital Contracts," *The Review of Economic Studies*, 70(2), 281–315.

Karpik, L. (1989). L'économie de la qualité. *Revue Française de Sociologie*, 30(2), 187–210.

———. (1996). Dispositifs de confiance et engagements crédibles. *Sociologie du travail*, 4, 527–550.

———. (2010). *Valuing the Unique: The Economics of Singularities*. Princeton: Princeton University Press.

Katz, J. A. (2003). The Chronology and Intellectual Trajectory of American Entrepreneurship Education (1876–1999). *Journal of Business Venturing*, 18, 283–300.

Kelley, P. C., and Lawyer, K. (1955). *How to Organize and Operate a Small Business.* New York: Prentice-Hall.

Latour, B. (1995). The 'Pedofil' of Boa Vista—A Photo-Philosophical Montage. *Common Knowledge,* 4(1), 145–187.

Leicht, K. T. and Jenkins, J. C. (1998). "Political Resources and Direct State Intervention: The Adoption of Public Venture Capital Programs in the American States, 1974–1990," *Social Forces,* 76(4), 1323–1345.

Mancuso, J. R. (1974). How a Business Plan Is Read. *Business Horizons,* 33–42.

Meade, N. (1978), "Decision Analysis in Venture Capital," *Journal of Operational Research,* 29(1), 43–53.

Miller, P. and Power, M. (1995). "Calculating Corporate Failure," in Dezalay Y. & Sugarman D., *Professional Competition and Professional Power: Lawyers, Accountants and the Social Construction of Markets* (pp. 51–76). London: Routledge.

Miller, P. and Rose, N. (1992). Political Power Beyond the State: Problematics of Government. *British Journal of Sociology,* 43(2), 173–205.

Musselin, C., and Paradeise, C. (2002). La qualité: Dossier-débat. *Sociologie du travail,* 44, 255–287.

Noone, C. M. and Rubel, S. M. (1970), *SBICs: Pioneers in Organized Venture Capital.* Chicago, IL: Capital Pub. Co.

Osgood, W. R. (1980). *How to Plan and Finance Your Business.* Boston, MA: CBI Pub. Co.

Osgood, W. R., and Curtin D. P. (1984). *Preparing your business plan with Lotus 1-2-3.* Englewood Cliffs, NJ: Prentice-Hall.

Osgood, W. R., and Curtin, D. P. (1985a). *Preparing Your Business Plan with Symphony.* Englewood Cliffs, NJ: Curtin and London.

Osgood, W. R., and Maupin, J. D. (1985b). *Preparing Your Business Plan: Multiplan on the DEC Rainbow,* Burlington, MA: Digital Press.

Osgood, W. R., and Wetzel, W. E. J. (1977). A Systems Approach to Venture Initiation. *Business Horizons,* 42–53.

Pinson, L. (2005). *Anatomy of a Business Plan.* Chicago, IL: Kaplan Publishing.

Porter, T. M. (1995). *Trust in numbers : the pursuit of objectivity in science and public life.* Princeton, NJ: Princeton University Press.

Rich, S. R., and Gumpert, D. E. (1987). *Business Plans That Win $$$. Lessons from the MIT Enterprise Forum.* New York: Harper and Row.

Schumpeter, J. A. (1911). *The Theory of Economic Development.* Cambridge, MA: Harvard University Press.

Stutely, R. (2007). *The Definitive Business Plan: The Fast-Track to Intelligent Business Planning for Executives and Entrepreneurs.* Harlow, UK: Pearson Education Ltd.

Sutton G. (2005). *The ABC's of Writing Winning Business Plans: How to Prepare a Business Plan that Others Will Want to Read—and Invest In.* New York: Warner Business Books.

Tarde, G. (1901). L'action des faits futurs. *Revue de Métaphysique et de Morale,* 2, 119–137.

Technimetrics (1973). *The Business Plan Package.* New York: Technimetrics Inc.

Timmons, J. A. (1975). Guided Entrepreneurship. *Business Horizons,* 49–52.

Timmons, J. A., Smollen L. E., and Dingee A. L. M. (1977). *New Venture Creation: A Guide to Small Business Development.* Homewood, IL: R. D. Irwin.

Vesper, K. H. (1993). *Entrepreneurship Education.* Los Angeles, CA: UCLA Entrepreneurial Studies Center.

Williamson, O. E. (1986). *Economic Organization: Firms, Markets and Policy Control.* New York: New York University Press.

Wofford, J. (2008). *The Business Plan Is Dead: How To Raise Capital in the New Economy.* Fremont, CA: Level Six Partners.

11 "A Picture Tells more than a Thousand Words"

Losing the Plot in the Era of the Image

Yiannis Gabriel

"His paintings don't tell stories," says, Griet, the central character in Tracy Chevalier's *The Girl with the Pearl Earring*, apropos of Johannes Vermeer's works (Chevalier, 2001, p. 91). As if to demonstrate the girl's lack of imagination (or her lack of awareness of intertextuality), Chevalier contrived to write a highly compelling novel inspired by Vermeer's painting by the same title. The novel's central character is a girl whose family has fallen on hard times as a result of her father's loss of sight. Once a skilled painter of Delft tiles, he was blinded in a kiln explosion. Griet has been her father's eyes, reporting for him what she sees. The novel starts with Griet, chopping vegetables in the kitchen and arranging them on a board according to color. It is her sensitivity to color and her ability to organize through color that impresses the painter. He hires her, first as the family's domestic servant, later as his assistant, his muse, and, eventually, his model for the famous portrait.

Reading the numerous readers' reviews in the Amazon web pages, one concludes that for the majority Chevalier has succeeded brilliantly in 'capturing the essence of the painting.' Maybe, we should add, her success mirrors Vermeer's success in 'capturing the essence of his subject.' This success is only partially repeated by the film of the same title which, in spite of some beautiful imagery, does not quite capture the psychological subtleties of the novel.

Who would nowadays dispute that a painting, an image, or a photograph tells a story. "Every picture tells a story" has become a widely accepted platitude today. The expression can be traced to the opening chapter of Charlotte Brontë's *Jane Eyre*. The heroine of the book, looking at Bewick's *History of British Birds* on a rainy day, explains

> *Each picture told a story[italics added]*; mysterious often to my un-
> developed understanding and imperfect feelings, yet ever profoundly
> interesting: as interesting as the tales Bessie sometimes narrated on
> winter evenings, when she chanced to be in good humour; and when,
> having brought her ironing-table to the nursery hearth, she allowed
> us to sit about it, and while she got up Mrs. Reed's lace frills, and
> crimped her nightcap borders, fed our eager attention with passages

Figure 11.1 Girl with a pearl earring. Painting by Johannes Vermeer.

of love and adventure taken from old fairy tales and other ballads; or (as at a later period I discovered) from the pages of Pamela, and Henry, Earl of Moreland. (Brontë, Chapter 1, 2006, p. 11)

For Jane Eyre, the illustrations of Bewick's book evoked stories of ship-wrecks, solitary rocks, wind-swept promontories and the vast expanses of icy Nordic landscapes. Today, as academics we have come to view most if not all pictures as telling stories. Indeed few would dispute that any image, a building, a tattooed human body, or even the gleaming surface of an automobile tell stories? We have become accustomed to reading stories in the most unstory-like texts, to treat them perfectly seriously as if they were stories.

In this paper, I would like to probe and question this view, namely that pictures tell stories. Of course, there are numerous narrative paintings inspired by particular stories. In the genre of 'continuous narrative,' for example, several episodes from a particular narrative are depicted in the same picture, and the main characters appear several times in different capacities. Thus, a representation of the martyrdom of John the Baptist may include different scenes, including his birth, Salome's dance, the saint's incarceration, his beheading, and his head on a silver platter (Andrews, 1995). Yet, it is possible to argue, as some artists do, that their paintings tell no stories, or that they, as artists, do not seek to tell stories. Of course, no one can stop readers or writers from reading and writing stories inspired by such paintings. I shall argue, however, that, *the attempt to read a story in every picture, every image or indeed any meaningful text is symptomatic of an era which has lost its ability to tell and to listen to stories.* This is what I shall describe as *narrative deskilling.* Narrative deskilling involves the inability to develop narratives with individualized characters and plots that grip the imagination and generate meaning. I shall argue that treating every picture as a story is a consequence of this deskilling. Having lost the skill necessary to create, tell and listen to stories, we lapse into viewing every sensical text as story. "Every X tells a story," where X becomes virtually anything. Try, for instance, "symptom," "brand," "accident," "building," etc.

Further, I shall argue that, in a spectacle-centered and media-dominated culture, stories are transcended by mass-produced images, some of which assume iconic standing. Such images possess considerable emotional and rhetorical power and may even claim to 'tell a story.' My argument, however, is that a line should be drawn between stories with characters and plots told by individuals singly or jointly and images or 'photo-stories' which rely for their effect on very different processes. My argument does not lament narrative deskilling, nor does it look back nostalgically at some time when 'proper stories' were told around the family hearth. What it does is to use narrative deskilling as the starting point for a sketching of new sense-making patterns, which are becoming increasingly preponderant today but also for an appreciation of the enduring and compelling power of stories with characters and plots. I conclude by suggesting that in our times, narrative deskilling is matched by the development of new skills. What we have lost in our ability to construct stories with beginnings, middle, and ends, characters, and plots, we have gained in an ability to read signs, accepting ambiguity, and multivalence; the ability to withstand confusion and cacophony, to filter out relevant information from a huge bombardment of noise, to decode difficult or non-specific signs and to endure multiple plots, and multiple storylines without clear beginnings or ends. Maybe, I shall argue, there is no deskilling without corresponding reskilling.

The argument I will develop is not one that I expect will find easy acceptance. The weight of opinion today among numerous scholars researching discourses, narratives, and stories suggests that we inhabit a narrative universe, where storytelling is the principal or even the only way of making sense of the world. This is in a characteristic reversal of an earlier argument, which was to view modernity, with its totalizing narratives of science, ideology, law etc., as leading to the end of storytelling (Benedict, 1931; Gabriel, 2000). Late modernity, by contrast has rediscovered and celebrated stories and storytelling. In a characteristic passage, Novak has argued:

> The human being alone among creatures on the earth is a storytelling animal: sees the present rising out of a past, heading into a future; perceives reality in narrative form. (1975, pp. 175–176)

Narratives themselves are also exalted and celebrated, not in their modernist mega-forms, such as theories, ideologies and doctrines but in their highly individualized, personalized, and privatized mutations—the petits récits as against modernity's grands narratives. Thus, Hardy:

> We dream in narrative, daydream in narrative, remember, anticipate, hope, despair, believe, doubt, plan, revise, criticise, construct, gossip, learn, hate and love by narrative. (1968, p. 5)

Building on such narrativist premises, theorists in our time have developed an elaborate set of arguments regarding the narrative base of experience, our ongoing attempts to develop coherent life stories, the contestation and denial of such stories, and the living out of such stories. In these arguments, the word story becomes a verb, indeed a transitive verb, denoting the work that goes into emplotting different episodes of experience and different incidents and events of personal and social lives. Storying emerges as an ongoing sense-making effort through which identities, relations and actions assume shape and significance. David Sims, for instance, has argued eloquently that

> We lead storied lives; we are continuously producing storied versions of what is happening in our lives, as well as revising the way that we tell the stories of earlier parts of our lives. We also spend much time plotting and imagining the next chapter in our lives. (2003, p. 1197)

Sims captures well the reflexive quality of storying—the author of the story and the story's central character co-create each other. At every moment the storyteller creates a protagonist, whose predicaments redefine the storyteller. In telling the story of my life, I make sense of past events and create a person living in the present as a continuation of the story. It is in this way that experience becomes digested, meaningful, and the basis of identity.

> The narrative tradition in research grew up in the belief that storytelling and experience are not separable. Experience is only made available, through memory, when it is turned into a story. (Sims, 2003, p. 1197)

Storying work is not easy—Kearney likens it to the work of the midwife who delivers a baby.

> From the Greek discovery of human life (bios) as meaningfully interpreted action (praxis) to the most recent descriptions of existence as narrative temporality, there is an abiding recognition that existence is inherently storied. Life is pregnant with stories. It is a nascent plot in search of midwives. (2002, p. 130)

And Sims points out that the story is created against resistances, both from internal and external audiences.

> We create stories about ourselves and our situation, and then proceed to live out some of them. Some of the stories we create, however, are contested, denied or simply ignored by others. We are on the verge of living out a story which features a major victory, a pinnacle to our achievements, or a rescue of some deserving cause, when someone else shows total disdain for our narrative of our lives by walking roughshod over the story we are creating. (2003, p. 1196)

Many authors believe that in our times, a variety of circumstances conspire to make the storying of our lives particularly difficult. Thus, Boje:

> Some experiences lack that linear sequence and are difficult to tell as a 'coherent' story. Telling stories that lack coherence is contrary to modernity. Yet, in the postmodern condition, stories are harder to tell because experience itself is so fragmented and full of chaos that fixing meaning or imagining coherence is fictive. (2001, p. 7)

The view that storying has become especially hard in our times is highly developed in Richard Sennett's work. He argues that new capitalism with its emphasis on flexibility, opportunism, and the powerful illusions of choice and freedom fragment life's narratives, denying them the continuity and coherence enjoyed by the narratives of yesteryear (Sennett, 1998, p. 31). Along similar lines, Brown (1987) has argued that personal narratives become problematic in an era when private lives and public conduct become detached from each other. These authors agree, however, that the emplotment of lives continues as a pressing need and that unplotted experiences are the source of malaise and alienation.

Nothing escapes from this line of argument which ultimately equates meaning with narrative, not even scientific theories. In a tour de force of narrative argumentation, Czarniawska demonstrates that many scientific theories, for instance, Hirschman's *The Passions and the Interests: Political Arguments for Capitalism Before Its Triumph,* emerge themselves as stories, with characters, plots, turning points, and so forth. Theory is the distillation of scientific writing, it is the name that we give to the plots of scientific genres—"theory is the plot of a thesis" (Czarniawska, 2004, p. 125).

To summarize then a very wide but fairly cohesive body of theoretical discourse, it is argued that nothing or more specifically no meaning exists outside narrative.

1. Human life and experience is lived in a storied manner, i.e., people endeavor to fit their experiences into story-like patterns, in short to emplot them.
2. By placing incidents in story-like patterns, people make sense of their experiences and establish some coherence in a potentially chaotic and meaningless world.
3. This process is reflexive, in other words in constructing their stories, people create themselves as individuals with histories and identities, i.e., the telling of the story becomes itself part of the story being told.
4. The telling of stories is not easy, since such stories are contested, denied, or ignored by audiences, internal and external.
5. This process has become especially difficult in our times, because of the fragmented or even chaotic qualities of contemporary lives.

At this point a few qualifications and perhaps even a few definitions may be in order. Is there a point in adhering to a distinction between story and narrative? I find this distinction to be quite a useful one. It seems to me that many different genres of text have narrative qualities, such as timed sequences of events, motivated characters, predicaments, recognitions, and so forth. Narrative texts may include most novels and films, ballads and legends, epic poems, chronicles and historical accounts, and so forth. Some pictorial texts, such as narrative paintings and strip cartoons, have narrative qualities. Stories too are narratives, but I would argue that not all narratives are stories. Stories are particular types of narrative governed by their own 'regimes of truth' and (as I have sought to show elsewhere, Gabriel, 2004) by a unique form of narrative contract between author and audience. This contract generally allows the storyteller poetic licence in return for a narrative that is verisimilar, but at the same time, has a plot. The narrative contract between a storyteller and his or her audience is quite different from that between a filmmaker, an epic poet, a historian, a chronicler, and their respective audiences. This is an important point, given that what I want to argue is that a painter, an image-maker, a spectacle orchestrator, and so forth, engage in different relations with their audiences, which may not necessarily involve plots or verisimilitude at all. In short, that they operate within realms of experience that may be unstoried and non-narrative (even though academic readers and others may treat them as stories).

If not all narratives are stories, not all texts are narratives. What is NOT a narrative? A question. And an answer. A question IS NOT a narrative. What happened to the cat that drank the green ink out of the bottle? A question may invite or augur a story, but by itself it is not a story. Moreover, a question may be answered in other non-narrative ways. When did the queen die? Contrast the answers: "She died in the year 1901." And "She died of shock when she heard that her much loved poodle had suddenly died" (poodle = her husband).

What then is the limit of narrative? What is narrative's 'other'? For a long time, I thought that facts and information (including generalizations, lists, tables, recipes, etc.) are far removed from narrative, in as much as their loyalty lies predominantly with accuracy, inviting very different types of 'reading' from narratives and stories. "Water boils at 100 degrees Celsius," or "the battle of Waterloo took place in 1815" would count as such factual statements. Of course, as the numerous accounts of the battle of Waterloo testify, facts can feed rich narratives and stories. Yet, outside of 'plots,' context and contestation, facts remain just information.

Facts, however, are far from the only things that are not narratives. Let me try some different answers. A noise is not a narrative. A sound may constitute a narrative, but it is not a narrative. The sound of a voice telling the story of Cinderella is performing a narrative, but sound itself is not a narrative. Likewise, a musical score, for instance, Bach's *Saint Matthew Passion* or Bob Dylan performing the *Ballad of Hollis Brown* are narratives, but many musical scores and musical performances are not narrative. What can be said of sounds, can also largely be said of images. An image by itself is not a narrative. An image or a painting such as *The Judgment of Paris* by Cranach or by Rubens may under certain circumstances evoke a narrative or a story, may illuminate a story or may even offer an interpretation of a story, but it is not a story.

Images, like sounds and like facts, can assume diverse relations with narratives. For example, images can inspire or feature in narratives. In Chevalier's novel, for instance, the painting by Vermeer, its inspiration, composition and consequences, are the narrative's driving force. Alternatively, images can function as icons standing for well-known and well-understood narratives. Symbolic pictures, like Byzantine and Russian icons, neither tell a story nor re-interpret it for us. Instead, they represent a story or a particular scene from it. As representations, the core quality of icons is that they are based on fixed, non-arbitrary relations between signifier and signified, in which the sign reproduces (or imitates) some of the qualities it signifies. Of course, there are many paintings which challenge or dislocate the relation of the signifier and the signified, offering new insights or interpretations of existing stories, framing, portraying, and highlighting features of the scene in ways that suggest particular interpretations. Thus a difference between Caravaggio's image of *Salome With the Head of Saint John the Baptist* and a Byzantine representation of the event is that the former offers an interpretation, whereas the latter does not. Thus, great paintings and works of art can undoubtedly suggest new meanings and interpretations to a story, inviting us to think of the story afresh. They do not, necessarily, 'tell' stories.

Image is the generic word I use for a text that is appropriated visually without the help of an alphabet. An image of a person captured on a security camera is just this, an image. The image of a sunset I am looking at is just this, an image. Pictures are particular types of image that have been composed by an author, such as a painter or a photographer. Spectacles or shows, for their part, are complex associations of images and pictures, often moving ones, produced by museum curators, television, film or theatrical producers, and so forth. What I have recently come to realize is that in spite of our academic fascination with images still and moving, films, advertisements, television programs, and so forth, we have been generally blind to their essentially unstoried qualities. What we have failed to recognize is that more often than not, images do not invite incorporation into a story or a narrative, but act as stand-alone emotional triggers, stimulating desires, arousing fantasies, prompting associations with other images. My argument is not that images and pictures exist in a vacuum or that they inhabit a different universe from the universe of words. I would not agree with Foucault's (1966/1970) argument at the opening of *The Order of Things: An Archaeology of the Human Sciences* that "pictures cannot be put into words" (see also Spence, 1984). On the contrary, we often find ourselves translating images into words and words into images with greater or lesser success. We equally often learn to 'read' images and words simultaneously, as we do in most drama and movies. An image of a happy person uttering an apology is very different from that of a glum face articulating the same words. As an opera lover, I recognize that music, words, and images can form a powerful discursive cocktail. What I am arguing, is that increasingly we, not as (discourse-) theorists but as spectators, come to appropriate images with or without words, incorporating them in our experience without necessarily seeking to turn them into narratives. As our daily universe has become saturated with images, jumping at us from our television sets, our magazines and newspapers, our computer screens and our digital cameras, our advertising billboards, and our shop windows, we have mostly given up trying to fit them into stories and have learned to accept them as spectacle pure and simple, pleasing, or annoying to the eye, evoking, prompting, comforting, upsetting, entertaining, or irritating. They are mostly part of a spectacular rather than a narrative universe.

The idea that we live in an era saturated by spectacle in which image reigns supreme is of course not new. Parodying Marx, Guy Debord opened his situationist manifesto with:

> In societies where modern conditions of production prevail, all life presents itself as an immense accumulation of *spectacles*. Everything that was directly lived has moved away into representation. (1977, paragraph 1)

Allowing for the obvious hyperbole, Debord's premise seems to be even more powerful today than in the 1960s when he made it the basis of his then fashionable critique. Numerous theorists, including Bauman, Ritzer, and Baudrillard, have since argued that spectacle has become the primary type of experience in late modernity, dominating every aspect of our public and private lives. Spectacle liquefies most forms of social exchange, colonizing politics, sport, religion, education, and so forth. What has changed since the situationist critique is the more nuanced evaluation that we accord spectacle, the less unequivocal equation of spectacle with passivity and stupefaction. Inspired by Bauman, Ritzer (1999), for instance, has argued that spectacle has led to a re-enchantment of the world in late modernity's cathedrals of consumption. Shopping malls, glass buildings, tourist resorts, sports venues, and theme parks, are all minutely planned and orchestrated shows, with spectators themselves becoming part of the display. Immense amounts of money are spent in advertising and packaging, films and television shows, magazines, and printed images. Spectacle becomes the archetypal experience of our time, offering "the promise of new, overwhelming, mind-boggling or spine-chilling, but always exhilarating experience" (Bauman, 1997, p. 181).

Spectacle stimulates every kind of emotional experience—horror, joy, anger, compassion, nostalgia, and so forth. Baudrillard who has pushed the argument furthest argues that we live in an era where only the spectacular counts as real—in short the dominant regime of truth is the regime of the simulacrum. He chillingly suggests that

> other people's destitution becomes our adventure playground . . . we are the consumers of the ever delightful spectacle of poverty and catastrophe and of the moving spectacle of our own efforts to alleviate it . . . when we run out of disasters from elsewhere or when they can no longer be traded like coffee or other commodities, the West will be forced to produce its own catastrophe for itself. . . . When we have finished sucking out the destiny of others, we shall have to invent one for ourselves. (Baudrillard, 1996, pp. 67ff)

Images then, like narratives, have their own regimes of truth. We respond differently to a painting, a cartoon, an advertisement and a photograph.

Some of these regimes may mirror those to which we subject narratives. We may, in other words ask the same questions of an image as we ask of a narrative: "Is it an accurate representation?" "Does it 'work?'" "Does it evoke another image?" "Has someone orchestrated it to create a specific effect?" and so forth. In many cases, the ways we answer such questions in relation to images are similar to the ways we answer them in relation to stories. For example, most advertising images, just like most advertising stories, are known to be idealized, exaggerated, and contrived, i.e., the result of careful doctoring, touching up, etc. Yet, at some level they are felt to be true. As Campbell has argued, such images are illusions, relying on our "ability to treat sensory data 'as if' it were 'real' whilst knowing that it is indeed 'false.' . . . It is this 'as if' response which is at the heart of modern hedonism" (1989, p. 82). Other images, are recognised as 'representations' of actual events, triggering a wide range of unstoried emotions which supplant moral judgement in what MacIntyre described as emotivism (MacIntyre, 1981). In this way, we treat images not as mere surfaces hiding underlying depths or 'capturing' a moment or an event. Instead, we use images to create reality, to define events, to constitute the world in which we inhabit. Images constitute many of our core experiences of the world and many of our core memories. Far from constantly constituting our lives as continuous narratives, I would argue that most of us, most of the time accept our lives as disorderly sets of photographic flashbacks, which have a disconcerting tendency of arriving uninvited to our consciousness, posing questions, evoking emotions and, occasionally, triggering off stories.

A few theorists have noted that as our culture becomes more ocular-centric, i.e., dominated by spectacles and images appropriated and experienced through the eye, many of our theories have become ocular-phobic (Jay, 1993; Kavanagh, 2004). We tend to assume that images are produced in the same way as narratives, are consumed in the same way as narratives and work in the same way as narratives. The idea of a text steamrolls those qualities that make each text unique, suggesting that every text is *read* in the same manner. We read our newspapers, we read the screens on our computers, we read photographs, and we read virtually any material object.

In a sense, it is perfectly appropriate to 'read' any cultural artefact that carries meaning. And it is perfectly true that images carry meanings. But as the anthropologist Grant McCracken argues the fact that images and objects may carry powerful symbolism does not alone turn them into stories (1988, p. 69f). Material culture cannot express the same nuance as language, it cannot generate plots, and it cannot portray reversals of fortune and can only at best create ambiguous characters. Of course, different images and spectacles are invested with symbolism; this is where the power of brands resides. But this symbolism, whether metaphoric or metonymic, is far from the symbolism of stories and narratives, with plots and characters.

As academics, some of us spend a lot of our time 'reading' literary or academic works. We may also spend much time 'reading' other artifacts crucial to our profession—images, documents, photographs, etc. We have lately started writing a lot about how people read, and this is something about which we know a lot, since we do it a lot. But we are making a mistake if we assume that everyone reads like us or indeed that we read everything the same way. Following the work of Eco and Rorty, for example, Czarniawska has done some extremely interesting work on the way we read texts, showing that both literary narratives and scientific monographs can be read in a 'semantic' or a 'semiotic' way (Czarniawska, 1997, 1999, 2004). In her own work, she offers several brilliant examples of reading. Hers is a high-caliber semiotic reading, in contrast to naïve or semantic readings, which are content with establishing the meaning of a text.

But are these two ways of reading the only possible ones or even the dominant ones? I would contend that even academics have different ways of reading texts—a student's artless essay is read differently from a paper under review for a prestigious journal or indeed a paper published by a prestigious journal. I would, in fact argue, other forms of reading exist— for instance, 'opportunistic' reading which neither seeks to discover what a text says (semantic reading) nor how a text comes to say what it says (semiotic text), but whether the text contains any particular element that may be useful for some other agenda. Consider too the purposeful reading we engage in when we seek a number in a telephone directory. Or indeed skim reading, which I suspect is more common among academics that either semiotic or semantic reading, when we just let our eye drift along the written page, letting it 'wash over us,' almost subliminally picking up some pieces of information. Close semiotic reading of theories, narratives, and images may be one way of engaging with them, but it is not the only or even the main one. The skills required for such reading take much time to develop and the results they yield are not consistently effective, as evidenced by clumsy interpretations and ridiculous inferences drawn by 'wild' or 'inexperienced' readers (Spence, 1984).

If written text can be read in many different ways depending on one's skills, one's circumstances, one's motives and the qualities of the texts themselves, other texts can be read in many different ways too. We will read an artistic masterpiece differently from a photograph on the front page of a newspaper or from the image on an advertising poster. The fact that, as theorists, we interrogate images and narratives in similar ways is a reflection of our own professional habits rather than the qualities of images and narratives themselves. In fact, I would argue that images and narratives do not 'work' in the same way. As spectators (rather than as theorists) most of the time we do not interrogate images, but like everybody else we let them wash over us, reading them almost subliminally. In our spectacle-centered culture, most of the time, people do not seek to emplot the image or the spectacle—but rather appropriate them visually. Our relation to image and spectacle is not logo-centric but ocular-centric, not trying to make sense of image through some notion of plot, unfolding story, and eventual conclusion, but as self-contained flashes to be read, experienced, and decoded in distinctly different ways from the ways stories and narratives are read, experienced, and decoded.

One of the most interesting differences in the ways in which images and narratives work concerns timing. An effective image can work almost instantaneously and subliminally, whereas an effective narrative, excepting one-liners, may require rather more time to unfold. An image may create a powerful emotion in a fraction of the time that a story can. The expression on a person's face, the tensions in their body, the lighting, and the perspective, can instantly communicate a mood, an emotion, or a moral tone. Images are often appropriated intertextually, by reference to other images.

But I would contend that the major difference between image and narratives and, in particular stories, lies in the *plot*. In his dazzling analysis of tragic plots, Aristotle famously identified three core features: (a) Peripeteia, i.e., the reversal of fortune (e.g., from happiness to misfortune or from being healthy to being sick); (b) Discovery or recognition (anagnorisis), i.e., movement from ignorance to knowledge, whereby the protagonists come to realize the true significance of events, accidents, omens, identities, and so forth; and (c) Suffering (pathos), the action of a destructive or painful nature, such as the perpetration of violence, the experience of physical or emotional pain and so forth. Aristotle rightly insists that this third ingredient of the plot, suffering, is the least significant, and rightly so. A man being constantly beaten up may be a horrible and disturbing spectacle or situation, but it is hardly a story. Prometheus bound on the Caucasus and Sisyphus pushing the rock up the mountain, by contrast, are highly tragic plots, since they entail both peripeteia (reversal from former glories) and recognition. And yet, it is suffering, this least significant of the plot figures that paintings, photographs, and other pictorial representations can 'imitate' rather than peripeteia and recognition. I would argue therefore that it is wrong to accuse our culture of gratuitous portrayals of violence—in a spectacular culture—this is the part of plot that can be portrayed visually.

Nor should it be thought that because image cannot portray peripeteia and recognition, it is less symbolically charged or less powerful that a story. On the contrary, in our spectacular culture it is often said that "a picture tells more than ten thousand words." It is interesting to contrast this cliché with the earlier one "Every picture tells a story." Although falsely ascribed to an old Chinese proverb, the expression was itself the product of high modernity with its spectacular, image-driven qualities appearing for the first time, according to my *Concise Oxford Dictionary of Proverbs*, in the 1920s. It was high modernity with its photographs and moving pictures, with its artificial lights and new forms of mass entertainment, and with its questioning of plots, characters, and narrative conventions that dislodged storytelling from its privileged position in the narrative universe signalling the coming hegemony of the image.

Narrative deskilling was part of a wider range of deskillings brought about by high modernity, which include undoubtedly the Taylorist deskilling, but also deskilling in a wide range of domestic, social, and political contexts. Why learn the violin to perform Beethoven's *Kreutzer Sonata*, when we can readily experience it, enjoy it, or discard it by listening to a recording of it? Why learn to cook and risk many disappointments when Marks and Spencer's will reliably provide high-quality meals with which to impress our friends? Why learn to weave when machines produce high-quality woven materials? And, for the purposes of the present argument, why learn to tell stories, weaving plots, when stories are available in every type of medium? And more importantly, when stories are far outshone and outsped in their ability to stimulate emotion, trigger symbolism, and change minds than photographs, images, and movies. Why develop stories of how beautiful or how powerful one is when one can invest in cosmetic surgery and expensive cars? Choosing a cosmetic surgeon, learning to program a digital versatile disc (DVD) player, or to use a digital camera, being able to play computer games on the Internet, and pressing keys with millisecond precision while also preparing tomorrow's homework, these are a few of the skills that have replaced the old ones.

Many of the old skills involved patient application, concentration, and slow learning. By contrast, the skills we acquire today involve speed, multi-tasking, short bursts of concentration, and quick gratification. This can be seen most clearly in the case of stories. If quick gratification has supplanted the skills entailed in the telling of stories, it has also supplanted the skills in patiently listening to stories of others, waiting for little clues regarding the imminence of peripeteia, or recognition. Instead, we allow images, noises, tastes, and sensations to wash over us. Even movies, which are capable of enormous narrative pyrotechnics, increasingly turn into visual and sound pyrotechnics, in the words of the great Greek filmmaker Theodoros Angelopoulos, treating their audience as shooting targets on which to practice.

Quick gratification is what most of us most of the time are after, and quick gratification can be obtained by simply seeing, listening or speed-reading. But quick gratification requires skills of its own. This is I think where late modernity has equipped us with remarkable new skills. These include

- learning to filter out much that is irrelevant noise and focusing on what creates a memorable emotional experience
- learning to tolerate uncertainty, lack of plot, and absence of closure
- learning to cope with pluri-vocality, with ill-defined characters and ambiguous moral messages
- learning to juxtapose, compare, and criticize
- learning to live experiences with ambiguous or opaque meanings, without closure
- learning to enjoy puzzles without permanent solutions

The key question that confronts us much of the time is not what Barbara Czarniawska suggests "What does this text say?" nor indeed "How does this text say it?" but rather "Is this a text?" and "Does it matter if it isn't?"

When I first started to develop the argument presented here, the gruesome pictures of Iraqi prisoner abuse at the Abu Ghraib prison and elsewhere were published, first on CBS, then Washington Post and the New Yorker and then they saturated the world media and cyberspace. Film of the beheading of an American hostage circulated on the Internet. The dread and horror of the pictures paralyzed my thinking processes for quite some time before raising age-old but still burning questions of morality, and politics, and colonial relations—they also, however, seemed to offer ample confirmation for both of the old clichés that "a picture tells more that a thousand words" and "every picture tells a story." Each picture of prisoner abuse had far greater effect than personal testimonies by witnesses and stories of prisoner abuse, which had been circulating for some time previously and also official reports that confirmed that the horrors portrayed by the pictures were no aberrations but endemic and systematic.

What I came to realize is that the images themselves told no stories, but rather acted as anti-stories, in two distinct ways. First, they torpedoed official narratives according to which the United States (US) and their allies, having failed to identify any weapons of mass destruction in Iraq, legitimated the invasion and subsequent occupation of the country by presenting these events as aimed at removing an abhorrent dictator and his callous regime with its record of human rights abuses from power. The symbolism of abuse being perpetrated by Americans and their allies in the very prison where Saddam Hussein's had tortured his victims is too obvious—different regimes, same prisons. In this way, the images acted as 'killer-facts' of the official narratives.

But images of prisoner abuse also functioned as anti-stories in a more radical way—they confirmed that stories are no longer a match for images in creating a climate of public opinion. As long as images of prisoner abuse have not leaked out of Guantanamo Bay detention camps, horror stories to former detainees may be ignored or discredited. It is not the story that has power as long as it can be dismissed as propaganda, exaggeration, or allegation. The image, however, even when contested (as in the case of photographic evidence of prisoner abuse by the British Royal Lancashire regiment) is incontestable, evidence of its hegemony in our times over any other type of text.

We are now deep in the era of spectacle. Some of us, not yet narratively deskilled or fighting a rear-guard action against narrative deskilling, may seek to interpret, deconstruct, or narrate the images that assault our senses. But we deceive ourselves to believe that we live our lives through narratives, that we routinely infuse it with meaning through stories or that we seek pleasure and fun in tales. To be sure, in the course of each day, we encounter numerous narrative fragments, still-born stories, opinions, fancies, and so forth. Occasionally, we encounter a story whose plot moves us, which 'resonates' with us. Swamped by images, pictures, and spectacles, we are more likely than not to forget it in a matter of days or weeks and quite unlikely to retell it to anyone. Newspapers peddle their own stories liberally supported by pictures, while around the clock newscasts urge us to stay with the "unfolding story" while excited reporters seek to keep our attention with liberal doses of opinion, speculation and interpretation. These are constantly interrupted by advertisements, which interject their own images or story fragments into our consciousness. Our consciousness is now saturated with image, and our memories are to a large extent visual ones. As Susan Sontag put it recently:

> The memory museum is now mostly a visual one. Photographs have an insuperable power to determine what people recall of events. . . . To live is to be photographed, to have a record of one's life, and therefore, to go on with one's life, oblivious, or claiming to be oblivious, to the camera's non-stop attentions. But it is also to pose. To act is to share in the community of actions recorded as images. . . . Events are in part designed to be photographed. (Sontag, 2004, pp. G2–G3)

Allow me to offer you one last illustration from the memory museum. This is a picture that many of you may have seen and may still remember. I wonder if you can guess how many years ago this picture was taken. The picture, known as *The Madonna From Bentalha*, was taken by the Algerian photographer Hocine who was awarded the prize for the best World Press Photo of 1997. The photograph is one that remained imprinted in my memory since then. It took me quite a long time to trace it on the Internet and my pleasure, if I can use such a word about such a picture, of finding it was considerable. My pleasure was even greater, when I discovered the story behind the picture, told by a reporter from *The Copenhagen Post*:

> On February 13 the Algerian photographer Hocine was awarded the prize for the best World Press Photo of 1997. The story behind the photo was of an Algerian woman grieving for her eight children killed in a massacre. A few days after the award was given the French press agency AFP and the organisation World Press Photo announced that in fact, the woman was grieving for her one brother and not her children. Eight months on, with the World Press Photo exhibition currently showing in Øksnehallen in Copenhagen, somehow the wrong story managed to be placed with the award winner photo, renewing the debate about the link between image and story.

The newspaper Politiken, which has arranged the World Press Photo '98 exhibition here, was quick to acknowledge its mistake. "Unfortunately we overlooked the disclaimer of the original caption text when we arranged the exhibition. It is Politiken's fault. I want to stress that neither World Press Photo nor Øksnehallen are to blame," said Søren Rud, footage manager at Politiken.

The mistake was pointed out by a journalist from another newspaper, Aktuelt. Rasmus Lindboe had visited the woman in Algeria and says that the photo, titled The Madonna From Bentalha, has destroyed her life. According to Lindboe, the woman feels humiliated and abused by the media, and that the photograph had caused her to be abandoned by her husband. She also lives in fear of her life, afraid that the authorities or religious fundamentalists will blame her for the bad publicity created by the Bentalha massacre (22 Sept. 1997).

The row about the truth of the story behind the photo has raised questions about the power of news pictures. The photo won the award because of its image of a grieving woman, and was a true representation of sorrow and mourning. In this way, the director of the World Press Photo Foundation, Árpád Gerecsey, stands by the prize-winning picture. "It is a very strong picture of a woman in grief. The photo documents that World Press Photo represents high quality photography," said Gerecsey to Politiken last week.

(*The Copenhagen Post online,* http://www.cphpost.dk/get/56475.html)

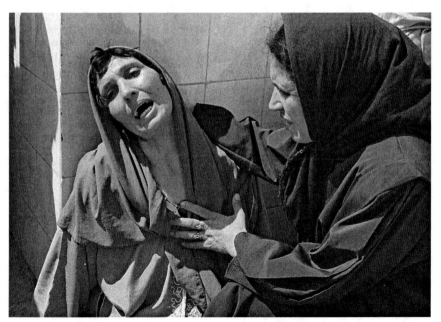

Figure 11.2   The Madonna from Bentalha. Photography by Hocine Zaourar.

Who now remembers the struggle whose tragic outcome the picture 'captures?' Who remembers the woman? Who remembers the facts, the story, the history?

For those interested, here is an account from the Amnesty International Web site:

In 1997, the civilian population has been targeted in an unprecedented manner. Thousands of men, women, children and elderly people have been slaughtered, decapitated, mutilated or burned alive in their homes. Babies and elderly people have been hacked to death. Pregnant women have been disembowelled. Most of these massacres were committed around the capital in the Algiers, Blida and Medea regions—in the most heavily militarized part of the country—and often near army and security forces barracks. Many massacres, often lasting hours, took place only a few hundred metres away from army and security forces' barracks.

Hundreds of men, women, children and even babies, were massacred in Rais and Bentalha, a few kilometres south of the capital, Algiers, on 28 August and 22 September, respectively. Both Rais and Bentalha are virtually surrounded by army barracks and security forces outposts, and survivors of the Bentalha massacre have reported that military troops with armoured vehicles were stationed a few hundred metres away as the massacre was taking place.

The massacres lasted for hours; yet despite the screams of the victims, sound of gunshots, flames and smoke from the burning houses, the security forces stationed nearby never intervened to come to the rescue of the victims, nor to arrest those responsible for the massacres, who got away on each occasion. In Beni Messous, near the most important barracks and security forces centre of the capital, more than 60 civilians were massacred. Neighbours telephoned the security forces who refused to intervene saying the matter was within the mandate of the gendarmerie.

Such testimonies add further weight to reports that armed groups who carried out massacres of civilians in some cases operated in conjunction with, or with the consent of, certain army or security forces units.

The Algerian authorities blame the massacres on the GIA (Groupe islamique armé—Armed Islamic Group) and other such groups, in the same way as they also blame other killings and abuses committed in the past five years on these groups. However, they have consistently failed to investigate, or to allow others to investigate, killings and other abuses blamed on both armed groups and security forces.

Armed groups, calling themselves "Islamic groups" have also continued to deliberately and arbitrarily kill civilians, often targeting the most vulnerable, including women and children, or carrying out indiscriminate bomb attacks in public places. Among those targeted by such groups are people from all walks of life, including relatives of members of the security forces, civil servants, journalists, artists, youths who had completed the compulsory military service, and people whom they accuse of being supporters of the government. In addition to killing civilians armed groups have also been responsible for abductions and torture, including rape, and for issuing death threats to individuals and groups of people.

It is time to return to our opening example. A painting of a young girl with a pearl earring is staring us sideways. Her lips are moist, slightly parted. A well-known painting by a notoriously unprolific painter. One that came to prominence as a result of an engaging novel and then a Hollywood film. It is now visited in its home by millions of visitors, intent on experiencing the original, having been moved by Chevalier's book. An Amazon reviewer of the novel, writes:

> I was attracted to this book for one reason. I was at the Maurithuis Museum at the Hague in the Netherlands in 1996 and saw Vermeer's "Girl with a Pearl Earring" and "A View of Delft" (both pictured on the book's dust jacket) in person. They are the most unforgettable paintings I have ever seen. Vermeer's paintings are incredibly hypnotic, drawing us into a time and place that no longer exists. By virtue of thousands of brush strokes, we are pulled into a time warp which places us into a scene the same surreal way that an old photograph does (Kusumoto, 2004).

The painting draws us indeed into a distant world. We are drawn into the world of a girl who has sat patiently for hours while a painter carefully and patiently lavished his brush strokes on the canvas. As a deliberate pose, it may strike us as anticipating our world of posing, images, and photo-stories. But such an interpretation would be very naïve. Griet's world is a very different world from ours. We can only surmise what such a world might have been like. But as numerous commentators have noticed, this is a world of stillness. It is a world whose tranquillity should not be confused with peace, and whose orderliness should not be confused with order. But it is a universe apart from the noisy, clamorous, and spectacular world of ours.

REFERENCES

Amnesty International (1997). "Algeria: Civilians caught in a spiral of violence amidst the indifference of the international community" News Service 189/97 http://www.amnesty.org/en/library/asset/MDE28/035/1997/en/20304a24-f884-11dd-b378-7142bfbe1838/mde280351997en.pdf (last accessed March 2011)

Andrews, L. (1995). *Story and Space in Renaissance Art: The Rebirth of Continuous Narrative.* Cambridge, England: Cambridge University Press.

Baudrillard, J. (1996). *The Illusion of the End.* Cambridge, England: Polity Press.

Bauman, Z. (1997). *Postmodernity and Its Discontents.* Cambridge, England: Polity Press.

Benedict, R. (1931). Folklore, *The Encyclopaedia of the Social Sciences*, Vol. 6. New York: Longman.

Boje, D. M. (2001). *Narrative Methods for Organizational and Communication Research*. London: Sage.

Brontë, C. (2010/1847). *Jane Eyre*. London: Penguin Books.

Brown, R. H. (1987). *Society as Text: Essays on Rhetoric, Reason and Reality*. Chicago: University of Chicago Press.

Campbell, C. (1989). *The Romantic Ethic and the Spirit of Modern Consumerism*. Oxford, England: Macmillan.

Chevalier, T. (2001). *The Girl with the Pearl Earring*. London: Plume.

Czarniawska, B. (1997). *Narrating the Organization: Dramas of Institutional Identity*. Chicago: University of Chicago Press.

———. (1999). *Writing Management: Organization Theory as a Literary Genre*. Oxford, England: Oxford University Press.

———. (2004). *Narratives in Social Science Research*. London: Sage.

Debord, G. (1977). *Society of the Spectacle*. Detroit, MI: Black and Red.

Foucault, M. (1966/1970). *The Order of Things: An Archaeology of the Human Sciences*. New York: Vintage Books.

Gabriel, Y. (2000). *Storytelling in Organizations: Facts, Fictions, Fantasies*. Oxford, England: Oxford University Press.

———. (2004). The narrative veil: Truth and untruths in storytelling. In Y. Gabriel (Ed.), *Myths, Stories and Organizations: Premodern narratives for our times* (pp. 17–31). Oxford, England: Oxford University Press.

Hardy, B. (1968). Towards a Poetics of Fiction: An Approach Through Narrative. *Novel, 2*, 5–14).

Jay, M. (1993). *Downcast Eyes: The Denigration of Vision in Twentieth-Century French Thought*. Berkeley: Univeristy of California Press.

Kavanagh, D. (2004). Ocularcentrism and Its Others: A Framework for Metatheoretical Analysis. *Organization Studies, 25*(3), 445–464.

Kearney, R. (2002). *On Stories*. London: Routledge.

Kusumoto, D. (2004) "Linking the Tangible to a Story We'd Like to Believe . . ." http://www.amazon.com/review/RO7718STCJFAU (last accessed March 2011).

MacIntyre, A. (1981). *After Virtue*. London: Duckworth.

McCracken, G. (1988). *Culture and Consumption: New Approaches to the Symbolic Character of Consumer Goods and Activities*. Bloomington: Indiana University Press.

Novak, M. (1975). 'Story' and 'Experience.' In J. B. Wiggins (Ed.), *Religion as Story*. New York: Harper and Row.

Ritzer, G. (1999). *Enchanting a Disenchanted World: Revolutionizing the Means of Consumption*. Thousand Oaks, CA: Pine Forge Press.

Sennett, R. (1998). *The Corrosion of Character: The Personal Consequences of Work in the New Capitalism*. New York: Norton.

Sims, D. (2003). Between the Millstones: A Narrative Account of the Vulnerability of Middle Managers' Storying. *Human Relations, 56*(10), 1195–1211.

Sontag, S. (2004, May 24). What Have We Done? *The Guardian*, pp. G2–G3.

Spence, D. (1984). *Narrative Truth and Historical Truth: Meaning and Interpretation in Psychoanalysis*. New York: Norton.

Afterword
Concluding Reflections: Imagining Business

Michael Lynch

I am grateful to Paulo Quattrone and the other editors for inviting me to write this brief commentary.[1] I do not intend to give an overview of common themes running through the many and varied chapters in the volume. Nor do I intend to write an 'underview' that purports to identify the background assumptions or common motives that underlie the chapters. Instead, I will briefly reflect upon the idea of 'imagining business,' on the basis of my continuing interest in practices and textual devices for rendering images in the natural and social sciences.

My own research has no direct connection to the fields of business and management. My home field of science and technology studies (STS) draws from philosophical, historical, and socio-cultural research on science, technology, and medicine. My disciplinary background is in sociology—specifically, ethnomethodology, the study of the routine production and organization of social life. Harold Garfinkel, the founder of ethnomethodology, is most widely known for his 'breaching experiments' systematic efforts to disrupt of 'business as usual' in order make tacit commitments and their associated practices visible. Consistent with that line of research, my work closely examines practices and technologies through which scientific phenomena are made visible and accountable (in a broad sense of being intelligible, sensually accessible, and demonstrable). Though I tend not to induce trouble deliberately into such practices, I find the regular emergence of trouble within such practices to illuminate 'usual business' that otherwise is likely to be taken for granted (so, in that sense, I have been studying 'business').

My interest in visualization goes back to research on microscopy and astronomy;[2] and most recently has been renewed in a study of nanoscience and nanotechnology. In that work, I pay close attention to how researchers produce 'renderings' of objects of study in order to make them visible, intelligible, and quantifiable. Rendering practices are material, in the sense that they produce *data* by working with biological specimens, chemical substances, and physical energies. To use a crude analogy, we can think of data as being like food—a cultural object created through organized, often industrialized, sequences of practice that start with 'raw' materials. As we know from food manufacture, the products we find on supermarket

shelves are so thoroughly bound up with histories of cultivation and manufacture that it is virtually impossible to trace them back to 'raw' or 'natural'
origins. Culturing toward manufacture starts very early in the game. To
cite a classic example, in his magnum opus on industrial mechanization,
Siegfried Giedion observes that the first assembly line that used overhead
rails for passing objects through a sequence of fixed work-stations was not
Henry Ford's assembly line, but the "disassembly line" of the 19th-century
slaughterhouse (Giedion, 1948). Efforts to implement standardized and
automated procedures in the slaughterhouse encountered the problem that
animal carcasses did not come in standard shapes and sizes. Such variability has partly been overcome, not only through innovation with rendering
machinery and processes, but also by selective breeding that designs the
carcass for the processes that render it into "food". A similar point can be
made about the chains of laboratory practice and associated instrumen-
tation that produce data from systematically inbred laboratory mice and
other model organisms, purified chemicals, and rectified energy sources.

Like all analogies, this one between food and data has its limits, but it
can encourage us to think that business studies may not be so far removed
from studies of science. Business studies have distinctive subject matter,
and are not just another field for applying STS ideas. Although I am not
very familiar with the field, I see some potential for those of us from STS to
learn from studies in this volume about what we have been talking about,
all along. I'll briefly mention a couple of areas that seem especially promising. These have to do with accountability and imagining.

ACCOUNTABILITY AND CREATING
SPACES FOR NUMBERS

In standard English usage, accountability has to do with responsibility and
governance: the effort to justify individual and organizational decisions
and actions by reference to rules, laws, and other formal standards and
expectations. Garfinkel gave the term a different twist when he proposed
that ethnomethodological studies would "analyze everyday activities as
members' methods for making those same activities visibly-rational-and-
reportable-for-all-practical-purposes" (1967, p. vii). Although this definition may seem opaque at first glance, one way to begin to understand it is
to think of the connection to the work of managing *accounts*, as in double-
entry bookkeeping for a business or other organization. In fact, according
to a biographical essay on Garfinkel, his conception of accounting derived
remotely from a business course on "theory of accounts" that he took in his
youth at University of Newark in preparation for going into the furniture
business with his father. The content of the course could just as well have
been named "qualitative accounting," as it had to do with the arts of setting
up budgetary categories and making categorical judgments about specific

sources of revenue, debt, and so forth (Rawls, 2002, p. 10). In other words, it had more to do with the work of setting up the nominal and categorical spaces in which quantities would be made visible and reportable, than with numerical reckoning practices themselves. Viewed in this way, accounting, is not just a matter of recording entries in spaces, but of composing things and shaping communicative actions so that they are account-*able*: record-able, arguably the same (MacKenzie, this volume).

According to this biographical account, Garfinkel derived general insights from his experience with this course on how accountability is central to the production of social order, and this led him away from his father's business and toward academic sociology. This conception of accountability relates to Paolo Quattrone's illuminating genealogy of accounting practices through the devices of classifying and stabilizing things and people (2008). And, as Barbara Stafford makes clear in her essay in this volume, such work also can make (potential) information invisible.[3]

In particular cases, accountability can be complex, contentious, politically-fraught work.

Justifiability is an important part of accountability, as images, reports, demos, and so forth, are placed in front of audiences, and subject to evaluations and audits. Accounts are pro-active as well as defensive—they anticipate skepticism as well as build hopeful scenarios—and while they attempt to project a favorable image of their creators, they do not try to give away too much.

Particularly salient in this volume, and no doubt in the field of business at large, is explicit attention to properties of numbers that are dismissed as irrelevant when we think of them as ideal mathematical forms, in a Platonic sense. Remarkably salient in economies, markets, and business activities is the strenuous, political work of making costs 'visible,' and establishing equivalences between what, initially, might seem unrelated. Markets are the economist's proxy for nature, as they appear to operate autonomously to create the equivalencies the economist analyzes.

Given the emphasis on numerical reckoning in accounts of business and market activities, 'count-ability' is an important aspect of account-ability.[4] Countability involves contextually variable displays: measures, charts, spreadsheets, and other organizational displays. Important features of such displays are traceability and translatability (Lezaun, 2006). Numbers and the administrative invocation of numbers become strong resources for assuring the stability of translations and the equivalences between different renderings.

IMAGINING

Visualization in business contexts has some things in common with visualization in the social sciences. It is often said that 'objects' of study in the social sciences are highly complex—so complex that, at least for the time being, there is little hope for developing maps, mathematical models, or concrete images comparable to those used in the natural sciences. Social scientists nevertheless make abundant use of charts, diagrams, and visual models, but their models tend to be abstract and the visual conventions they use tend to be simplified—often consisting of words in boxes connected by single- or double-headed arrows. In some cases, especially in more theoretical fields, conceptual diagrams and charts seem to be little more than visual ornaments in texts that could easily be deleted without losing much of what is already said in words (Lynch, 1991). Models and charts used in business (though often more colorful that their social science equivalents) often have a similar abstract 'conceptual' design. However, one thing that the contextual use of such charts and conceptual diagrams makes clear is that their intelligibility and pragmatic value has little or nothing to do with their point-by-point correspondence to some existent "thing". Instead, they express hopes, represent ideals, and project imagined possibilities. Once we are alerted to such features, we also can see that they are commonplace in the natural sciences as well, and this insight can encourage us to put aside any expectation that scientific data should represent what *is*, whereas business charts, models, figures, and other images represent what *might be* (often requiring a liberal dose of imagination). Although scientists do often make diligent efforts to compose highly accurate maps, models and measures of the things they study, they also spend much of their time composing images of imaginable and (arguably) possible realities. Many published scientific images are *expressions* of imagination rather than displays of evidence that prove the case for what was previously hypothesized.

Consider the broad and amorphous field of nanotechnology. As the term suggests, nanotechnology includes scientific and engineering projects that work with phenomena at a scale of 1–100 nanometers (a nanometer is one billionth of a meter). An instrument such as the scanning tunneling microscope (STM) can be likened to a probe such as a stylus or a blind person's cane that runs across a surface and transmits signals that can be translated by computer programs into two- and three-dimensional images and models (Daston and Galison, 2007, pp. 363ff; Mody and Lynch, 2010). One important property of these probes, and of the fields that deploy them, is that they can be used to push or pull atomic and molecular entities, in order to arrange them in patterns. Numerous online image galleries present inscriptions, drawings, and sculptures produced at (or near) the nanoscale.[5] Instead of showing monochromatic, difficult-to-resolve images produced through the translation of instrumental signals to topographic fields, many widely circulated images and animations of nanoscale objects are made with computer graphics to depict nanobots (nanoscale robots) composed of assemblies of atoms. These 'atoms' often resemble color-coded ball-and-stick models. They have shiny (seemingly hard or plastic) surfaces, and often are depicted with linear-perspective conventions that imply illumination, shadow effects, and a distinct angle of view. Images of nanoscale phenomena are (and have been criticized for being) promissory and promotional, rather than empirical.[6] But, once we open our expectations to possibilities other than a correspondence to some empirical object, we can begin to realize that such images perform jobs other than revealing natural configurations. In short, they are expressions of imagination that promote a nascent, transdisciplinary field by vividly depicting (as though present) what imaging and manipulation of molecular objects may someday create. Even a 'view' of impossible objects—impossible, because the illusion of a '"standpoint' and of light and shadow effects is out of the question for nanoscale objects that are subject to quantum forces and are smaller than the wavelength of visible light—creates a template for further imagining and research.

Imagination is often ascribed to human psychology, but when we examine images, we can begin to identify how imagining is performed in publicly accessible spaces afforded by communicational media. Possible and impossible forms are made vividly present through the artful use of graphic materials, surface configurations, and conventions. The illusionist art of the Renaissance, creating dazzling hyper-realistic scenes in which angels and mortals exist on the same plane—a plane that becomes endowed with depth, illumination, and perspective through artful manipulation of the viewer's gaze—is still very much alive in the 21st-century future-oriented world of nano-imaging. The use of glossy images and animations that seemingly place viewers inside an imagined world is hardly novel for advertisers. Although it may be disconcerting to find that such 'slick' imagery has a prominent place in the promotion of a transdisciplinary movement in science and engineering, there are relatively benign as well as sleazy aspects of this particular moment in the global convergence between business and science. Vivid imaginings, even when dismissed as impossibilities, can have a leading role in setting up expectancies for what a future 'thing like that' should look like. Ball-and-stick and space-filling models of molecular machines work to supplement and concretize mechanistic metaphors that otherwise would be expressed through theories or verbal analogies, and they can even provide visual images for enframing empirical realizations performed through work with microscopes and other tools that translate data into pictures.[7] In this respect, a routine practice for imagining business—using diagrams and charts to 'depict' possible futures to work towards—identifies a no-less-routine, but occasionally transgressive, way of imagining science.

CONCLUSION

Those of us who have a home in STS are happy to see connections form between our interests and those in other fields. For the past three decades, what started out as 'science studies' has had a history of expansion into studies of technology, medicine, science and mathematics education, feminist and gender studies, economics, information studies, and now business and management studies. Described from a parochial point of view, this expansion involves a transfer of STS concepts, arguments, ideas, and methods to other fields. However, what I'm suggesting in these brief comments is that STS is not simply a source of expertise or theory with which to 'bless' other fields in a Catholic expansion. STS is not a privileged administrative center, but more of a focus of interest and source of suggestive exemplars. Those of us who identify with that field stand to be, and hope to be, instructed by work in other fields that take up themes that we recognize, but which develop and transform them in ways we had not imagined. This volume takes a large step toward realizing that possibility.

NOTES

1. This commentary is based on my "Concluding Reflections," at the First Workshop on Imagining Business: Reflecting on the Visual Power of Management, Organizing and Governing Practices (Saïd Business School, Oxford, UK, June 26–27, 2008).
2. For work on microscopy, see Lynch (1985); and on digital imaging in astronomy, see Lynch and Edgerton (1988).
3. For a brilliant study that focuses on the dynamics of showing and hiding features of an innovative technology at a trade exhibition, see Catelijne Coopmans (2011).
4. On methods of counting human and nonhuman 'things', see Martin and Lynch (2009).
5. Such galleries are the subject of ongoing research I am conducting with Kathryn de Ridder-Vignone. The research was supported by National Science Foundation, Science and Society Award No. SES-0822757.
6. For a collection of articles on the prominent orientation toward the future in nanotechnology, see Fisher, Selin, and Wetmore (2008). For a criticism, see Pitt (2006).
7. For an insightful account of how molecular models lead researchers' expectations about what molecules might look like, see Myers (2009).

REFERENCES

Coopmans, C. (2011) Face Value: New Medical Imaging Software in Commercial View. *Social Studies of Science*, 41(2), 155–176.
Daston L. and Galison, P. (2007) *Objectivity*. Cambridge, MA: Zone Books.
Fisher, E., Selin, C. and Wetmore, J. M. (Eds.) (2008) *The Yearbook of Nanotechnology and Society: Volume 1: Presenting Futures*. New York: Springer.
Garfinkel, H. (1967) *Studies in Ethnomethodology*. Englewood Cliffs, NJ: Prentice Hall.
Giedion, S. (1948) *Mechanization Takes Command: A Contribution to Anonymous History*. Oxford: Oxford University Press.
Lezaun, J. (2006) Creating a New Object of Government: Making Genetically Modified Organisms Traceable. *Social Studies of Science*, 36(4), 499–531.

Lynch, M. (1985) Discipline and the Material Form of Images: An Analysis of Scientific Visibility. *Social Studies of Science*, 15(1), 37–66.

———. (1991) Pictures of Nothing? Visual Construals in Social Theory. *Sociological Theory*, 9(1), 1–22.

Lynch, M. and Edgerton, S. Y. (1988) Aesthetics and Digital Image Processing: Representational Craft in Contemporary Astronomy. In G. Fyfe and J. Law (Eds.), *Picturing Power: Visual Depiction and Social Relations* (pp. 184–220). London: Routledge and Kegan Paul.

Martin, A. and Lynch, M. (2009) Counting Things and People: The Practices and Politics of Counting. *Social Problems, 56*(2), 243–266.

Mody, C. C. M. and Lynch, M. (2010) Test Objects and Other Epistemic Things: A History of a Nanoscale Object. *British Journal for the History of Science*, 43(3), 423–458.

Myers, N. (2009) Conjuring Machinic Life. *Spontaneous Generations: A Journal for the History and Philosophy of Science* 2(1), 112–121.

Pitt, J. (2006) "When is an Image not an Image?" In J. Schumer and D. Baird (Eds.), *Nanotechnology Challenges: Implications for Philosophy, Ethics and Society* (pp. 131–141). Singapore: World Scientific Publishing.

Quattrone, P. (2008) "Books to be practiced: Memory, the power of the visual and the success of accounting" presentation at the "Imagining Business" workshop, Saïd Business School, Oxford; June 26.

Rawls, A. (2002) Editor's Introduction, to H. Garfinkel, *Ethnomethodology's Program: Working out Durkheim's Aphorism* (pp. 1–64, at p. 10). Lanham, MD: Rowman & Littlefield.

Contributors

EDITORS

Chris McLean is a Senior Lecturer at Manchester Business School and a member of the Centre for Research on Socio-Cultural Change (CRESC). Her research interests focus on the area of organizing, images and performativity. She has been involved in a variety of empirical research projects using an ethnographic style of investigation and she is currently exploring practices of organizing within the newspaper printing industry and mental health care.

Paolo Quattrone is Professor of Accounting and Management Control at IE Business School, Madrid and hold academic posts at the Universities of Manchester, Carlos III (Madrid), Siena and Oxford. He has been a Fulbright New Century Scholar at the University of Stanford and visiting professor at the University of Kyoto and HEC (Paris). His research spans from the history of administrative practices in religious Orders to information and management control technologies in large organisations, major programmes and universities.

François-Régis Puyou is assistant professor in management accounting and a member of the Centre for Financial and Risk Management at Audencia Nantes Management School. He is also associate researcher to the "Centre de Sociologie des Organisations" at Sciences-Po Paris where he defended his PhD on management accounting practices as governance processes in large multinational corporations in 2009.

Professor Nigel Thrift is the Vice-Chancellor of the University of Warwick since July 2006 and one of the world's leading human geographers and social scientists. He is academician of the Academy of Learned Societies for the Social Sciences, and a Fellow of the British Academy.

CONTRIBUTORS

Franck Cochoy is professor of sociology at the Université de Toulouse and member of the CERTOP-CNRS. His work on the sociology of markets focuses on the different mediations that frame the relation between supply and demand, such as marketing, packaging, self-service, trade press, etc. He is the author of Une histoire du marketing (La Découverte, 1999) and Une sociologie du packaging ou l'âne de Buridan face au marché (Presses Universitaires de France, 2002). His most recent publications in English appeared in *Theory, Culture and Society, Marketing Theory,* and the *Journal of Cultural Economy and Organization.*

François Cooren is a communication scholar, past president of the International Communication Association (2010-2011) and editor-in-chief of *Communication Theory* from 2005 to 2008. He is chairman of the Department of communication of the Université de Montréal, where he is full professor. His research mainly focuses on organizational communication in mundane and emergency situations. He is part of what has come to be known in the field as the Montreal School of Organizational Communication, which proposes communication as the "site and surface" of organizations, meaning that the latter emerge from and are maintained by communication processes.

Barbara Czarniawska is Professor of Management Studies at Göteborg University, School of Business, Economics, and Law (Gothenburg Research Institute). Her work is interdisciplinary, combining organization and management theory with other social sciences such as anthropology in order to understand organizations as complex cultural entities. Her work based on the method of the narrative approach has been innovative. Her publications cover such themes as managerial work, organizational learning and change, city management, and gender inequality. She has worked as Visiting Professor in several European and United States (US) universities, and she is, among other things, a member of the Swedish Royal Academy of Sciences, the Swedish Royal Engineering Academy, the Royal Society of Arts and Sciences in Göteborg, and the Finnish Society of Sciences and Letters.

Jane Davison is a Professor in Accounting at Royal Holloway, University of London. She is a chartered accountant (ICAEW) with City of London auditing experience within a major firm and an academic background and continuing research interests in the fine arts. Her principal work is on accounting and the visual. It aims at developing interdisciplinary theoretical frameworks together with close empirical analysis of the visual in financial reporting, accountability and governance, using approaches from philosophy, literature, and the fine arts.

Yiannis Gabriel is Professor of Organizational Theory and Deputy Dean of the School of Management at Bath University. Yiannis is known for his work into organizational storytelling and narratives, leadership, management learning, psychoanalytic studies of work, and the culture and politics of contemporary consumption. He has used stories as a way of studying numerous social and organizational phenomena including leader-follower relations, group dynamics and fantasies, nostalgia, insults and apologies. More recently, Yiannis has carried out research on leadership and patient care in the hospital sector and on the experiences of sacked leaders and senior professionals. He is the author of ten books and has been editor of *Management Learning* and associate editor of *Human Relations*. His enduring fascination as a researcher lies in what he describes as the unmanageable qualities of life in and out of organizations.

Martin Giraudeau is a lecturer in the Department of Accounting at the London School of Economics & Political Science. He received his Ph.D. in 2010 from the University of Toulouse, for a dissertation entitled: *The Making of the Future: A Historical Sociology of Business Plans*. His research, at the crossroads of economic sociology, business history and accounting, has been published in *Sociologie du Travail, Long Range Planning*, and the *Journal of Cultural Economy*.

Joanne Locke is a senior lecturer at University of Birmingham in the UK. She has published in a range of areas including international account-ing, linguistic analysis of accounting standards, and journal rankings. Currently Joanne's main area of interest is in the standardizing effects of computerized systems of reporting such as Enterprise Resource Plan-ning (ERPs) and eXtensible Business Reporting Language (XBRL). My most recent publications include a 100-page monograph for ICAEW on aspects of digital reporting initiatives, which make use of recent develop-ments in regulatory policy and in digital communication technologies. In addition to the ICAEW report, two articles have been published in high-quality international journals. Joanne has published in *European Accounting Review, Accounting Organizations and Society, The Brit-ish Accounting Review, Critical Perspectives on Accounting, Interna-tional Journal of Accounting,* and *Accounting Forum*.

Alan Lowe's current research projects are around financial reporting, trans-parency, and accountability. I have recently co-authored a 100-page monograph for Institute of Chartered Accountants in England and Wales (ICAEW) on international aspects of digital reporting. A coherent meth-odological frame can be seen in much of my research, which uses a socio-technical perspective in order to explain the impact of accounting and other related information technologies. This includes research and publications in enterprise resource planning and casemix systems in the health sector.

Other research interests include the impact on management accounting systems of changes in management philosophies, methods of performance measurement, issues related to the management of intellectual capital, and the application of qualitative research methodologies. Recent publications have appeared in: *Accounting Organizations and Society, Accounting Auditing and Accountability Journal, British Accounting Review, Critical Perspectives on Accounting, European Accounting Review, Information Technology and People, Management Accounting Research,* and *Organization Studies and Organization.*

Michael Lynch is a Professor in the Department of Science & Technology Studies at Cornell University. His research is on discourse, visual representation, and practical action in research laboratories, clinical settings, and legal tribunals. His most recent book, *Truth Machine: The Contentious History of DNA Fingerprinting* (with Simon Cole, Ruth McNally & Kathleen Jordan; University of Chicago Press, 2008) examines the interplay between law and science in criminal cases involving DNA evidence. He is Editor of the journal *Social Studies of Science,* and past President of the Society for Social Studies of Sciences (4S).

Donald MacKenzie works in the sociology of science and technology and in the sociology of markets. He holds a personal chair in sociology at the University of Edinburgh, where he has taught since 1975. His most recent books are *An Engine, Not a Camera: How Financial Models Shape Markets* (MIT Press, 2006); *Do Economists Make Markets? On the Performativity of Economics* (Princeton University Press, 2007), co-edited with Fabian Muniesa and Lucia Siu; and *Material Markets: How Economic Agents Are Constructed* (Oxford University Press, 2009). Currently, his main research (in conjunction with Iain Hardie) is on credit derivatives and the credit crisis.

Wanda J. Orlikowski is the Eaton-Peabody Professor of Communication Sciences at MIT, and Professor of Information Technologies and Organization Studies at MIT's Sloan School of Management. Her research focuses primarily on the sociological aspects of technology and work. She is particularly interested in the dynamic relations between information technologies and organizations over time, with emphases on organizing structures, cultural norms, communication genres, and work practices. She recently led a multi-year project (funded by the National Science Foundation) on the social and economic implications of Internet technologies in organizations. She is currently examining the sociomaterial entailments of distributed collaboration. Dr. Orlikowski has served as a senior editor for *Organization Science* and currently serves on the editorial boards of *Information and Organization, Information Technology and People,* and *Organization Science.*

Jonathan E. Schroeder is the William A. Kern Professor of Communications at Rochester Institute of Technology. He has held visiting appointments at Wesleyan University (Center for the Humanities), Göteborg University, Sweden (Center for Consumer Science), University of Auckland, New Zealand (Center for Digital Enterprise), Bocconi University in Milan (Program in Fashion, Experience, and Design), and Indian School of Business, Hyderabad. Schroeder has published widely on branding, communication, consumer research, and identity. His current research involves four intersecting areas: aesthetic leadership, branding, ethics of representation and visual communication. He is the author of *Visual Consumption* (Routledge, 2002) and co-editor of *Brand Culture* (Routledge, 2006). He is editor in chief of *Consumption Markets and Culture,* and serves on the editorial boards of *Advertising and Society Review, Critical Studies in Fashion and Beauty, European Journal of Marketing, Innovative Marketing, International Journal of Indian Culture and Business Management, Journal of Business Research, Journal of Historical Research in Marketing, Journal of Macromarketing,* and *Marketing Theory.*

Susan V. Scott is a senior lecturer in the Information Systems and Innovation Group, Department of Management, at the London School of Economics and Political Science. Her research focuses on technology, work, and organization from a management studies perspective. Susan has developed a major body of research examining the role of information systems in the transformation of work practices within the financial services sector. She has published on the implementation of information systems for risk management; electronic trading; the strategic organization of post-trade services; organizational reputation risk; enterprise resource planning and best practice. She is currently involved in research projects exploring the sociomateriality of service innovation and teaches a core Masters course in qualitative research methods for the ISI Group. Her background includes a BA in History and Politics (School of Oriental and African Studies, SOAS), MSc in Analysis, Design, and Management of Information Systems (London Scool of Economics, LSE), and a PhD in Management Studies (University of Cambridge).

Barbara Maria Stafford is the William B. Ogden Distinguished Service Professor, Emerita, at the University of Chicago. Her work has consistently explored the intersections between the visual arts and the physical and biological sciences from the early modern to the contemporary era. Her current research charts the revolutionary ways the neurosciences are changing our views of the human and animal sensorium, shaping our fundamental assumptions about perception, sensation, emotion, mental imagery, and subjectivity. Stafford's most recent book is *Echo Objects: The Cognitive Work of Images* (University of Chicago Press, 2007).

Consuelo Vásquez is assistant professor at the Department of Social and Public Communication at the University of Quebec at Montreal (UQAM). Her work is associated to the Communicative Constitution of Organizing approach (CCO), through which she addresses issues related to spacing and timing, organizational movement and other forms of collective representation in communication. She is an active member of the research group Language, Organization and Governance of the University of Montreal. She is also member of the Chair in Public Relations and Marketing Communications and the Research Center for Health Communications at UQAM.

Index